Eternal Encouragements

A Six-Month Devotional

David A. Jones
II Peter 3:18

Eternal Encouragements

A Six-Month Devotional

By David A. Jones

XULON PRESS

Xulon Press
2301 Lucien Way #415
Maitland, FL 32751
407.339.4217
www.xulonpress.com

The author would enjoy hearing from you at davidjones@frontier.com.

Printed in the United States of America

Paperback ISBN-13: 978-1-66283-983-2
Ebook ISBN-13: 978-1-66283-984-9

Table of Contents

Acknowledgements

The Stonerise Network (Stonerise Healthcare) provides an essential and broad range of transitional care services to patients in West Virginia and southeast Ohio, including transitional and skilled nursing care centers, therapy, home health, and hospice care. As a faith-based company, they also make available spiritual resources to their constituency through a chaplaincy program and daily devotionals. I am very grateful to the leadership of Stonerise for the privilege of serving as their Manager of Chaplaincy Services and for the opportunity to write these devotionals during the 2020-2021 covid pandemic season. I am also thankful for their permission and encouragement for me to publish them in this format.

With even deeper gratitude I also acknowledge God's special gift to me of my wife, Debra, who has walked with me through over 47 years of life and ministry for the Lord and who continues to provide generous daily doses of God's eternal encouragements to me. I lovingly dedicate this book to her.

Introduction

I t is my desire and prayer that each reader of these devotionals will be led to trust Jesus Christ as Savior from their sins and to begin a close walk with the Lord. I trust that what is included here will provide some spiritual meat and potatoes from God's Word on which to feed and nourish your spiritual health and growth and will enable you and your family to love the Lord and to serve Him daily. Extra Scripture references in most pieces will provide for further study and I trust you also will find at times some things that will bring hearty joy and laughter to your day, as well. By God's grace and for His glory, I share these with you.

David A. Jones

Book Summary

Conceived and birthed during the early weeks of the 2020-2021 Covid pandemic, the writing of a series of encouraging daily devotionals was requested by the leadership of Stonerise Healthcare, a faith-based administrative services company in West Virginia. The author, serving as Manager of Chaplaincy Services with them, eagerly complied.

However, as a pastor, he desired to take the readers a bit deeper into the Scriptures, leading them to develop a personal relationship with God. He wanted to help them to understand God's Word and to encourage them to walk by faith in every area of their lives. He believes that is the way to survive and even thrive during the deep and dark valleys of life, such as our worldwide pandemic. By doing so, we can then know the special wisdom, comfort and encouragement that comes directly from our loving, eternal God.

Author Bio

David Jones is an ordained pastor who has served in four independent Bible and Baptist churches in New York, Pennsylvania, and West Virginia for about 39 years. He is a graduate of Lancaster Bible College and Baptist Bible Seminary and currently serves part-time as Manager of Chaplaincy Services for Stonerise Healthcare, headquartered in Charleston, West Virginia.

David and his wife, Debra, have one son, who with his wife, have blessed them with three young grandchildren. They happily reside near each other in Ohio.

David has also written "Dollars and Biblical Sense", "A Biblical Guide to Caregiving" and five other mini-books, training manuals on caregiving subjects, for individual or small group use.

Encouragements #1

So, What Are "Eternal Encouragements"?

"The eternal God is thy refuge, and underneath are the everlasting arms..." (Deut. 33:27) "For thus saith the high and lofty One that inhabiteth eternity, whose name is Holy; I dwell in the high and holy place, with him also that is of a contrite and humble spirit, to revive the spirit of the humble, and to revive the heart of the contrite ones." (Isaiah 57:15)

Let's begin this series by clarifying its title.

FIRST – "Eternal" speaks of a timelessness, a present sense of existence without beginning or end. It lasts forever.

1. God is eternal, always existing. He already existed "in the beginning" when He created time, space, and matter. (Gen. 1:1; Deut. 33:27) He will continue to live forever.
2. He is described as inhabiting eternity. He dwells there. He fills it. (Isaiah 57:15) Being above and beyond our physical world He is not bound by it or limited to it. But He has invaded this world to bring salvation and His daily grace to man.
3. His Word, the Bible is eternal; it will endure forever and forever remain true and trustworthy. (I Peter 1:23-25) It is God's truth, wisdom, and plan, for man.

SECOND – God has made us in His image for eternity. Life is not limited to this world. After our bodies die, our soul will continue on and last forever somewhere. (Gen. 1:26)

1. Solomon wrote that God has placed eternity in our hearts. (Eccl. 3:11)
2. God, knowing our sinful state will bring us eternal suffering, loved us and provided freely a salvation, a rescue from sin through Christ's sacrificial death on the cross and the guarantee that we will live forever with the Lord (John 3:15-16; 10:28-30; I Thess. 4:13-18).

So, with these "eternal encouragements" (devotionals) I don't want to share human wisdom or the shallow theories of our world. I desire to remind you of the God of eternity and share with you His eternal Word to encourage you with His love, truth, and wisdom that, as you make use of it, will encourage and help you with the daily challenges of life and prepare you for an eternity with the Lord.

Are you overly burdened today with situations that are discouraging and draining you? Notice our verses at the top again. Something else is described there as being eternal. "...underneath are the everlasting arms." He can hold you and never let you go. Talk to Him today about your pain; let Him carry you and care for you through this day.

For Prayer Today
- Ask God to remind you that today's sufferings won't last forever; for the Christian, they are not eternal.
- Thank Him for providing deliverance from sin and eternal blessings throughout the future.

Personal Notes and Responses

Shut-in but Not Shut-Up

"And Paul dwelt two whole years in his own hired house, and received all that came in unto him, preaching the kingdom of God, and teaching those things which concern the Lord Jesus Christ, with all confidence, no man forbidding him." (Acts 28:30-31) "But I would ye should understand, brethren, that the things which happened unto me have fallen out rather unto the further-ance of the gospe; so that my bonds in Christ are manifest in all the palace, and in all other places..." (Phil. 1:12-14)

The book of Acts is an action-packed book as it tells the pow-erful story of the dramatic birth and growth of the church and the exploits of the followers of Christ as they risked their lives, facing persecution, imprisonment, and death to share the good news of the gospel. One of those early church heroes was the apostle Paul who traveled many miles, established and encour-aged many churches, while suffering incredibly many trials. (Read II Cor. 11:22-33 for his record of these trials.)

The book of Acts ends with the verses above. (Please read them again.) Paul was actually a prisoner of the Roman government at that time, under house arrest for two whole years; he had to "shel-ter-in-place"-for two years!

I would think that would have been frustrating to this busily active follower of Christ, to be stuck at home for so long. But he was allowed to have visitors, possibly many of them being Roman sol-diers and guards or friends from the Roman church and he took every opportunity to continue to preach and teach about Jesus. He may have been shut-in but he never did shut-up!

Most people today or at other times in their lives, maybe due to illness, age, or disability may find themselves confined some-where or simply unable to do a lot of the things they used to do. Let me encourage you to do whatever you can do. Paul couldn't

4

travel or talk to large crowds so he taught individuals who came to him. God has given me lots of time at home presently and I have the opportunity to write devotionals and send them out to others. Perhaps you can read, write some memories of your past that your family will enjoy, work on a craft or art work that you can give away, or call someone to check on them. Let them talk and be a good listener. Spend time in prayer. Don't allow what you can't do to keep you from doing something you can do. You will be encouraged by doing something for others. I don't want you to miss that special blessing.

For Prayer Today
- Ask the Lord to give you some ideas to occupy your time. Then spend some time each day involved in it.
- Pray again for the many first responders and health care workers who probably have very little personal time at home right now. Pray for their health, safety, stamina, and wisdom. Pray for their families who are sharing the stresses of these times.

Personal Notes and Responses

Our Greatest Need

"For God so loved the world, that he gave his only begotten Son, that whosoever believeth in him should not perish, but have everlasting life... He that believeth on the Son hath everlasting life: and he that believeth not the Son shall not see life; but the wrath of God abideth on him." (John 3:16, 36)

As I continue the privilege of taking eternal truths from an eternal God and sharing them with eternal souls to prepare them for their eternal future, today's edition is among the most important one of all.

I was about six years old when I trusted Jesus as my Savior. I had received a children's Bible correspondence course and when the first lesson arrived, my dad sat down with me and worked through it together. It was on the "Steps of Salvation", the basic A, B, C's of it. The gospel message is simple enough for a child to understand and respond to it. I share it with you in that same simple format.

So how can a person be saved from their sin and receive the eternal gift of salvation, forgiveness of sin, and membership in God's family?

A. **Admit that you are a sinner** and cannot save yourself. No amount of good works, ceremonies, rituals, baptisms, church memberships, perfect attendance records, or family connections can solve the sin problem. They do not remove our sin which brings us guilt and death, physical and spiritual separation from God forever. (Romans 3:23; 6:23; Eph. 2:8-9)

B. **Believe that Jesus Christ actually took my punishment on the cross, suffered in my place to pay for my sin and to provide salvation for me.** To "believe" means "to trust, to rely on" Jesus to be my Savior. To accept what He did for me on the cross by His love and grace and to trust Him

6

alone to save me results in my forgiveness and welcome into the family of God. "But as many as received him, to them gave he power to become the sons of God, even to them who believe on his name:" (John 1:12; Acts 16:30-31)

C. **Call on the Lord Jesus Christ to save you.** Personalize your faith in Christ by talking to God in prayer, telling Him that you admit your sinfulness and repent of it and are right now placing your faith in Jesus Christ to save you and make you a child of God. Ask Him to help you walk with Him all your life and to use you for His purposes all your days. Thank Him for loving you and for providing the free gift of salvation for you. (Romans 10:9-10, 13; 6:23; II Cor. 5:17)

That day in September of 1958 I learned those truths and prayed to trust Christ and receive His gift of eternal life and a personal relationship with Him. On that day I became a newborn in God's family and have been growing steadily all these years, by His grace, as I have walked with Him. I urge you to consider this very seriously as the consequences of rejecting Christ are eternally severe. God loves you and wants to save you. This is, indeed, a life-or-death matter. Forever.

For Prayer Today
-   If you have never done so before, please think about the above truths and seriously consider talking to God and asking Him to save you from your sins and to make you a child of God.
-   Thank God for so great a salvation! This should always be one of our greatest "eternal encouragements"!

Personal Notes and Responses

ETERNAL ENCOURAGEMENTS #4

"It was a Dark and Stormy Night..."

"All Scripture is given by inspiration of God, and is profitable for doctrine, for reproof, for correction, for instruction in righteousness: that the man of God may be perfect, throughly furnished unto all good works." (II Timothy 3:16-17)

Do you recognize today's title? It is actually the first line of a novel that was being written by a certain "literary character" who never was able to finish his book. I don't think he ever got much beyond the second sentence, "Somewhere a door slammed."

I love to read and in my present semi-retired status I am doing a lot of it. But there is one book above all others that I recommend highly to you today. Its opening line is also well known and it says this, "In the beginning, God created the heavens and the earth." What a start!

The eternal God is the author of the Bible, as seen in the verses above. It's an amazing book for many reasons. God used about 40 different men to actually do the writing over a period of about 1600 years. It was written on 3 continents, originally in 3 languages. The human writers did not know most of the others, were of different backgrounds and eras, occupations, educational and social status, and yet as God inspired and guided their writings and brought them together, the result was a complete and accurate record of God's truth for mankind. God not only created humanity, He chose to communicate with us! In a book!

The Bible is described as
- a lamp and light for our path (Psalm 109:105)
- as wisdom from God (Psalm 119:30)
- as milk for new believers (I Peter 2:2)
- as meat or solid food for growing believers (Heb. 5:12-14; I Cor.3:1-2)

- as water that can cleanse and refresh (Eph. 5:25-26)
- as more valuable and desirable than gold (Psalm 19:10)
- as sweeter than honey in the honeycomb (Psalm 19:10)
- as the seed that stimulates faith and draws us to the Savior (Rom. 10:17; II Tim. 3:14-15; I Peter 1:23; Luke 8:4-15, esp. verse 8)
- as that which can benefit the believer in all the ways seen in II Tim. 3:16-17!

Bottom line for today is simply this, in all you can do or can't do in your current situation, please DO NOT NEGLECT THIS BOOK. Think about all you'd miss!

For Prayer Today
- Ask God to help you and your family spend time reading God's Word each day. Then do so.

Personal Notes and Responses

ETERNAL ENCOURAGEMENTS #5

"The Hip Bone's Connected to the Thigh Bone, the Thigh Bone's Connected to the ..."

"For as the body is one, and hath many members, and all the members of that one body, being many, are one body: so also is Christ...If the foot shall say, Because I am not the hand, I am not of the body; is it therefore not of the body?...But now hath God set the members every one of them in the body, as it hath pleased him." (I Cor. 12:12-18)

Remember that song? That "spiritual" was loosely based on Ezekiel 37 where the nation of Israel is described as dried up and scattered bones that one day God will gather together and restore to life and health for His use. They would then, finally "hear the word of the Lord." (37:4)

Are you feeling rather "disconnected" these days?

In I Corinthians 12, God tells us that the family of God, the church, is like a body with Christ as the head (Colossians 1:18) and all the members are body parts that He fits together for His use. Read carefully 12:12-27 and take note of several truths.
   1. It is God who places the different members of the body together, for His pleasure (12:18).
   2. However large or small you may see your part to be in the body of Christ, the church needs you (12:14-17). You cannot say, "They don't need me!"
   3. You need the body of Christ. The hand cannot say to the foot, "I don't need you." You cannot say about the church, "I don't need them." (12:19-24)
The body of Christ, the church should act like a body so that "there should be no schism (division) in the body; but that the members should have the same care one for another. And whether one member suffer, all the members suffer with it; or one member be honored, all the members rejoice with it." (12:25-27) Much

of the eternal encouragement that God can provide for you can come through your local church family, if you are practically connected to it.

We have endured seasons when church families could not meet together. But we are still one body though physically disconnected from each other. What have you done or what can you do in future such seasons to demonstrate your oneness with other believers? You still need them and they still need you. Possibly much more than ever.

Let us "Hear the Word of the Lord" on this matter! Now join me in song, "...to the leg bone...the leg bone's connected to the ankle bone..."

For Prayer Today
- Be much in prayer for other members of your church that they will remember the oneness that they have with others and that they are not alone.
- Ask God to help you "reconnect" with a few from your church; send a note, make a phone call, pray over the phone with them, check on some elderly or weakened individual, ask someone to pray for you, etc.
- Pray for your pastor(s) and their families and be a source of eternal encouragement to them.

Personal Notes and Responses

The Sacredness of the Family

"...It is not good that man should be alone; I will make him an help meet for him." "Whoso findeth a wife findeth a good thing, and obtaineth favor of the Lord." "Lo, children are an heritage of the Lord: and the fruit of the womb is his reward..." (Gen. 2:18; Proverbs 18:22; Psalm 127:3)

Someone said, "I was watching my 5-year-old granddaughter play with her toys and saw that she was staging a wedding. She first played the role of the mother who assigned specific duties to others, then suddenly she became the bride with a teddy bear groom. She picked him up and said to the "minister" presiding over the wedding, 'Now you can read us our rights.' Without missing a beat, she became the minister who said 'You have the right to remain silent; anything you say may be held against you; you have the right to have an attorney present. You may now kiss your bride.'"

How precious and how much fun it can be to be raising children in the warm womb of a family who deeply loves God and each other. Unfortunately, families today are often deeply stressed and troubled, seriously damaged or shattered completely. Personal hurts and disappointments, financial burdens and employment busyness, and many other factors have robbed families of the love, joy, and peace that God intended for them.

As I wrote this, most of us were under quarantine in those days and spending much more time with our family members than we have in many years. How did you do with that? Many found it to be very stressful and challenging.

Do you realize how special, how sacred, "family" really is? The whole concept was birthed in the heart and mind of God as one of His greatest ideas to provide lasting blessing, security, unselfish love, joy, and peace to mankind. No family or individual within it is in any way perfect, far from it. But in this special supernaturally endorsed relationship within the commitments of love and togetherness we can, with God's help and direction, face the storms of life victoriously and with incredible joy.

I'll have more to say about this later. For now, I beg you, please do not allow the present crises or future ones to drive you further apart from your family members. Do not let irritable selfishness prevent you from thinking of the good you can bring to others closest to you in those times. Be patient with each other, quick to forgive and to draw closer to each other and to God as you spend time together in His presence, as well.

Your family is very valuable and precious in God's sight. May it be for you, as well. Enjoy them and help each other to walk through any challenging times together!

For Prayer Today

- I know that many who read these may be alone, single, divorced, or bereaved of a spouse. Please spend time praying for the families of today. So many of them don't know the joy and peace that God can bring to them.
- If you are "estranged" from family due to hurts, anger, bitterness, etc. pray that God will work in you first to humble yourself, forgive others, etc. and then pray for your family to draw closer together again in the days ahead.
- Those of you who are in the middle of chaotic and challenging times with your family due to this virus, ask the Lord to give patience and wisdom, ideas for caring for and entertaining your family members as well as worshipping and serving the Lord together.

Personal Notes and Responses

Eternal Encouragement #7

Count Your Blessings!

"Bless the Lord, O my soul: and all that is within me, bless his holy name. Bless the Lord, O my soul, and forget not all his benefits:" (Psalm 103:1-2)

Today's title is not just a cliché. It is also a hymn title that is probably known by many of us. The tune has a happy cadence to it and urges us to "Count your many blessings. Name them one by one. Count your many blessings, see what God has done."

In my recent reading of the autobiography of evangelist Gipsy Smith from the late 1800s-early 1900s he reports learning that hymn from a little girl who sang it to him in an infirmary. He then began singing it in many of his crusades, popularizing it so that it became the most popular song in London in 1900. He said, "Wherever one might go, in the streets, in the trams, in the trains – someone was humming or whistling 'Count Your Blessings'. The boys pushing their barrows along, the men driving their horses, and the women rocking their cradles,–all had been caught by the truth and melody of the hymn."[1]

Can you imagine that? It's hard to imagine our secularized society doing so today but how about those who claim to be Christians and have come to know the blessings of God personally? Are we singing that hymn? Better yet, are we counting our blessings?

Psalm 103 comes to my mind whenever I think of that song. When I was of elementary age our pastor's wife had us memorizing the entire passage (22 verses), one verse per week and I can still quote it almost perfectly over 50 years later.

Please read slowly the entire Psalm. You will find a very special catalogue of God's blessings that He provides for those who trust

---

[1] David Lazell, *Gipsy Smith – From the Forest I Came* (Chicago: Moody Press, 1973) 162-163

Him. Both physical blessings and spiritual blessings are listed. Allow this passage to encourage you as you focus on how good God is and has been to you. I also have a few other suggestions.

1. Remember how the game of Boggle is played? How about this? Around the dinner table with your family (or on the phone or online with a friend), read through Psalm 103 and each of you list as many blessings from God as you can, maybe with a 2 or 3 minute time limit. Then one by one each of you read your list aloud and each of you check off those items that you had recorded as well. See who "wins" with the most blessings left over. Have some fun with this.

2. Challenge one of your children to research the distance referred to in verse 12. I'm sure your tech-savvy kids can take this on. Have them report to the family on it and discuss the importance of its answer for those who know the Lord. If you know the answer, don't give it away.

3. A greater challenge is to ask the entire family or your friend(s) to work together to memorize the entire chapter. Work on it individually and then recite as much of it as you can often to check up and encourage each other with the project.

4. Find the words to "Count Your Blessings" learn it and begin singing it often, individually, as a family or with friends.

"...and forget not all His benefits..."! (Psalm 103:2)

For Prayer Today

- Another challenge is to fill your prayers to God today with only praise and thanksgiving. Seriously, it is harder than you think. But, as you do so, you will find your heart filling with eternal encouragement from the Lord.

Personal Notes and Responses

ETERNAL ENCOURAGEMENTS #8

Hopeless or Hopeful?

"But I would not have you to be ignorant, brethren, concerning them which are asleep, that ye sorrow not, even as others which have no hope. For if we believe that Jesus died and rose again, even so them also which sleep in Jesus will God bring with him... For the Lord himself shall descend from heaven with a shout, with the voice of the archangel, and with the trump of God: and the dead in Christ shall rise first: Then we which are alive and remain shall be caught up together with them in the clouds, to meet the Lord in the air: and so shall we ever be with the Lord..." *(I Thess.4:13-18)*

I've been doing some personal grieving lately as a gentleman I've known for 20 years has passed away due to this virus. He and his wife were part of a church I served as a pastor in WV and he was a resident of a nursing home where I served as a chaplain. I've been on the phone with his wife several times in the last few days as we have grieved together. But our sorrowing also had a very real component of hope, that positive assurance and confidence of seeing our loved one again and the certainty of a glorious future together.

Across our world today, many thousands of families are heartbroken with grief as they've had to bid farewell to dearly beloved family members and friends. Others are painfully waiting with anxiety and fear about their uncertain future. What hope is there for these folks? On what basis can any of us have peace and joy with these disastrous realities darkening and threatening our lives?

The passage that is quoted above acknowledges that grieving is appropriate but that some do so with absolutely no hope while others have every reason for hope. Those are the ones who are trusting in Christ for their own salvation. Several wonderful reasons for hope are found in the verses quoted above.

1. **Because of Christ's resurrection** – "…if we believe that Jesus died and rose again…" By dying for our sins and then rising from the grave, Jesus conquered death, removed its sting, and guarantees that life goes on with Him. Death is not the end. We will live on beyond our physical death.

2. **Because of Christ's return** – "…even so them also who sleep in Jesus will God bring with him…For the Lord Himself shall descend from heaven…then we which are alive and remain shall be caught up..." Christ promised His disciples that He would one day return for them and rapture them to heaven. (John 14:1-6) What an event that will be!

3. **Because of the reunion** that will take place–"…shall be caught up together *with them* in the clouds, to meet the Lord in the air and so shall we ever be *with the Lord*." We may be physically separated from our loved ones now but at the rapture we will join them again; we will be "with them" and "with the Lord" forever. What a family reunion that will be!

The writer closes the passage in verse 18 by saying, "Wherefore comfort one another with these words." Let's do so for one another in these difficult days. And when we meet folks who lack this assurance, let's share with them the good news of how to be sure of this hope, as Jesus did in that upper room. (John 14:1-6).

For Prayer Today
- Pray fervently for those who are dying, that they may trust the One who died for them so that they can be saved.
- Pray for the families and friends who have or are losing loved ones and entering seasons of deep grief and sadness. Pray for their comfort and strength and that they may find hope and peace in the Lord as well.
- Pray for pastors and other religious leaders, for funeral directors and their employees as they seek to serve the bereaved during this season of heavy restrictions, limitations, and protocols.

Personal Notes and Responses

ETERNAL ENCOURAGEMENTS #9

"Lord, How Long?"

"How long wilt thou forget me, O LORD? For ever? how long wilt thou hide thy face from me? How long shall I take counsel in my soul, having sorrow in my heart daily? how long shall mine enemy be exalted over me?" (Psalm 13:1-2)

I think we'd all agree that we can stand some inconveniences, some pain, some disappointment for a time, a brief time. But things get really difficult and complicated when those trials that arrive in our lives, unpack their luggage and move in for a long time, especially when they give no indication as to when they'd be leaving. Or, if they will ever depart.

In our passage above, David asks about this time element four times. He admits to how he feels as he wonders how long will all this last? As we endure difficult times and much time passes without relief we often begin to get discouraged in our soul and begin to consider thoughts that are contrary to God's Word and his promises. Are you feeling or thinking any of the following things that David expressed here?

1. How long will I be forgotten, Lord? I certainly don't feel like You are thinking of me or remembering my tough circumstances. (13:1)
2. How long will I be forsaken, Lord? Why have You turned your face away from me? I feel lonely and abandoned by You. (13:1)
3. How long will I be frustrated inwardly, struggling with sorrows and my inability to figure things out? (13:2)
4. How long will I feel like a failure, like I'm losing battles while my enemy is triumphing over me? (13:2, 4)
5. How long must I be fearful of possible impending death? (13:3)

Three Thoughts for Today:
1. God doesn't mind His children asking such questions. He wants us to cry out to Him in our agony and confusion and express the burdens on our hearts. Don't hesitate to ask, even the hard questions of Him. He understands our struggles and genuinely loves and cares for us.
2. God often uses long periods of time to accomplish things in our lives and sometimes the tools He uses are painful. We shouldn't expect quick band-aid fixes for all our problems. But we can know that He is at work and that He cares. Notice David's expressions of continued faith in God in 13:5-6.
3. One type of fruit that God wants to grow in us is that of "long-suffering". Not short-suffering. He wants to develop in us the capacity to endure long periods of hardship so that we keep maturing and being equipped to help others who may be suffering-long around us now or later. (Gal. 5:22-23; II Cor. 1:3-4)

For Prayer Today
- In prayer, do not hesitate to get real with your Heavenly Father and share your feelings and fears with Him. But do so in faith, trusting Him to care for you.
- Pray for others you know who have been suffering for a long time that God will accomplish His purposes for them and also give them strength and courage for each day.
- Pray that God will use you to encourage some of these long-term sufferers.

Personal Notes and Responses

Music 101

"Praise ye the LORD. Praise God in His sanctuary: praise Him in the firmament of his power. Praise him for his mighty acts; praise him according to his excellent greatness. Praise him with the sound of the trumpet: praise him with the psaltery and harp..." (Psalm 150:1-3)

Have you ever wondered where music came from and who started humming or singing first, figuring out the chromatic scale (which is totally beyond me), etc.? God, being the creator of all, must be credited with music's creation, as well. Apparently, there was music in heaven (Ezekiel 28:13) and when God created man in His image, He graced man with the ability to hear distinctive notes and tones, and gave him vocal chords that could express musical sounds and a mind that could develop and play various instruments.

Music played an important role in the dedication of the temple and in all the worship of God that took place there (I Chron. 25:1-7; II Chron. 5:11-14). The biblical David was not just a shepherd, warrior, king, and fugitive, but he was also a musician who made musical instruments, especially harps and psalteries, (I Chron. 23:5) and wrote songs (many of the Psalms, Israel's hymn book) that were sung at times of worship, individual and corporate. Solomon also wrote over 1,000 songs (I Kings 4:30-32). And, in the New Testament we are told that one evidence of being under the control of the Spirit of God is that we would be "Speaking to yourselves in psalms and hymns and spiritual songs, singing and making melody in your heart to the Lord" (Eph. 5:19). God is a God of music and He appreciates musical forms and expressions of worship.

I call to your attention one episode in musician David's life. King Saul was often troubled with depression, dark moods, and evil spirits. He learned of the excellence of David's musical abilities and called on this young man to play his harp for the king. And, on several occasions, David's music was effective in soothing and calming the king (I Sam. 16:14-23). (Now, music is not a total cure-all for, twice David had to dodge javelins that were hurled at him (due to Saul's jealous anger and bitterness toward him). But we all know how effective music can be in affecting our moods and attitudes.

So, are you using music in your home during this stressful time? May I suggest that you use, not just our pop-culture's newest and wildest pieces, but try playing some worshipful sacred music, some light classical music, some Sousa-style band music, etc. If you are a couple or have children, sing some hymns and gospel songs together, learn and play instruments together, learn the words of a few favorite hymns, etc. Don't live in a dreary silence or with a televised, chaotic noise. Fill your home with great music and let it encourage your heart.

Early on Easter morning, since we are not permitted here yet to gather others for any purpose, Debra and I got up early, went a short distance to a beautiful overlook and in the semi-darkness had our own Sunrise Service, singing several hymns together, reading Scripture, and praying together. A very cold but precious time. Even the birds joined us in song!

Do not ignore the God-given resource of playing, singing, or listening to uplifting and God-honoring music during these stressful seasons. And, don't throw any javelins at anyone.

For Prayer Today
- Sing your praises and requests to God today. Use hymns or gospel songs that you can personally and honestly express to God. He will be pleased and honored.
- Pray for many others who may be living in lonely silence (or noise). Ask God to give them special joy through music. Perhaps contact them and suggest such.

Personal Notes and Responses

Have Your "Needs" Changed?

"But my God shall supply all your need according to His riches in glory by Christ Jesus." (Phil. 4:19)

I am remembering an old Disney movie in which the Don Knotts' character is wandering aimlessly through a hot, barren desert weakly crying out *"Water...I need water,"* when he sees up ahead an oasis and eagerly staggers toward it and upon reaching a pool of water, throws himself into this mirage and lands solidly on hardened, dusty earth. Upward he struggles and begins moving again for quite some distance, crying out *"Water...I...need...water!"* Once again, he finds what he thinks is a pool of clear, refreshing water, dives into it only to find it the hot and dry desert floor. He starts out again continuing his cry, *"Water...I...need...water"* and this time finds another such scene, but he isn't going to be fooled this time and begins to just stride through it but splashes down into a real pool of water. Moments later he surfaces, gagging and gasping and crying out, *"Air!...I...need...Air!"*

So, have your needs changed in light of this virus? (Maybe not quite as dramatically as Don's did.) Are you discovering that much that you had highly valued as your needs, you suddenly can indeed do without? We often have been guilty of mixing up our real needs with our wants. Sometimes those pleasures and treasures become even much more important. We invest so much time, money, and effort into them, we depend on them, we love and value them, and may admit that they have almost become gods to us as we have built our lives around them.

A missionary friend of ours wrote recently that, perhaps this virus and its effects on us all "...is revealing our... addiction to comfort and control and is exposing what is really in our soul. Maybe it is exposing the gods we (really) worship: our health, our hurry, and our security. Now that the Lord has removed many of the attractions and distractions that once replaced Him in our lives, may we take this time to humble ourselves, pray, and seek His face. God is more than enough and all that we need."

From the verse above, for the believer, God does know our real needs and has promised to provide for them "by Christ Jesus". Our greatest need is to know and trust Him.

Another powerful passage on this is Hebrews 13:5. "Let your conversation be without covetousness; and be content with such things as ye have. For he hath said, 'I will never leave thee, nor forsake thee.'"

So, have you been recognizing a change in your value system? Are you discovering new values and treasures that may be of far greater worth than many of the things we are now forced to do without? Do you know what your real needs are? Are you trusting the Lord to provide them through your personal relationship with Him?

For Prayer Today
- Ask God to help you examine your own heart to help discover your true value system. Is your life all about sports, politics, pride, food, your job, pleasure, money, etc.? Are you coveting, chafing, craving, or complaining about what you no longer can do?
- Ask God to reveal to you the greater valuables that you have around you in your family, your faith, and your friends.

Personal Notes and Responses

The Love of God

"...that Christ may dwell in your hearts by faith; that ye, being rooted and grounded in love, may be able to comprehend with all saints what is the breadth, and length, and depth, and height; and to know the love of Christ, which passeth knowledge..." (Ephesians 3:17-19)

Sometimes when troubles come and stay, when repeated disappointments discourage us, when our goals and interests continue to be thwarted, we may begin to question the love of God. "If God really loved me, He would do this or that. If God really loved me, He wouldn't have allowed this or that to happen to me."

The Bible makes clear that "God is love." (I John 4:7-8) Let's notice several things about this truth.

1. We are to **Receive and Grow in God's Love**. (Romans 5:8; 6:23; John 3:16) We are to understand that even as sinners, God's love reaches out to us with the offer of His gift of salvation through Christ. When we believe in Christ as Savior, we then receive His love gift of eternal salvation and His love begins to grow in us. (Gal. 5:22-23)

2. We are to be **Rooted and Grounded in God's Love** (Eph. 3:17-19) This speaks of a gradual but deepening grounding in knowing and appreciating God's love for us. We are to discover that His love is infinite, expansive, and exceedingly personal and practical. It is beyond our full understanding, even as Paul prays that we will grasp the dimensions of it, its width, length, depth, and height. We are to be progressing in knowing the unknowable. Wow! Such knowledge should become foundational, as a deep root system in our lives keeping us strong and steady, even and especially during the fiercest storms of life.

3. We are to be **Resting in and Re-Gifting God's Love to others.** (I John 3:16-18; 4:11-12) Trusting in God's love

can drive away our fears and anxieties. (I John 4:16-21; II Tim. 1:7-8). That can then free us up to focus on others and their needs as we try to love them in practical ways with God's special kind of over-the-top brand of love.

From my teenage years to this present day, my favorite gospel song is still "The Love of God". I can still hardly read or sing the third stanza without being overwhelmed and moved toward tears as I think about these words.

> "Could we with ink the oceans fill and
> were the skies of parchment made.
> Were every stalk on earth a quill
> And every man a scribe by trade.
> To write the love of God above
> Would drain the oceans dry.
> Nor could the scroll contain the whole
> Though stretched from sky to sky."

I believe the author of this song, F.M. Lehman (1917), may have been meditating on Eph. 3:17-19. Let's do the same.

For Prayer Today

- As you think through this Eph. 3 text again, express your thanksgiving to God for loving you and caring for you, even in these troubled times. Confess any doubt you may have had about this and trust Him to stabilize you through these and any future storms of life.
- Ask God to help you take some of His love and express it to those closest to you and to some who are farther away. Ask Him to help you guide your family or friends creatively to do the same.

Personal Notes and Responses

I Don't Like Change!

"Therefore if any man be in Christ, he is a new creature; old things are passed away; behold all things are become new." (II Cor. 5:17)

I really don't. I mean, I'm ok with small change, loose change, if you will, and I do change my clothes rather often. But that's about it. Our furniture never moves from where we originally placed it. I order the same favorite item in most restaurants every time. When my shoes wear out, I wear them into the shoe store and almost demand another pair of the exact same color and style.

I've always been a little suspicious of those folks who seem to need to change almost everything all the time. Like there is something innately wrong with them, some radical condition that welcomes flexible superficiality but will eventually lead them into emptiness and despair. In contrast, being content with no or little change in one's life, for me, comfortably fits in with predictability, confidence, stability, organization and, of course, maturity. Someone once said "Come weal or woe, my status is quo", and I'm ok with that.

BUT, as I've discovered over the years, God is into change. Really. Big time. Check out the verse at the top again and note that when we trust Christ as Savior, God immediately makes us something brand new – a new creation and then He starts us on a path where the old will disappear and all will become new. Wow!

In II Cor. 3:18 we read, "But we all, with open face beholding as in a glass the glory of the Lord, are changed into the same image from glory to glory, even as by the Spirit of the Lord." As we study His Word and live in light of it, He will be transforming our heart and life to be more and more like Jesus Christ. That's what spiritual growth is all about. It is about change; a gradual and total inward and outward make-over.

One of the clear evidences that a person is genuinely a Christian is that God has made some changes in their lives, their attitudes, priorities, appetites, etc. If you claim that you are saved but you keep living exactly like you did before your decision, then you might question the validity of your decision. God changes His children. He grows and matures them. He accepts them as they are when they come to Him but He will not let them stay in that condition. He will bring lots of changes into their character and lifestyle.

So, where might God be wanting to change some things in your life right now? We are living in a dramatically changed world presently and for people like me, it's quite a ride when everything is so different. Many of us have time on our hands to consider what God may want to do with us. Is there anything in your life that should change to make you more and more like your Savior? God wants to change you. Welcome and cooperate with His wonderful work in doing so. You will bring glory to God and good to others as they more and more see Christ in you.

For Prayer Today
-   Ask God to point out any areas of your life that need to change. As He brings things to mind, ask for wisdom and help in cooperating with His desires in your life.

Personal Notes and Responses

ETERNAL ENCOURAGEMENTS #14

Used, Abused, and Confused

"He healeth the broken in heart, and bindeth up their wounds."
(Psalm 147:3) "...because the LORD hath anointed me to preach
good tidings unto the meek; he hath sent Me to bind up the bro-
kenhearted, to proclaim liberty to the captives, and the opening
of the prison to them that are bound...to comfort all that mourn...
to give unto them beauty for ashes, the oil of joy for mourning,
the garment of praise for the spirit of heaviness...that he might be
glorified." (Isaiah 61:1-3)

The woman, Hagar, is a sad representative of our title today, unfortunately as are so many men, women, and children today.

Hagar's story in Scripture begins in Genesis 12:10-16 when
Abraham and Sarai ran to Egypt during a famine in their own
land. I believe that Hagar joined their family at that time as a servant. Next, we find her being used as a "surrogate" mother as once
again, Ab and Sarai couldn't trust God's timetable to give them the
promised male heir. Soon after Ishmael was conceived, tensions
and strife filled the household between all three adults and at one
point, after being harshly dealt with, Hagar flees into the wilderness in despair. Later she returns to their home. (Genesis 16:1-16).

Maybe 15+ years later, the issues are rekindled again as Isaac is
born of Abram and Sarah (17:15), as God had promised, and the
two brothers find themselves in conflict. Sarah, once again erupts
in anger and bitterness and this time orders her husband to cast
Hagar and her son out of the household for good. Into the wilderness they go again, this time with a mother's loss of hope that her
young son will live very long. (Gen. 21:1-21)

I realize that these are just two snapshots of her life, but the
truths that she learned during them can be helpfully encouraging
for us today.

In the first episode as God "finds her" in her wilderness valley, she learns that "Thou art the God that seeth me" and basically grants Him that new name. She realized that **God is alive and sees and knows** what she was going through (16:6-16). Years later as they were banished from the security of the home, while totally broken-hearted and believing that Ishmael would soon die, as she distanced herself from his cries, she learned that **God also hears and responds** to those in desperate need (21:15-21) with promises and provisions.

I've read and been told by authorities who know that during this intense season of house-bound relationships, loss of jobs, increasing tensions, etc. that domestic violence and abusive activities are on a precipitous rise. Those who are addicted to substances or sinful distractions are taking their personal crises out on anyone in the household within reach. These situations are devastatingly serious – and criminal.

If you find yourself in these circumstances, please know that God sees and knows your situation. Maybe others don't know, but He does. Then cry out to Him often, even audibly, plead for His protection, provision, and wisdom. Ask Him to intervene. Then call on any appropriate legal authorities who are available to help you in these crises. (Police, Hospitals, Help-Lines for addictions, suicide, etc.) God does care for you and has placed helpful resources around you. Ask Him for guidance in your next steps.

For Prayer Today
- Pray fervently and often for those who find themselves in abusive and dangerous situations, including children (Matt. 18:1-1), for their protection and for adequate help for these crises. Ask for God's specific intervention and involvement in "healing the broken-hearted and binding up their wounds."
- Pray for the addicted and the abusers that they will be humbled and will cry out to God for help. Pray for religious leaders in each area to be called on that they might be helpful in leading these sin-sick and broken people to come to Christ

and to be delivered from their sinful lifestyle. Where needed, pray for justice to be done.

Personal Notes and Responses

The Winter Coat Episode

"Therefore take no thought, saying, What shall we eat? or What shall we drink? or Wherewithal shall we be clothed? (For after all these things do the Gentiles seek:) for your heavenly Father knoweth that ye have need of all these things. But seek ye first the kingdom of God, and his righteousness; and all these things shall be added unto you." (Matthew 6:31-33)

It all started when I was probably around 8 or 9. We had just finished dinner and, as was our family custom, dad read a portion from the Bible, a page from "Our Daily Bread," and then got ready to lead us in prayer. He first inquired, "Is there anything we should be praying about?" Mother replied that she needed a new winter coat. A few minutes later, dad's usually long-winded prayer was loudly interrupted by someone pounding on our back door. Upon opening the door to a neighbor, whose first words were, "Anna Mae, can you use a new winter coat?", I sensed my whole being just freeze in place as she presented mother with a brand new coat. How could this be? Is this a miracle or something? I was shocked and totally mesmerized by it.

Does God really do this kind of thing? Think about what He went through that day, first getting that woman to go shopping (probably not that hard at all). But then to get her to notice and purchase a beautiful coat, get her home and suddenly prompt her to give it away, to drop her other bags inside her door, run across the yard, through the hedge and up to our door in time to interrupt dad's prayer with God's quick provision – incredible! Just a coincidence? No way! But in the following years I came to realize that God just wasn't providing some needed winter-wear for my mother; he was changing a little boy's life!

About 5th grade I began to sense a call to the ministry and then as a teen I kept wondering if God could and would do the same kind of thing for me. How would I afford Bible College and all the necessities of life? I knew all the Bible stories about God miraculously providing for His people. But that was so long ago. What about me today? Repeatedly came to my mind mother's coat story.

As a teen I began to study all that the Bible says about money and read so many missionary stories of how God provided faithfully for them. I read books on finances by Christian authors who clarified and illustrated what God wants to do for His children who walk with Him. It became one of my favorite truths of the Bible and I have preached and taught and written about it for over 40 years. And now Debra and I have dozens of personal encouraging and entertaining stories about how God has abundantly provided for us over these years.

In these days in which our national and local economies are being weakened and seriously threatened, when employment status for so many is uncertain or has already been curtailed or lost, as national, corporate, and personal debt is overwhelming, my believing friend, do not worry. If you have trusted Christ for your eternity, you can also trust Him for your needs here and now. Please read Matthew 6:19-34 and be encouraged about what you see there. Your Savior promises to provide all our basic needs as we put Him and His kingdom first in our lives. And I know that He is really good at doing so!

For Prayer Today
- If you have a personal relationship with Christ, I strongly urge you to gather your immediate family together often and pray together for whatever your specific needs might be at that time. Ask God for His wisdom, His provision, and His daily care. Let your children and grandchildren in on these prayer times and rejoice together as God responds. (I am so glad that I was "at the table" that night!

Personal Notes and Responses

That Bitter Weed

"Follow peace with all men, and holiness...looking diligently... lest any root of bitterness springing up trouble you, and thereby many be defiled..." (Hebrews 12:14-15) "Let all bitterness, and wrath, and anger, and clamor, and evil speaking, be put away from you, with all malice..." (Ephesians 4:31-32)

Some of my worst times of sadness and discouragements throughout about 50 years of ministry have been the all-too-frequent discovery of people who claim to know Christ but who are no longer attending any church and are not outwardly serving Him. Like a doctor who can readily diagnose a patient after seeing thousands with identical symptoms, and after listening to their stories, I became quick to discern that their heart's garden had become choked with weeds, the deep taproots of bitterness. The problem was complicated by whenever I'd get close to using that "B" word, they would usually flare up in anger and loudly deny that they were bitter. Like a physician's patients who don't want to hear that "C" word out of fear, these people react deeply to the "B" word out of defensive anger. Often, they would then reject any further attempt by me to help them.

This is so tragic. When their hearts should be flourishing with beautiful, heaven-grown love, joy, peace, patience (with people and circumstances), gentleness, goodness, faith, humility, and self-control, we find disgustingly dry stalks of selfishness, defensive suspicion and distrust, anger, resentment, pride, and resistance to the Spirit of God.

What is bitterness and how does it sprout and grow? Often the seed is planted when someone is hurt, wronged, or disappointed by another. But the recipient, instead of ignoring, forgiving, or fixing the slight responds with anger, often boiling up on the inside. Over time, by continually stirring up the memory of it and by telling others of the injustice with gossipy attempts for sympathy, they too become defiled by this sinful attitude. Such anger continues to build and may be expressed in many ways (see Eph. 4:31) but it ultimately results in cold bitterness against the person, a hardening of the "hearteries" toward others, maybe even all Christians, and a withdrawal from church and service for the Lord.

Read again the verses at the beginning of this piece. God expects that every form of anger, every stage of bitterness be rooted out of our lives so that we can return to the full experience of God's grace and spiritual health. Emotional or psychological weed whackers won't do the job; this process must dig deep. In our next devotional we'll see exactly how this can be accomplished. Read ahead one verse to see the answer now in Eph. 4:32.

But for today, how is the garden of your heart? Are you angry or bitter about how anyone has treated you? Are you resentful and stirring up malice toward someone? Are you avoiding family members or fellow Christians, etc. because of this bitter root in your heart?

For Prayer Today
- If God has revealed or reminded you of harboring and growing such wrong attitudes toward others, please confess those attitudes to God as sin and claim His cleansing and forgiveness. (I John 1:9)
- Ask Him next to reveal to you how your stinky weeds have affected others. Ask His help in going to these people with sincere apologies. Then ask God to help you to take the next step – to forgive those difficult people of the wrongs they have done to you.

Personal Notes and Responses

The Freedom of Forgiveness

"Let all bitterness, and wrath, and anger, and clamor, and evil speaking, be put away from you, with all malice: And be ye kind one to another, tenderhearted, forgiving one another, even as God for Christ's sake hath forgiven you." (Eph. 4:31-32) "...But if ye forgive not men their trespasses, neither will your Father forgive your trespasses." (Matt. 6:14-15)

In our previous devotional we saw how devastating the root of bitterness can be in our hearts and how it gets there. Someone has said that living with resentful anger and bitterness toward someone is like carrying around in your pocket a flask filled with deadly poison. Then, every time you remember or cross paths with the object of your anger, you take out the flask and take a swig of its contents, while smugly hoping that it will do that other person serious injury. But the reality of it is that it is only killing you, one deadly sip at a time.

So how do we root out this bitter weed? There is only one sufficient way. It is the way of forgiveness. You must first confess this sinful attitude you've harbored to God and gain His forgiveness. Then, with His help you must forgive the one who hurt you. This generally involves three steps.

1. Forgiveness involves **the removal** of the offense between you. With your will you must remove it; choose to throw it out of the way. Don't let it remain between you and your offender any longer. Don't wait for them to apologize. Don't wait till you feel like doing this. Your emotions may take some time to catch up with your obedience to God about this but just do so.

2. Forgiveness then involves **the refusal** to ever bring it up again. Promise not to hold it over their head again, not to refer to it or remind them or anyone else of it.

3. Forgiveness then allows for **the renewal** of the relationship. What was once broken can now be made whole. This is not always possible; maybe the person has died or perhaps resists getting close again. But a sincere attempt should be made. As the renewed relationship grows over time, the old offense may slowly fade from our memories.

Forgiveness doesn't mean you will forget the offense but it will free you from its control over you. Forgiveness may allow you to focus on the victory over the offense and rejoice over it. Forgiveness does not mean that the offender may get away with any wrong behavior. If that person does not confess it as sin, God will still hold him accountable for it and will bring justice to bear on him. Trust God to handle it. Genuine forgiveness on your part will restore fellowship with God and allow His wonderful fruit, His love, joy, peace, etc. to sprout and grow in your heart. The coldness will melt; the hardness will soften; your compassion for others will expand; your awareness of what God can do will be shared with others for their benefit. Your garden will be weeded; your spiritual health will be whole again. Your joy will be full.

The greatest reason why we should be quick to forgive others is that through what Jesus did on the cross for us, **God has forgiven us everything** when we trusted Christ as our Savior (Eph. 4:32). How in the world should we think that we should withhold forgiveness from someone else who has slighted us? Please read the story that illustrates this truth in Matt. 18:21-35. Do you want to experience God's torturers? (18:34-35)

Do you really want to spend the rest of your life in misery and anger, sipping the poison of that bitter weed? Really? Forgiveness is the way to really live, my friend.

For Prayer Today
- Thank God for His very generous forgiveness of all your sins through Jesus Christ.
- Ask Him to help you be generous and quick to forgive those who hurt you.

- Ask God to help you teach your children and grandchildren how to handle the hurts of others and the meaning and importance of forgiveness.

Personal Notes and Responses

ETERNAL ENCOURAGEMENTS #18

He That Has a Hearing Aid to Hear, Let Him Hear!

"So then faith cometh by hearing, and hearing by the word of God. For whosoever shall call upon the name of the Lord shall be saved. How then shall they call on Him in whom they have not believed? and how shall they believe in him of whom they have not heard? and how shall they hear without a preacher?" (Rom. 10:17, 13-15) "Verily, verily, I say unto you, He that heareth my word and believeth on him that sent me, hath everlasting life, and shall not come into condemnation; but is passed from death unto life." (John 5:24)

My limited experience with hearing aids goes back quite a long time. When I was teaching in a Christian school in the 1970's I had a 5th grade student with a speech impediment due to her severe loss of hearing. She would show up at my desk every couple of days to get new batteries for her hearing aid which I kept stored there for her.

In recent years in my nursing home ministry, I have frequently dealt with people who needed them but weren't using them, had forgotten them, had them turned off, claimed to have lost them or had them stolen, broke them, needed fresh batteries, etc. Upon request, I've rooted in trash cans and dresser drawers for them, crawled under some beds to retrieve them, very gingerly reached through some blankets and spreads for them, etc. Yes, I've even been asked to help insert them into someone's ear. I tried on two occasions, but brushing aside some woman's hair to insert something the right way into her ear carefully so nothing is forced out the other side, I'm sorry, I just couldn't bring myself to do it. (I wanted to say, "Just call an aide. I think that's why they are called that. They've had a lot of experience with hearing aids!")

But in my years of ministry I have learned about the ultimate importance of hearing. When it comes to spiritual issues, to eternal matters, the ability to hear is vital. Worldwide, man cannot be saved without hearing the gospel message that Christ died for their sins and that trusting in Him is the only way of salvation. Actually, when the gospel is communicated, saving faith can be generated in the soul of the hearer, helping them to understand and to believe the gospel. This is why Christ commissioned His followers to go to every nation on earth to proclaim that important message.

Unfortunately, there are so many who choose not to hear it, who rejected this wonderful message even in Jesus' day as He said, "... for this people's heart is waxed gross, and their ears are dull of hearing, and their eyes they have closed; lest at any time they should see with their eyes, and hear with their ears, and should understand with their heart, and should be converted, and I should heal them." (Matt. 13:13-15) Then He said, "But blessed are your eyes, for they see: and your ears, for they hear." (13:16)

Are you among those who eagerly welcome the hearing of the Word of God and are tuning in often to the preaching, teaching, and reading of God's Word?

Are you among those who are helping others around you or others far away on some mission field to hear clearly God's truth that brings salvation and blessing to all?

"He that hath an ear, let him hear what the Spirit saith unto the churches." (Rev. 2:7, 11, 17, 29; 3:6, 13, 22)

For Prayer Today
- Ask God today to open the spiritual ears of people who need to hear and understand the gospel. Pray for missionaries all over the globe who are trying to share this message with others.
- Pray for the many preachers and pastors whose messages are going out to many people daily through radio, TV, the

internet, that their voices will be heard by many who will then turn to Christ.

Personal Notes and Responses

"When My Heart is Overwhelmed..."

"Hear my cry, O God; attend unto my prayer. From the end of the earth will I cry unto thee, when my heart is overwhelmed: lead me to the rock that is higher than I. For thou hast been a shelter for me, and a strong tower from the enemy. I will abide in thy tabernacle for ever: I will trust in the covert of thy wings." (Psalm 61:1-4)

Life does get overwhelming sometime, doesn't it? We say, "When it rains, it pours" indicating some angst-driven attempt at accepting all this "injustice". We say, "God isn't supposed to give us things we can't handle, but, I don't know, He thinks I can handle more than I think I can!" We say, "I just can't take any more!" as we move toward serious despair.

The Psalmist knew something of those feelings. Please take note of his prayer in Psalm 61. He calls it a "cry"- one of "deep agony". He wasn't just "saying his prayers", he was distressed and desperate. He does the right thing – crying out to God.

1. **Notice the Crises** Behind His Cry (II Sam. 13-18)
    The personal consequences of his adultery with Bathsheba and the murder of her husband play out tragically – one son rapes his sister – another son, Absalom kills the rapist and flees from David – David's baby dies – Absalom and father are painfully estranged from each other for several years – when superficially reunited Absalom steals the kingdom from his father and David and his men have to flee into the wilderness – battles are fought – beloved son Absalom is killed – and David is overwhelmed with grief and sorrow.

2. **Notice the Content** of the Cry (Psalm 61:1-7)
    He cries out to be led higher to his Rock-solid God whom he asks to harbor him, to hide him, and to help him,

desiring protection from his enemies, and daily provision of his needs – all from God's mercy, truth, and grace.

3. **Notice the Confidence** of the Cry (Psalm 61:5-7; I John 5:14-15)

   By faith, David was certain that his cry was being heard and that God would respond to his needs and enable him to continue to carry out his God-given responsibilities for His people.

4. **Notice the Commitments** with the Cry (61:2, 4, 7)

   In light of God's grace, David sees a future for which he makes several promises; he determines to continue to cry to the Lord, to trust Him, to abide in His presence, to sing His praises forever and to daily keep his commitments to serve the Lord.

Overwhelming trials are often used by God to get our attention, to humble us, to position us to look to Him, and to deepen our walk with Him so that He can continue to use us to serve Him and bless people. He is not done with His people. We will continue to serve Him. By His grace, may that be true for all of us.

For Prayer Today

- Are you currently "overwhelmed"? I understand. So does God. Don't hesitate to cry out to the Lord audibly, asking specifically for help, expressing your continue faith in Him, and praising Him for being your God
- Pray the many around you who are very discouraged and possibly moving toward despair, both those who are ill and those who are struggling to care for many others. Our batteries do get drained sometime; we need God's power and grace.

Personal Notes and Responses

Is There a Doctor in the House??

"Luke, the beloved physician, and Demas greet you." (Col. 4:14)
"Only Luke is with me..." (II Tim. 4:11) "There salute thee Epaphras,
my fellow prisoner in Christ Jesus; Marcus, Aristarchus, Demas,
Lucas, my fellow laborers." (Philemon 23- 24)

My wife and I were reading Colossians 4 this morning in our devotional time together and as soon as I read "Luke the beloved physician" in verse 11, I was moved and... well, what followed was this devotional.

Dr. Luke was a Gentile Christian who grew up in and around Antioch. From eyewitness accounts and the inspiration of the Holy Spirit he penned the account of Jesus' earthly life that bears his name. Very soon thereafter he wrote "The Acts of the Apostles", very much a sequel to the former book, detailing much of what God did through His Spirit after Jesus's ascension into heaven. He wrote both tomes to Theophilus, another Gentile friend in order to set in order and to verify the events around Jesus that had been taught.

Most General Practitioners and other levels of medical specialties focus on the well-being of our physical bodies. Interestingly, among the four Gospel writers, Luke says the most about the humanity of Christ, His physical side. Right from the beginning Luke writes about the announcements of the forecasted conceptions of Jesus and of John the Baptist. Then we are told about where Jesus was born, in what He was wrapped, and of His first earthly cradle. He even deals with His circumcision 8 days later. (Makes you wonder if he was an OBGYN.)

Luke goes into more detail than the others describing the medical conditions and durations of the infirmities from which Jesus healed people. He mentions often Jesus' hunger, weariness, etc. And in the book of Acts he traveled with the Apostle Paul during several seasons of his journeys (16:10-17; 20:5-15; 21:1-18; 27:1-28:16), entering into spiritual ministry while possibly tending to Paul's "thorn in the flesh" (II Cor. 12) or possibly the medical needs of others.

We all certainly benefit much from his meticulous and polished two-part account of the ministries of Jesus and then of the Holy Spirit through the apostles. Today all that doctors and nurses must record voluminously on charts and electronically must remain private. Praise God that He used a very attentive and thorough medical doctor to write these accounts that were meant to go public, even global.

Paul apparently deeply appreciated Luke's partnership in the ministry, even his accompanying Paul on some of his risky and dangerous trips. This morning I caught myself wondering if I have ever considered my doctor "beloved" by me.

I don't have the words to express myself on this subject adequately, but we all should recognize the incredibly valuable contribution our medical personnel in every field are making on our behalf in these days. Globally and locally. Their medical challenges have become increasingly complicated as they have boldly stepped up and return to the trenches day and night to do hand-to-hand combat with this unforeseen virus and many other life-threatening conditions. They struggle with exhaustion, fear and anxiety; they deal with all kinds of deeply troubled people, and they feel very personally each loss of life, with each grieving family. They worry about their own family's safety as they come and go daily, etc.

Do we consider any of them "beloved"? I know that Paul and Luke were close friends but our medical heroes need our love, support, and gratitude, as well. Are we providing it?

For Prayer Today
- Pray for the vast numbers of these faithful responders to all medical crises. Then pray specifically for those you know

personally. Ask God to give them rest, wisdom, safety, effectiveness in their work, etc.
- Spend time thanking God for these special people and all the medical resources we have in our country.

Personal Notes and Responses

Getting Old(er)

"LORD, thou hast been our dwelling place in all generations. Before the mountains were brought forth, or ever thou hadst formed the earth and the world, even from everlasting to everlasting, thou art God...The days of our years are threescore years and ten; and if by reason of strength they be fourscore years, yet is their strength labor and sorrow; for it is soon cut off and we fly away." (Psalm 90:1-2, 10)

On this very day, as I write this, I am celebrating my 68th birthday. Under the restrictions from the threat of this virus, here at our retirement community we are not yet permitted to have guests inside our dwellings so, this morning at 7:20 our son showed up with my current favorite breakfast concoction from a local restaurant and we sat, safely distanced, on our front porch, enjoying each other's fellowship – in 32 degrees of temperature! My heart was warmed even more when David's wife and our 3 grandchildren (ages 6, 2, and 1) called to sing "Happy Birthday" to me – Grandpop, Be Bop, or Pop-Pop-De-Doodle-Lop. How special is that?!

Ah, yes, birthdays can be so special but they are also reminders that we are indeed aging and the longer that goes on, the harder things seem to get.

I have for decades called Psalm 90 the "Birthday Psalm" and have read it so many times each year to elderly friends in their homes or in nursing homes on their special day. The Psalm begins acknowledging that no one can know how old God is because He is eternal; He lives from eternity past on throughout eternity future. It then speaks of how tenuous might be our lives as sinners living before this holy God to whom we will have to give an account someday. The uncertainty and brevity of life is mentioned followed by some **specific instructions on how to age well**, how to make our latter years really count, for us and others. Please read the entire Psalm and pay close attention to the last few verses as described below.

We are first instructed to "number our days" (90:12)– to compute them, evaluate them, give account of them, to take them and their diminishing potential seriously so that we might do the following:

1. **Keep learning**. – "Teach us" the value of our days. (90:12) Do not waste the precious days you may have left.
2. **Keep living** out God's wisdom – "that we may apply our hearts unto wisdom". (90:12) Make and follow Godly-wise choices; obey and serve Him.
3. **Keep "laughing"** (my word). – "O satisfy us early with thy mercy; that we may rejoice and be glad all our days. Make us glad…" (not just on our "*Happy* Birthday" but all our days, every one of them). (90:14-15)
4. **Keep leaning** on the Lord – "Make us glad according to the days wherein thou hast afflicted us, and the years wherein we have seen evil". (90:15) Yes, life gets harder but we can trust God to help us and to bless us through it all.
5. **Keep leaving** a legacy, a testimony of the gracious works of God that can impact children and grandchildren "Let thy work appear unto thy servants, and thy glory unto their children" (90:16-17).

As we all age, let's not take the grumpy route. Let's not fill our minds with negative things. Let's draw close to God and keep growing in Him. Let's put His joy and peace on display every day. Let's depend on Him for everything and then let's talk about His great and wondrous works in our lives – to our little ones who may treasure and remember our timely talks with them about the Lord.

For Prayer Today

-   Pray about whatever aches and pains you may have due to getting older, not necessarily that God take them all away, because He might not do that, but that He will help you to handle things by trusting His grace for each day.

- Pray for patience as you may be trying to care for elderly people who are suffering. Ask for extra compassion and love for them and toward them.

Personal Notes and Responses

ETERNAL ENCOURAGEMENTS #22

Passing On the Faith

"And also all that generation were gathered unto their fathers: and there arose another generation after them, which knew not the LORD, nor yet the works which he had done for Israel." (Judges 2:10) "...which he commanded our fathers, that they should make them known to their children: that the generation to come might know them, even the children which should be born who should arise and declare them to their children: that they might set their hope in God, and not forget the works of God, but keep His commandments..." (Psalm 78:5-7; see also 78:1-4)

I have actually no way of measuring these things but I have read several times and been told repeatedly that this present generation of children may very well be the most unchurched and spiritually ignorant generation in the history of the USA. Church leaders, Sunday School teachers, Vacation Bible School workers have been saying that due to broken and scattered families today, not only can they often not determine a child's real name or address, they cannot identify the name or number of "parents" that child has or with whom he may be living on any given day. As a result of this level of brokenness where very few efforts seem to be made to introduce these children to God, these little ones know absolutely nothing about the Bible, who Jesus Christ is, or any of the common Bible stories.

This simply underscores what Judges 2:10 and Psalm 78 report, that each new generation is birthed without a clear knowledge of the true God and they need to be informed about Him, introduced to Him by people who know Him. Without that influence and being totally immersed in a sinfully secular and selfishly driven culture, they will continue to live in a dark world in which they will accept the values of that culture and suffer the consequences of living life apart from God.

Whose responsibility is it to pass on the faith to each new generation? Obviously, it is the job of parents who love the Lord and live by His Word to do so. Occasionally, I will be ministering to grieving believing parents over their teen or adult children's evil choices or lifestyle. They will usually cry to me, "I don't understand; we raised our children in the church and look what happened!" I sometimes say to them with compassion, "Oh, really? I'm so sorry to hear that. You raised them in the church? Oh my, that's not where we are to raise them."

Of course, the church should play an important role in helping parents raise their children but where did we get the idea that 1-3 hours a week in church is the guarantee that a child will "turn out right"? Where is that taught in the Bible? We are to raise our children in the bright light of God's Word in the home, in the family setting. Seven days a week, not 3 hours elsewhere. Even doing this is no guarantee of what decisions our maturing children will make in their lives but the responsibility to lovingly teach them God's Word and to live it out in front of them 24/7 is the responsibility of parents and grandparents. Let's not ever forget this.

In our current world, where sometimes churches are unable to gather groups of children together and minister to them, it is even more important that godly families are doing so. I urge every Christian home to prioritize this in your daily schedule now. Tell them what God has done for you. Have contests of memorizing important Bible verses. Teach them the stories and principles of God's truth. Teach them to pray and pray with them daily about specific matters. Help them to obey God's Word in practical areas. Lead your children to trust Christ, then to love the Lord and others around them daily.

Please don't allow the extra time at home together right now to be all about controlling or entertaining your children. How about passing on the faith as a key objective? You might use Deut. 6:1-9 as a pattern to follow in this important endeavor. Start a new habit and continue it in the years ahead, with eternal hope.

For Prayer Today
- Pray much for the children of our world today to be protected from evil and to have godly adults around them who will teach them about God and the Bible.
- Pray for parents and grandparents to be obedient to this calling in their lives.

Personal Notes and Responses

Guilt and Grief at the Grave

"And when Joseph's brethren saw that their father was dead, they said, Joseph will peradventure hate us, and will certainly requite us all the evil which we did unto him...forgive, I pray thee now, the trespass of thy brethren, and their sin; for they did unto thee evil: and now, we pray thee, forgive the trespass of the servants of the God of thy father. (Gen. 50:15-21) "He that covereth his sins shall not prosper: but whoso confesseth and forsaketh them shall have mercy." (Proverbs 28:13)

After many years of estrangement from his family, God cleverly brings his family together in Egypt. After a hearty reunion, crowned with Joseph's forgiveness of his brothers, he moved his family to be near him in Egypt so that he could generously provide for them (Gen. 45:1-13). His father, Jacob then lived in Egypt for 17 years till he died (Gen. 47:27-31; 50:1-14). Now read again the verses above to see the brother's initial reaction to his death.

Seventeen years after Joseph forgave his brothers and had since then provided continuously for them, they were still haunted by their guilt over what they had done to him and sought, though a bit indirectly, to remedy that.

Personal sin of any kind brings consequences, one of which is this thing called guilt. It is an inward heaviness that reminds us, even judges us for what we have done. It drives friends and families apart. It robs people of sound sleep. It nags at our conscience about the need to make things right. It burdens us with shame and fear and can complicate our lives in many ways as we respond wrongly to it.

Guilt is often in attendance at funerals. Grief is so painful enough. Add years of stale guilt to it, blend it into superficial reunions with estranged relatives, and try to serve it as a side dish at a funeral luncheon and it can spoil all the other food. I have personally officiated at many dozens of funerals where these realities were sadly and obviously present. Lots of guilt-fed regrets are often shared. A bit late.

As the death toll numbers continue to rise astronomically, is there anyone with whom you have serious sin issues that remain unconfessed or unforgiven? Have you accepted the forgiveness of God and others? The process of communicating may be more complicated right now but through whatever method you can use, please seek to make things right with those who need to hear from you. Don't drag guilt to their funeral or yours. Instead come to know now the peace and joy of forgiveness and restoration. Our eternal God can bring you this wonderful encouragement!

For Prayer Today
-   Pray that damaged relationships will be restored during this unique time and that even at times of loss, there will be guilt-free peace and comfort known.
-   Thank the Lord that when we confess our sins to Him that He will always grant forgiveness and cleansing to our lives (I John 1:9).

Personal Notes and Responses

ETERNAL ENCOURAGEMENTS #24

"Good Night. Sleep Tight. Don't Let the Bed Bugs Bite."

"It is vain for you to rise up early, to sit up late, to eat the bread of sorrows: for so he giveth his beloved sleep". (Psalm 127:2) "I will both lay me down in peace and sleep: for thou, LORD, only makest me dwell in safety." (Psalm 4:8)

So, does today's title ring any bells? (Alarm bells maybe.) Parents used to say that to their kids as they settled them into bed at night. Does that invoke pleasant thoughts that could relax anyone's heart? I would have laid awake swatting at those unseen insects or scratching myself raw. It doesn't help at all now that we have magnified images of those ugly critters. None of them were even smiling when their picture was being taken!

Or how about this? Parents had taught children to pray, "Now I lay me down to sleep. I pray the Lord my soul to keep. If I should die before I wake, I pray the Lord my soul to take." "W h a t!!??? You mean I could die tonight!!??..." "Yes, dear. Now let's all sing, "… When the bough breaks, the cradle will fall, down will come baby, cradle and all." Who wrote this stuff?! Lullabies? I don't think so!

Today, long nights of sound sleep for most people are very rare and there are certainly many reasons for it. From the verse above, the phrase "to eat the bread of sorrows" doesn't refer to a heavy, late night snack but to what may be eating you. (See Psalm 6:1-7, esp. vs. 6.)

Let me share a few Scriptural suggestions.
1. Don't try counting sheep. They may be slow but they all look alike. It's really hard to keep track of them. Instead, talk to the Shepherd, praising Him for all that He is and talking about your troubles as David did in Psalm 3:1-6. Verse 5 says "I laid me down and slept; I awaked; for the

LORD sustained me. I will not be afraid..." Commit to God all that is on your heart nightly.

2. As you recline for the night, talk to yourself, examine your own heart and do any needed business with God "...and be still." (Psalm 4:4)

3. Do not carry anger into bed with you. Try to settle things, if you can, before sundown. Apologize or forgive. (Psalm 4:4; Eph. 4:26-32)

One night Daniel didn't find himself confined among microscopic bedbugs but among large, hungry lions. I think he slept well because He trusted in God but the one who put him there was in sleepless agony all night. (Daniel 6:16-18) And that's your bedtime story for tonight. Sleep well, my friends. ZZZzzzzzzzzzzz.

For Prayer Today

- Let's pray for the many who are exhausted from their labors and problems or who are frightened by their circumstances, that they will find good rest by trusting in the Lord.

Personal Notes and Responses

_____

ETERNAL ENCOURAGEMENTS #25

"Crowd Control"

"And Jesus went about all the cities and villages, teaching in their synagogues, and preaching the gospel of the kingdom, and healing every sickness and every disease among the people. But when he saw the multitudes, he was moved with compassion on them because they fainted, and were scattered abroad, as sheep having no shepherd..." (Matthew 9:35-38)

During these days here in Ohio, as our state authorities have been reopening the business establishments and restaurants gradually. Suddenly, the ghost towns of Walnut Creek and Berlin near us were repopulated with "newly freed" numbers of people eager to resume some semblance of normality in their lives.

"Crowd control" is now a growing concern of the authorities who are yet seeking to prevent the further spread of this virus. We hear daily of the need for continued social distancing in establishments, controlled pacing of movements of people, folks waiting outside till the store's number of customers drops below the limit, long, slow lines at drive-thru's (DQ especially!), etc. But as people return in droves, such crowd control becomes quite a challenge.

But sometimes I struggle with another type of "crowd control". And every time I read the extended passage above, I am convicted of my lack of "self-control" whenever I see a crowd. I confess that, all too often, when I see a crowd of people who are in my way, ahead of me, and slowing me down, I am moved in my spirit also; I can be deeply stirred with irritation, frustration, impatience, or a critical attitude. Sometimes, even a DQ Blizzard can't cool me down! And that's bad!

Then I read that when Jesus saw the crowds, He was deeply moved with... compassion! And I feel so guilty. He responded with tender care because He really knew their great needs. They were weary, scattered, and without a shepherd. Verse 35 tells us He also cared enough to address their medical needs.

Let me just challenge us all. When we are confronted with multitudes of people around us, let's recognize that some of them are heavily burdened and very weary of life and its challenges. Some are experiencing serious brokenness. Some have lost loved ones, some feel hopeless, some are battling illnesses, and many are anxious and fearful. Some need to know our Savior. Let's think that way about people around us; let's pray that way for them; let's respond as Jesus did.

For Prayer Today
- Specifically ask God to give you the "eyes of Christ" through which you can see and be moved by the real needs of people in today's world.
- Ask God to bring some needy people across your path that you might pray for them or provide some measure of witness and practical love for them.

Personal Notes and Responses

ETERNAL ENCOURAGEMENTS #26

So, How are You Handling Life?

"Fret not thyself because of evildoers...Trust in the LORD, and do good...Delight thyself also in the LORD...Commit thy way unto the LORD; trust also in him...Rest in the LORD, and wait patiently for him...Fret not thyself in any wise to do evil." (Psalm 37:1-8)

This is such a uniquely challenging time in our lives, one we will forever remember and talk about to our grandchildren and their children, certainly. But what will we tell them when they wonder how we handled it all, about how we survived it?

Will our testimony be full of our worries and fears, our sleepless nights, our impatience and irritable anger with one another, our diatribes against our government? Will we trumpet to them our grandiose schemes and plans and how we toughed it out on our own? How we bravely won some toilet paper victories and such? Big tough guys that we were!

How should we be handling life? What different stories could we tell?

In these early verses of Psalm 37 we find instruction about how life is to be handled. Notice what God recommends here, what He commands.

1. We are to FRET NOT. – We are not to go through life with a troubled, displeased, agitated, envious or angry attitude. (Psalm 37:1-2, 8)
2. We are to FAITH IT. (37:3-7) How do we do that?
   a. Trust in the Lord. – to rely on Him, to depend on Him with all of life and then to invest in doing good instead of evil. (37:3, 8) Praying always.
   b. Delight in the Lord. – Enjoy your relationship with God. Love and worship Him. Honor, obey, and serve Him with joy. Enjoy the pleasure of bringing Him delight.

c.   Commit thy way to the Lord. – Roll your hopes and plans over on to Him, your agenda, your schedule, your responsibilities, everything daily.

d.   Rest in the Lord and wait patiently for Him. We cannot know real rest and peace until we trust, delight, and commit to Him everything.

Did you notice who is featured in this passage? It isn't you or me, or even others; it is the Lord, our wonderful and loving Savior who wants to care for us. Let's build our daily lives around Him and rest in His gracious love and care. Then, in the future we can talk of all His faithful caring provision and help throughout this time and we can direct our little ones to trust the Lord with their daily lives, as well.

For Prayer Today
-   Tell the Lord everything that is on your heart, turn it over to Him, asking that His will and wisdom be done in your life situations today. Do so with any family you might have with you, as well.
-   Rejoice in God's goodness to you today and rest in knowing that His care of you and your circumstances will continue through the night into tomorrow.

Personal Notes and Responses

Benefits of Trusting the Lord with Your Life

"The steps of a good man are ordered by the LORD: and he delighteth in his way. Though he fall, he shall not be utterly cast down; for the LORD upholdeth him with his hand. I have been young, and now am old; yet have I not seen the righteous forsaken, nor his seed begging bread...For the LORD loveth judgment, and forsaketh not his saints; they are preserved for ever..."(Psalm 37:23-28)

This is a follow-up of our previous devotional in which we were instructed to make the Lord the center of our lives, trusting Him, loving Him, committing our plans to Him, and resting in Him. If this sounds a bit much to you, you may be asking, "What's in it for me? What will all this religious sounding advice really accomplish for me and my family?"

From that same Psalm (37) come the words quoted above. It just scratches the surface of all the blessings we receive when we trust Christ as our Savior and then walk with God. But summarized, we can say that it introduces us to a very personal relationship with a loving God who has a plan for us and desires to care for us throughout life and eternity. Among other things, we can discover practically these four truths which are found in the verses above.

1. **God's Guidance is Intentional** (37:23, 31) We discover that God has a plan for our lives and we experience His daily direction and wisdom for our path, far better than any GPS device. He orders, guides, and enables us to know and do His will, fulfilling His purposes for us. Tremendous reasons to live!

2. **God's Grip is Powerful** (37:24-25, 28) He will not abandon us even when we fall; He holds us tightly by His hand from which no one can remove us. We are kept

saved and securely held by His power and He will get us safely Home. (John 10:28-30; I Peter 1:3-5; Jude 24) That's incredible security!

3. **God's Grace is Provisional** (37:25-26; II Cor. 9:8) This continues to be so incredible to me; God desires and has the ability to meet all our needs. As our Father, He loves to provide good things for His children (Matt. 7:7-11).

4. **God's Guarantees are Eternal** (37:27-29) No "Warranty Expiration" calls or emails will ever come from God. What He has promised and provided for us will be true forever! God isn't just "Ever-Ready" but "Forever-Ready" to follow through on His promises.

As I look back over 68 years of my life, I can thoroughly "vouch" for these wonderful realities and for so much more. I am so very grateful!

For Prayer Today

- If you have never yet repented of your sin and placed your trust in Jesus Christ to save you, please consider doing so today. Don't continue trying to go through life without Him as your Savior and Lord.
- Thank God for the truths about Him you've read today. Worship Him as the wonderful God that He is. Then trust Him with every detail of your life, daily.

Personal Notes and Responses

ETERNAL ENCOURAGEMENTS #28

Chester the Cricket

*"Remember now thy Creator...while the evil days come not...and
the grinders cease because they are few...and he shall rise up at
the voice of the bird...also when they shall be afraid of that which
is high...and the almond tree shall flourish, and the grasshopper
shall be a burden, and desire shall fail...and the mourners go
about the streets." (Eccl. 12:1-6)*

Many years ago, as a pastor I was helping to care for a very elderly
church member who had just lost her husband. In her rather fresh
grief, she began to tell some friends that God had provided her
with a new friend she called Chester. Some of us reacted with concern over such a declaration; it was certainly too soon and rather
suspicious. Moments later she'd tell people that Chester was actually a cricket that found its way into her apartment and when
she'd hear his chirping, she would talk back to it. Though she
could never actually find where it was hiding, she was enjoying
his companionship.

One day when visiting her I heard Chester and tried to locate
for her his secretive location. Moments later I had to comically
inform her that what she was hearing was actually her smoke
detector chirping as its battery power had run down. The dear lady
was mature enough that we both laughed ourselves silly over it
and Chester's story still lives on (especially since I've just resur-
rected it). Adding fresh batteries effectively killed him off, but her
grieving his demise was comparatively brief.

I just thought of Chester again last week as I was reading
Ecclesiastes 12, including Solomon's poetic and somewhat
humorous description of old age. He describes how our limbs
weaken and shake, how we walk stooped over, how chewing is
difficult with fewer teeth, how our eyesight dims, our hearing

diminishes , our appetites lessen, our hair turns white, our fears multiply, and even insects can become a burden to us.

Why does he mention all of that? Well, he begins the chapter with "Remember now thy Creator in the days of your youth..." before we get older and time is running out. He continues the warning in verse 6 "... or ever the silver cord be loosed, or the golden bowl be broken...then shall the dust return to the earth as it was..."

Whether you are still "youthy" or elderly or somewhere between the two, it is most important to build your life around knowing your Creator personally and living for Him. Like Solomon, I urge you to do so.

And, whenever you hear or see a cricket, may the reminder of our imaginary friend, Chester, put a smile on your face!

For Prayer Today
If you are seriously struggling with any of the older-age matters that Solomon addressed in this passage, ask God to help you with those needs or to provide someone who can bring some aid your way.

Personal Notes and Responses

Lonely Grief

"And Ruth said, Intreat me not to leave thee, or to return from following after thee: for whither thou goest, I will go; and where thou lodgest, I will lodge: thy people shall be my people, and thy God my God: where thou diest, will I die, and there will I be buried: the LORD do so to me, and more also, if ought but death part thee and me." (Ruth 1:16-17)

So very many people today are deeply grieving losses of family members, homes, jobs, pets, wealth, losses of health or independence, mental clarity, contact with others, etc. Such painful shocks to one's mental and emotional well-being cut deeply and often last a long time. Complicating the "recovery" is that remaining survivors often desire solitude and loneliness and yet are in great need of help and support from God and others nearby. Suppressing their grief can do them much harm. Sharing it with others who care can be very beneficial.

Though we do need to show appropriate respect for a person's privacy and their desires early on, we must realize that the grieving person desperately needs some frequent, even if brief, interaction **with** caring friends who know the Lord.

Romans 12:15 says, "Rejoice **with them** that do rejoice, and weep **with them** that weep." And "…but that the members should have the same care one for another. And whether one member suffers, all the members suffer **with it**." (I Cor. 12:25-26)

Jesus wept, not because of a friend's death but when He saw and heard the tears of family and friends weeping. He identified **with them** and shed actual tears **with them**. (John 11:28-38) And even Job's friends, though they probably stayed too long and said way too much, their arrival at Job's side "to mourn **with him** and to comfort him…they lifted up their voices and wept" (Job 2:11-13) illustrates this point dramatically.

The passage at the beginning of this article is often recited at weddings and, somewhat ironically like a Hallmark movie, there is a wedding at the end of this short story. But these beautiful words of faithful devotion and promised presence were said, not to some handsome beau, but to a grieving and bitter mother-in-law after the losses of her husband and two adult sons and in the midst of a nation-wide famine–by a sensitive and caring daughter-in-law, vowing to stay **with her**. Wow!

I urge us all, let's not allow the grieving among us to grieve alone. Let's stay close and in-touch, and by including them in our lives as we are able, let them see what God can do for them, just as Ruth and Naomi were to discover.

For Prayer Today

- With losses mounting and grieving almost everywhere, ask the Lord to "heal the brokenhearted and to bind up their wounds." (Psalm147:3) Pray specifically for those you know.
- Ask the Lord for wisdom, creativity, and respectful boldness to call, write, visit, treat, invite, or otherwise show personal care to a grieving person nearby, even for the "long-term". Then, please do so. Even a little bit of care goes a long way!

Personal Notes and Responses

Rare Prayers

"And this I pray, that your love may abound yet more and more in knowledge and in all judgment; that ye may approve things that are excellent; that ye may be sincere and without offense till the day of Christ. Being filled with the fruits of righteousness, which are by Christ Jesus, unto the glory and praise of God." (Philippians 1:9-11)

Have you ever stopped to evaluate the nature of your prayer list? Sometimes they begin to look like long shopping lists of all kinds of items that we repetitively request from God each day. When I was quite young, I heard my dad pray every night at our devotional times for a long list of relatives and neighbors by name that they might come to Christ – a very good thing. But sometimes when we children were asked to pray, we just recited that long list and often forgot to remove the names of those who had passed away, thoughtless and "vain repetitions" most certainly.

Even during most church prayer meetings, it could be observed that a large percentage of our requests deal with physical matters, our health, safety, financial concerns, etc., all of which do matter to God and for which He so desires us to call upon Him. But, if you've ever studied the prayer lists of Bible characters, you may discover that their prayer items were rarely physical but focused much more on spiritual matters. Check out the verses above.

Paul tells us four items for which he was praying for the Philippian Christians:
1. That their love would keep growing but with the boundaries of true knowledge and wise discernment – that their love would continue to expand for God and others in appropriate ways and directions

2. That their decisions and choices would be made after evaluating options for that which is morally excellent, not just good, better, or "ok"
3. That they would be sincere – honest and pure inwardly and outwardly, genuine, not deceitful or hypocritical before God and man
4. That they would be producing righteous fruit for the praise of God

Think about these prayer requests. Have any of them made it onto your prayer lists? If not, you can begin to pray for them *for me* as I daily need all four of them. I will be grateful!

For Prayer Today

- Add the above 4 items to your prayer list and pray them for specific people you know might be in need of them.
- Add other items that are more inward and spiritual and begin focusing on them as you pray.

Personal Notes and Responses

Life's Most Important Question... and Answer

"And if I go and prepare a place for you, I will come again, and receive you unto myself; that where I am, there ye may be also. And whither I go ye know, and the way ye know. Thomas saith unto him, Lord, we know not wither thou goest; and how can we know the way? Jesus saith unto him, I am the way, the truth, and the life: no man cometh unto the Father, but by me." (John 14:3-6)

"So you are saying that this guy nicknamed "Doubting Thomas" was the one who asked life's most important question? Really? So, what again was his question?"

Jesus had just informed His disciples that He would soon be leaving them to go Home to His Father's house but would one day return to take them there. The essence of Thomas's question was, "How does a person get to heaven?" I ask you, my readers today, "Are you sure that you know the right answer?"

Please note that Thomas prefaced his question with a humble statement, "Lord we do not know where you are going; how can we know the way?" He admitted not knowing and being confused and concerned about the subject. Unfortunately, so many today aren't interested or think that they know the right answer to this critical question.

Many believe that being a good person will get them there, making sure that their good works outweigh their bad ones. Some believe that their parents' religious habits and traditions or their grandmother's prayers will be sufficient. So many believe that their own religious activities and ceremonies, baptism, communion, confirmation, church attendance, or deeds of charity will earn their acceptance with God. Many believe that there are many different ways to get to God. Unfortunately, none of the above answers are correct and trusting in any of those ideas will actually exclude a person from heaven!

There is only one correct answer to this question. Jesus answered, "I am the way, the truth, and the life; no one can get to heaven but through Me." The way there is a Person, a Savior named Jesus Christ. He came to earth in human flesh so that He could suffer, bleed, and die, taking our much-deserved punishment so that through His death and resurrection He can save us from our sin, birth us into His family, and take us Home with Him someday.

The Bible clearly says that our eternal salvation does not come by human effort but by God's gracious provision of a loving Savior. When we repent of our sin and place our trust in Jesus Christ alone to save us, He does just that. There is no other right answer to that most important question. Please do not get it wrong! (See Acts 4:12; John 3:15-18, 36; 10:28-30; Eph. 2:8-9; Romans 3:23; 6:23)

If you have doubts or questions about this, like Thomas, don't be too proud or fearful to ask them. It really is a matter of life or death.

For Prayer Today
- If you recognize your sinful condition and your need of a Savior and desire to place your trust in Him to save you, tell God that in a sincere prayer of repentance and faith in Christ.
- If you already are a believer in Christ, ask Him to help you explain the message of this devotional with someone else who needs to know the only right answer to life's most important question.

Personal Notes and Responses

God and Government – and Me

"Let every soul be subject unto the higher powers. For there is no power but of God: the powers that be are ordained of God. Whosoever therefore resisteth the power, resisteth the ordinance of God: and they that resist shall receive to themselves damnation...For he is the minister of God to thee for good...For he is the minister of God, a revenger to execute wrath upon him that doeth evil..." (Romans 13:1-7) "I exhort therefore, that, first of all, supplications, prayers, intercessions, and giving of thanks, be made for all men; for kings, and for all that are in authority; that we may lead a quiet and peaceable life in all godliness and honesty." (I Timothy 2:1-2)

It is in Genesis 9 that we first find God entrusting to mankind the responsibility to govern themselves. Then throughout the Old Testament we find multiplied episodes depicting His sovereign control and use of various national governments and their officials for His purposes. He even crafted one particular nation, Israel, to fulfill some of His most unique plans for and through them. God is seen raising up civil leaders and putting them down. He is seen involving tribes and nations in warfare with victories and defeats. He is seen sending pestilences and famines, catastrophes and brokenness to entire populations, often as judgment for their wickedness. God is sovereign over and deeply involved in working in and through human governments for our good and His purposes.

In our verses above, the three primary purposes of civil government are to protect all citizenry (from enemies, criminals, viruses, catastrophes, etc.), to praise and reward the good, and to punish the evil doer. These men and women, including often our first and faithful responders are "God's ministers (servants) attending continually to this very thing." (13:4, 6)

No earthly government does things right all the time. No human authority is perfect or above making terrible choices, establishing bad laws, allowing injustices to prevail, or failing to fulfill their purposes. That is why our faith must not be in human offices or efforts but in the Supreme King of kings and Lord of lords Who rules over all. May we continue to trust God as we serve Him as grateful and godly citizens of this country, while supporting and praying daily for all who lead and serve our greatly blessed nation.

For Prayer Today

- Thank the Lord for our country, for the freedoms that God has granted us and which our nation still upholds and protects, and for all the blessings we know as citizens.
- Pray much for all our governmental leaders in all levels of office and for our law enforcement community, our military, our firemen and women, medical personnel, and many others who lead and protect our nation. Pray for their safety, for divine wisdom, for care and compassion, for their families, etc.

Personal Notes and Responses

ETERNAL ENCOURAGEMENTS #33

Troublesome Trials

"My brethren, count it all joy when ye fall into divers temptations; knowing this, that the trying of your faith worketh patience. But let patience have her perfect work, that ye may be perfect and entire, wanting nothing. If any of you lack wisdom, let him ask of God... and it shall be given him...receive with meekness the engrafted word...But be ye doers of the word, and not hearers only, deceiving your own selves." (James 1:2-12, 21-22)

Very similar to the book of Proverbs in the Old Testament, the New Testament book of James is exceptionally practical and down-to-earth. At its very beginning, James bluntly jumps right into a difficult problem that most of us face often. The issue is "How are we to respond when difficult problems enter our lives?" The answer is five-fold and is clearly and directly stated.

1. **Rejoice** when trials come. (You have to be kidding!) We are to "count it"or compute it as something worthy of joy, not because it makes sense, is pleasant or good in itself, or based on our limited knowledge or understanding, but on something we should or *do know*. "…knowing that…" (James 1:1-3)

2. **Recognize** "that the trying of your faith worketh patience" or endurance (1:3). God is using trials to grow us, to produce in us certain qualities and capacities for our growth toward maturity. We can rejoice, knowing that God has not abandoned us but that He may be using different tools on us to accomplish new and better things in us. He is at work.

3. **Remain** under the pressures that have come your way. (1:4, 12) "Let patience have her perfect work that ye may be perfect and entire wanting nothing." Don't cut and run; don't quit or give up; don't rebel and resist. Remain; give God time to work in and on you. Trials can help us endure and endurance can help us mature as we see God growing

us and building us up to serve Him. Running away will cripple us and stunt our growth instead of mature us.

4. **Request** wisdom and help from God in prayer (1:5-8). Do not lean on your own understanding and try to fix or figure everything out. Ask God by faith for His perspective on the troubles and be assured that He will provide.

5. **Receive** eagerly **and Respond** obediently to the wisdom and direction God's Word may give to you (1:19-25). Practically "do" whatever God indicates you should do, including reaching out to others who may also be troubled, something which God may be equipping you to do. Do not deceive yourself by ignoring God's wisdom. Use it in your situation.

Trials come to all of us in different quantities and intensities. When (not if) they come, I urge us all to take these commands seriously and by faith to apply them obediently to our tough situations. I know this isn't easy. (See Rom. 5:1-5; 8:18-39 for extra encouragement with this.) Let's pray for each other about this.

For Prayer Today
- Ask God for His help in understanding these points from James 1 and for the strength to obey them when troubles come.
- Pray for others whom you know are struggling and reach out to help them.

Personal Notes and Responses

ETERNAL ENCOURAGEMENTS #34

"Please, Won't You Be My Neighbor?"

"Withhold not good from them to whom it is due, when it is in the power of thine hand to do it. Say not unto thy neighbor, Go, and come again. and to morrow I will give; when thou hast it by thee. Devise not evil against thy neighbor, seeing he dwelleth securely by thee." (Proverbs 3:27-29) "He that despiseth his neighbor sinneth: but he that hath mercy on the poor, happy is he." (Prov. 14:21) "...And the second is like unto it; Thou shalt love thy neighbor as thyself..." (Matt.22:34-40)

Beside the opening brief weather report from "the neighborhood," perhaps, Mr. Fred Roger's literary legacy to us all might be the question serving as our title today. I suspect that this very question is on the hearts of a lot of people in our world. Even your very nearest neighbor may be inwardly asking it of you.

We have never lived among so many neighborly neighbors as we do now in our retirement community here in Ohio. Even during this sequestered time as we take frequent walks on our campus, we are getting to know lots of people. Many of them are lonely widows and widowers. Quite a number have burdened hearts about family members who are struggling with issues or who may just "never" call or visit. Many are facing medical challenges with uncertain futures. Many have had to say "good-bye" to former family, friends, or jobs and hobbies that they have loved for many years.

I must confess to not being really good at this. Unfortunately, throughout my busy "ministry years", I have rushed by our neighbors to get to some appointment elsewhere far more often than I have lingered outside to chat with someone next door. I have waved at them with a friendly smile frequently but have failed miserably to really care enough to get to know them and invest good time with them. Some neighbors we've had have been

..."challenging..." and avoiding them was my easy response. Debra has done far better with this as she has connected with many over yard work, pets, baked goods, etc. But not me. Guilty as charged.

But now I have absolutely no excuse. Our neighbors are everywhere; I have time on my hands, as do they. Everyone seems so very outgoing and cheerful. We take a lot of walks. About a month ago during an evening stroll, we stopped and had good conversations with 13 different neighbors! When we got home, I was exhausted but excited, confessing again that I had never done anything like that before and how incredible it was.

How are your neighbors doing? Do you know? I strongly suspect that they may be in need of a bit of care or encouragement. They may not be singing Fred's song, but they may be silently yearning for a "neighbor".

For Prayer Today

-   Pray for your neighbors by name and ask the Lord to reveal how you might get a bit closer to them, to discover any needs, and to offer some of God's love to them.

Personal Notes and Responses

ETERNAL ENCOURAGEMENTS #35

Don't You Be; *Please Don't* You Be...
My Neighbor!

"Be not a witness against thy neighbor without cause; and deceive not with thy lips. Say not, I will do so to him as he hath done to me: I will render to the man according to his work." (Prov. 24:28-29) "Go not forth hastily to strive, lest thou know not what to do in the end thereof, when thy neighbor hath put thee to shame. Debate thy cause with thy neighbor himself; and discover not a secret to another: lest he that heareth it put thee to shame, and thine infamy turn not away." (Prov. 25:8-10)

This title popped into my head a few weeks ago when my wife and I were reading Proverbs together and noticed several warnings about not being a bad neighbor, someone others would dread to have live nearby. With apologies this time to the late Fred Rogers, let's consider these warnings from God's Word.

Neighbors can be a source of stress or difficulty sometimes and, as believers, we need to avoid being that way as we seek to "love our neighbors as ourselves" as Jesus commanded. So, what should we strive to avoid in our neighborliness?

1. Do not be nasty or feisty with your neighbor. Do not plan him any harm. Do not carry a chip on your shoulder, just begging him to knock it off, because you are looking for a fight. (Prov. 3:29-30; 25:8)

2. Do not appear friendly on the outside but deceitfully plan to take him to court over something. Do not plan to "get even" or to seek vengeance for some wrong that has been done to you. Don't pick up someone else's cause against your neighbor. (Prov. 24:28-29; 25:8)

3. When there is a problem between you, do not talk to others about it but go directly to the person involved and seek to settle matters privately. (Prov. 25:8-10) Do not gossip and

smear your neighbor's character or reputation in the minds of others.

4. When you are enjoying your neighbor's kind hospitality, do not linger there too long; don't overstay your visit and wear them out so they dread the next time your paths cross. (Prov. 25:17)

5. When you discover that a neighbor has a need, do not withhold or postpone helping them if you can help. (Prov. 3:27-28) Jump in right away with some aid.

Jesus told the "Good Samaritan" story to answer the question, "So, who is my neighbor?" His response revealed more about how to be a good neighbor. But among the first two characters who crossed the stage in that early scene were two religious people who saw the desperate need, crossed the street and avoided the opportunity to help. That's how not to be a good neighbor!

For Prayer Today

- Ask God to make you the kind of neighbor He can use in your community.

- If you are embroiled in neighborhood tensions, small border disputes, pet poop problems, unkind communications, prejudices, etc., confess anything on your part that may be sin and ask God to help you love your difficult neighbor as you already love yourself. (And be ready for what God may do.)

Personal Notes and Responses

The Calmness of Contentment

*"But godliness with contentment is great gain...and having food
and raiment let us be therewith content." (I Timothy 6:6-8) "...Not
that I speak in respect of want: for I have learned, in whatsoever
state I am, therewith to be content. I know both how to be abased,
and I know how to abound: every where and in all things I am
instructed both to be full and to be hungry, both to abound and to
suffer need. I can do all things through Christ which strengtheneth
me." (Philippians 4:11-13)*

One of the most excruciatingly painful things my wife and I had
to do during the months of preparing to relocate to Ohio has been
this thing called "downsizing". "Radical surgery" is the more
accurate term. We were shocked and embarrassed at all we had
accumulated over the years and how hard it was to let it go as
we attempted to shoe-horn our way into an 1100 sq. ft. 4 room
cottage here.

We unloaded lots of stuff in two massive and successful yard sales,
sent over two truckloads of stuff to Charleston area thrift shops,
then another couple loads to such a shop near us here. I gave away
several thousands of my books, even "forcing" many of them on
my chaplains and pastoral friends. Our son's family "inherited
early" many items, etc.

An early discovery in our time here is that we could indeed live
without all those things; we do not need them at all. Our shopping
excesses for "more" have disappeared. A quiet, calming contentment has been growing in our hearts ever since. Refreshing. Freeing.
Encouraging. Invigorating. Simplifying. Motivating. Exciting.

In our passages above, Paul admits that becoming content is a
learning process. We are not born content and our lusts, desires,
and appetites are easily inflamed by marketing efforts and prideful

comparisons with others throughout our lives. Note a couple lessons that Paul had learned about this subject.

1. **Contentment prevents** greed and covetousness which are serious sins that never satisfy. (Phil. 4:11; I Tim. 6:6-10; Psalm 106:13-15; Col. 3:5) A lust for money and a love of money are dangerous desires in all the evil directions.

2. **Contentment provides** life-learning for the extremes of life. (Phil. 4:11-12) Because he learned to be content, he could handle properly times of fullness or hunger, times of prosperity or poverty without anxiety or fear.

3. **Contentment is possible** by leaning on Jesus Christ. (Phil. 4:13; Heb. 13:5-6) In this passage, "I can do all things through Christ which strengtheneth me" has direct reference to him being able to handle such financial extremes with contentment through Christ's help.

Is it time to evaluate your "wish list" or your "gotta have this" list? Why not take time to do so in light of today's lesson?

For Prayer Today

- Ask the Lord to help you experience the truth of Heb. 13:5-6. "Let your conversation be without covetousness; and be content with such things as ye have. For He hath said, 'I will never leave thee nor forsake thee.'"
- Thank the Lord that, as believers, we have Jesus Christ who will provide all we need and who will never leave us!

Personal Notes and Responses

DANGER AHEAD!!!

"A wrathful man stirreth up strife: but he that is slow to anger appeaseth strife." (Proverbs 15:18) "A soft answer turneth away wrath: but grievous words stir up anger."(15:1) "Hatred stirreth up strifes: but love covereth all sins." (10:12) "...but the fool rageth, and is confident. He that is soon angry dealeth foolishly..." (14:16-17) "Make no friendship with an angry man; and with a furious man thou shalt not go: lest thou learn his ways, and get a snare to thy soul." (22:24-25)

Every time the subject of anger is raised in a class or sermon, someone always reminds us that God gets angry; Jesus demonstrated anger. Yes, that is true but the anger of the Godhead is without sin. It is righteous and just anger meted out appropriately to guilty recipients. It is holy justice. Our anger is usually stimulated by bothersome irritants, tainted with selfish motives, and can develop into vindictive vengeance. It is anger that is not dealt with properly but grows over time, metastasizing into bitterness, wrath, evil speaking and malice and brings about serious destruction instead of forgiveness and restoration. (Eph. 4:26-32)

Lots of Bible narratives illustrate anger's dangers. Cain killed his righteous brother out of anger (Gen. 4:1-5-15). To avenge the assault of Jacob's daughter Dinah, her brothers devised a calculated plan to deceive the guilty man and his father, killing them and every male in their city and totally plundering it (Gen. 34). Moses threw an angry tantrum toward God's people and lost his opportunity to enter the Promised Land. (Numbers 20:1-13; Psalm 106:32-33). King Nebuchadnezzar, in "rage and full of fury" overheated by 7 times the furnace resulting in incinerating several of his own men while God delivered His three servants alive (Dan. 3:8-25).

I'm sure that many of us have regretted our words and actions expressed in moments of anger or rage toward our spouse, family, co-workers, friends, or neighbors. In our nation and across the globe many people are wrestling with many anger-fueled issues and serious problems and the effects are often catastrophic. Anger is so very dANGERous! It's not a solution but always a problem.

God's answers to this sin's treacherous destructiveness are found in the Scriptures. On this subject, the book of Proverbs alone gives much counsel about diminishing anger and applying God's wisdom to our daily lives. Can't we begin doing this in our personal lives now and then help others to do the same?

For Prayer Today
- Read again Ephesians 4:26-32 and ask God to help you live out His commands about anger and forgiveness.
- Pray for our citizens, law enforcement officers, business owners, city councils, preachers, etc. to cease human efforts to solve our problems and to seek God's wisdom for each situation.

Personal Notes and Responses

ETERNAL ENCOURAGEMENTS #38

Let's Do the Math

*"Grace and peace be **multiplied** unto you through the knowledge of God, and of Jesus our Lord, according as his divine power hath given unto us all things that pertain unto life and godliness, through the knowledge of him that hath called us to glory and virtue: whereby are given unto us exceeding great and precious promises: that by these ye might be partakers of the divine nature, having escaped the corruption that is in the world through lust. And beside this, giving all diligence, **add** to your faith..." (II Peter 1:2-5)*

Multiplication – Remember memorizing those "times tables" and reciting them endlessly in class? I do and I also distinctly remember how amazed I was when I realized how large a number you got when doing this multiplying action of two small numbers. 9 x 9 = 81! 12 x 12= 144. Wow! Amazing and a bit overwhelming to this simple-minded child.

As a Christian, our passage tells us that God's grace and peace is similarly multiplied toward us, including all things that pertain to life and godliness and His exceedingly great and precious promises. These arrive as oceanic waves, one upon another to us, "grace for grace". (John 1:16). His gracious provisions, promises, blessings, and assurances continue to multiply exponentially for us each day. Amazing and abundant! Wow! Praise the Lord!

Addition God does the multiplying so we can do the adding. We are to cooperate with Him in a process of obedient growth and productivity that honors Him. With a focused diligence we are to add to our initial faith in Christ virtue (moral excellence), knowledge, self-control, patience, godliness, brotherly kindness, and love. (II Peter 1:5-8) In connection with the fruit that the Spirit of God wants to produce in our lives (Gal. 5:22-23) are our efforts, by God's grace, to grow in all these areas. As we mature in these inward qualities, they will become evident and examples to all of what God can accomplish in a life that is walking with Him.

Subtraction If we profess to know the Savior but our lives, over time, are lacking these qualities, we may become aware of other missing realities. "But he that lacketh these things is blind, and cannot see afar off and hath forgotten that he was purged from his old sins." (II Peter 1:9) Lack of spiritual growth and fruit along with the loss of spiritual memory and diminished spiritual sight should cause one to question the reality or the health of their relationship with Christ.

I urge you, if the sum total of your testimony is far less than what it should be, it is time to recheck your "figures" to make certain of your personal relationship with the Savior. (See II Peter 1:10-11)

For Prayer Today
- Ask God to recheck your figures and to show you what corrections may need to be made in your life. Ask Him to help you to really trust Him as Savior and then to walk with Him daily.
- Think about the abundant blessings and provisions God has provided for us through Christ and spend time thanking and praising Him for them all.

Personal Notes and Responses

A Drive-By Shouting...

"...the tongue of the wise is health."(Prov. 12:18) "Heaviness in the heart of man maketh it stoop: but a good word maketh it glad." (Prov. 12:25) "Let nothing be done through strife or vainglory... Look not every man on his own things, but every man also on the things of others." (Phil. 2:3-4)

Actually, the complete title of this piece is "A Drive-By Shouting, and Honking and Waving, and Cheering, and Thanking", but I just had to be a bit clever with the shortened version above, (of course).

On our retirement campus, in addition to independent living homes, there is a large retirement center and a separate nursing care facility with an Alzheimer section. Recently, we were invited to participate in a drive-by parade of sorts to entertain and encourage the sequestered residents and staffs of these facilities. I'll admit to inwardly scoffing a bit at the idea, feeling it a bit silly, but when the day arrived, Debra and I participated.

A good number of cars and golf-carts slowly circled the buildings, honking our horns, waving wildly, and shouting words of greetings and encouragements. Residents and staff had gathered at windows and doorways to receive our celebratory support. As we circled around the nursing home and approached the retirement center, the large number of folks on its porches and balconies cheering us on and waving home-made signs of gratitude for our efforts moved some of us to tears.

After making two slow laps and then heading home, I was stunned by the deep, pleasurable joy that was swelling in my heart. This little outing cost nothing, lasted about 10 minutes, but brought great blessing to both givers and receivers. A tiny bit of care impacted so many in big ways.

The other day our doorbell rang during breakfast and a neighbor lady presented us with a beautiful, off-white rose, the very first from her garden. We were so surprised and deeply moved and we have continued to enjoy its beauty and her love on our table all week. A family with small children, friends of our son's family, beautifully painted 5 small rocks, each one decorated with pictures of each of our family member's special hobby or interest, then under cover of darkness one night, they hid them in our son's yard. In the morning they telephoned our family to announce a scavenger hunt for those 5 special stones. What a fun time our kids had on the search and they all treasure their own special stone, a reminder of friends' love.

It's been a challenge to be hunkered down and secluded during these months and it has led many of us to think only of ourselves, our safety, our needs, and our desires. Have you reached out to anyone else to surprise them with a gift, a card, a call, a prayer for them over the phone, an encouraging text or email, etc.?

Jesus said, "It is more blessed to give than to receive." (Acts 20:35) I say, "Amen!"

For Prayer Today
- Ask the Lord to remind you of someone who could use some surprise encouragement today and to motivate you or your family to "deliver it".

Personal Notes and Responses

Things More Valuable Than Money

"Happy is the man that findeth wisdom, and the man that getteth understanding. For the merchandise of it is better than the merchandise of silver, and the gain thereof than fine gold. She is more precious than rubies: and all the things thou canst desire are not to be compared unto her..." (Prov. 3:13-18) "A good name is rather to be chosen than great riches, and loving favour rather than silver and gold." (Prov. 22:1) "For what is a man profited, if he shall gain the whole world, and lose his own soul? or what shall a man give in exchange for his soul?" (Matt. 16:26)

For the last ten years, my wife has been managing the financial matters for her now 99 year-old mother in Pittsburgh. She also maintains our checkbook while I keep a close watch on our family budget, tracking every penny and evaluating all things financial monthly. Now that we are almost on the proverbial "fixed income", the need to remain financially conscious may be more important than ever. With the recent painful downsizing that we've done and now our plans to update our wills, it is so easy to allow this financial focus to limit our view of things that are far more valuable. "What might they be?" you might ask.

The Bible actually mentions several great valuables that are not financial in nature and that far exceed the worth of anything physical. Let's concisely list them.

1. **God's Wisdom and Understanding** (Prov. 3:13-18; 16:16; Job 28:12-19) This is the ability to see everything from God's perspective, from His viewpoint. Incredible! This is attained by investing time in His Word and prayer.

2. **The Fear of the Lord and of His Word** (Psalm 19:7-11; Prov. 2:1-5; 19:23) This is an attitude of holy reverence and respect for God and His Word, taking them very seriously as our guide for all of life.

3. **A Good Reputation** (Prov. 22:1; 19:1; Eccl. 7:1) Many have destroyed this and their families in their lust for the almighty dollar. What a waste!

4. **Our Genuine Faith in Christ Surviving Tests and Trials** (I Peter 1:3-7) We try to avoid trials but they have great value to our growing faith.

5. **A Virtuous Woman, Wife, and Mother** (Prov. 31:10-31) I say a seven-fold "AMEN" to that!

6. **The Eternal Soul of a Person** (Matt. 16:24-26; Luke 12:13-21-a truly tragic story!) Do not miss this one. One day you will die and leave everything else behind. Please make sure you are ready for that day by trusting Christ as your Savior.

For Prayer Today

- Ask God to help you to evaluate your list of things that you value most and see how many of the above items are on that list.

- Ask Him to recalibrate your value system so that every day you are treasuring and making conscious investment in the things that really have lasting value.

Personal Notes and Responses

Are You Sinking Beneath the Waves?

"...Fear not: for I have redeemed thee, I have called thee by thy name; thou art mine. When thou passest through the waters, I will be with thee; and through the rivers, they shall not overflow thee... for I am the LORD thy God, the Holy One of Israel, thy Saviour..." *(Isaiah 43:1-3)*

My parents had that passage on a beautifully painted glass plaque hanging above a door-way in our kitchen. That door was one that we kids avoided at almost all costs. It was the door-way into our basement and we dreaded every thought of going down there.

There was very little stored down there but occasionally we were sent down on some mission for the folks and discomforting dread always gripped our young hearts. The dim light at the top of the stairs illuminated enough of the handrail-free steps to reveal the cob webs and spider webs that adorned the downward passageway. Damp smells assaulted our breathing attempts as the cold, naked walls had shed their coats of paint and plaster long ago. If we needed to yank the chain on the bulb that hung in the back of the basement, its swinging moves just caused the dark shadows around us to come alive and drove us back upstairs as fast as possible.

Oh yes, there was also the water. It accumulated down there frequently and often the sump pump decided not to get out of bed to do anything about it. Its gasping or squeaking didn't help our morale down there either when it decided to suddenly express itself in our jittery presence.

Thus, the plaque over that doorway. My parents thought it was an amusing way to greet the plumber, "When you pass through the waters, I will be with you..."

God does send us into stormy deep waters at times but He promises to control their effects on us as well as to be present with us during the storm. He doesn't always keep us out of troubles, but He promises to be present with us in them.

Notice that core thought in this verse and others like it. "When thou passest through the waters *I will be **with thee**.*" Similar to David's expression, "...though I walk through the valley of the shadow of death, I will fear no evil, for Thou art **with me**." As Jesus prepared his disciples for their coming challenges, He reassured them that His Spirit would **be in them and abide with them forever**. (John 14:16-17) Later, when He commissioned them to a worldwide ministry, he said, and "Lo, **I am with you alway**, even to the end of the world." (Matt. 28:18-20)

If you know Christ as your Savior and you are overwhelmed by troubles and fears, please know that your Savior is with you; do not doubt it. You don't have to ask Him to come and be with you; He is present and available to help you in your crisis. Peter found that out one day during his stroll...on water. (Matt. 14:22-36)

For Prayer Today
- If, as a believer, you find yourself drowning in severe trials, please call out to your Savior for His help; He is ever-present with you and cares for you.

Personal Notes and Responses

Giving is Godly

"God that made the world and all things therein, seeing that he is Lord of heaven and earth...neither is worshipped with men's hands, as though he needed any thing, seeing he giveth to all life, and breath, and all things..." (Acts 17:24-25) "He that spared not his own Son, but delivered him up for us all, how shall he not with him also freely give us all things?" (Romans 8:32) "...as his divine power hath given unto us all things that pertain unto life and godliness..." (II Peter 1:3) "Thanks be unto God for his unspeakable gift." (II Cor. 9:15)

Unfortunately, in a lot of religious circles yet today, the subject of "giving" is still "touchy". Some preachers avoid addressing it completely and some parishioners avoid attending if it is addressed. That is so sad...and wrong. Yes, some clergy overdo it with the subject and thus, discourage folks from giving. Some organizations have destroyed their credibility by misuse of funds and other abuses. All of that diminishes the true blessings of giving. So, what is my point today? Actually, two points.

God is a Giver. He is continually a very generous giver. In addition to the Scriptures above, give these verses serious grateful consideration. "Every good gift and every perfect gift is from above, and cometh down from the Father of lights..." (James 1:17). "And God is able to make all grace abound toward you; that ye, always having all sufficiency in all things, may abound to every good work." (II Cor. 9:8) The wealthy are not to trust in their wealth, "...but in the living God, who giveth us richly all things to enjoy..." (I Tim. 6:17) I believe that God loves to give (Matt. 7:7-11) and gives because He loves. (John 3:16; 4:9-11)

When we give like God does, we become more like Him. His generosity toward us is purposeful; it is not only to meet our own needs but that so we can then be generous to others. I Timothy 6 continues, "...that they do good, that they be rich in good works, ready to distribute, willing to communicate..." (6:18).

In this challenging season in which we have been encouraged to "hunker down", we may have also been tempted to hide, hoard, to hang on to our things and to hover over them. Please remember that needs abound everywhere around us. The Scriptures command us to give to our own faith community, to the poor and needy, to global mission opportunities, as well as to our own families. There are many helpful social agencies, food banks, rescue missions, etc. that deserve our support. With a generous God who is eager to continue to provide for us, let's not forget that He desires us to share with others some of what He has given us. (II Cor. 8:1-15)

For Prayer Today
- No one can help everyone but ask the Lord to lay on your heart or on that of your family some nearby needy person or family, some mission or agency that can use your help, and then begin giving, even in some small way to them.
- Thank God sincerely for His daily generosity to you.

Personal Notes and Responses

ETERNAL ENCOURAGEMENTS #43

Brewster the Rooster

"An high look, and a proud heart...is sin." (Prov. 21:4) "These six things doth the LORD hate: yea, seven are an abomination unto him: a proud look..." (6:16-17) "The fear of the LORD is to hate evil: pride, and arrogancy, and the evil way, and the froward mouth, do I hate." (8:13) "He that is of a proud heart stirreth up strife..."(28:25) "A man's pride shall bring him low..."(29:23) "When pride cometh, then cometh shame..." (11:2) "Pride goeth before destruction and an haughty spirit before a fall." (16:18) "...God resisteth the proud, but giveth grace unto the humble." (James 4:6)

My wife is an animal person; she loves them all and was delighted that she could help care for several goats and chickens in a pen and small barn at the back of the nursing home here. Debra is in her element. But there is (was) another resident there, one very beautiful and stately rooster that I unofficially named "Brewster". (I was thinking of Brutus or Bluto but Brewster has a nice ring – or clang to it.)

Like the description of Lucifer in Ezekiel 28:17, this bird's "...heart was lifted up because of thy beauty" (I suspect) and he strutted his stuff proudly around his small dominion. If you walked the length of the pen on the outside, he would match you step for step the whole distance as if he built the fence himself, single-"clawedly", and was daring you to stick one toe inside it. He always had a lot to say and interrupted or drowned out every other conversation in the area. He crowed his opinions loudly, though wearily repetitive, and could be heard all over our campus (even rudely before most people were out of bed. Can you imagine that?

With his arrogant attitude, his people skills were severely lacking even with loving, gentle, kind people like my wife. He flew up at her twice and surprised her with two painful pecks on two other occasions. He had begun pecking the backs of the chickens raw when the decision was made that he had to move on. (We'll skip the moment of silence.)

And I always thought that peacocks were the poster-animal for pride! They're not even in the running.

I plan to deal with this subject again later but this fresh illustration was just crowing to be written now. I won't elaborate here but dare I ask these questions? (Yes, I do.) Does this bird, as described, remind you of anyone you know? Better yet, do you identify with any of its characteristics personally? (I'm not speaking of red-haired people here.)

Take some time with the above Scriptures about the seriousness and sinfulness of such pride and make whatever adjustments you may need to make.

For Prayer Today
- Pray that God will deliver us from the sin of pride, that we will humble ourselves and allow God to guide our every step.
- Pray for those who struggle in this area; that they will learn the incredible blessings of humility and of all God's graciousness toward the humble.

Personal Notes and Responses

Grumbling or Groaning?
–There is a Difference!

"And when the people complained, it displeased the LORD: and the LORD heard it; and his anger was kindled..." (Numbers 11:1) "Do all things without murmurings and disputings: that ye may be blameless and harmless, the sons of God, without rebuke, in the midst of a crooked and perverse nation, among whom ye shine as lights in the world..." (Phil. 2:14-15) "...the children of Israel sighed by reason of the bondage, and they cried, and their cry came up unto God...And God heard their groaning, and God remembered his covenant...and God looked upon the children of Israel, and God had respect unto them." (Ex. 2:23-25) "I am weary with my groaning; all the night make I my bed to swim; I water my couch with my tears." (Psalm 6:6)

With little or no effort, we daily maintain a long list of things about which we often grumble and complain. Like worry, we often respond this way to almost everything. However, "grumbling" is forbidden. Fortunately, there is another legitimate option. Let's try "groaning". Let's note their basic differences as seen in Scripture.

Grumbling
- expresses our dissatisfaction or disgust with whatever God is doing or allowing in our lives
- is often driven by attitudes and emotions of selfish irritation or anger
- frequently is announced publicly to others in pride and arrogant frustration, seeking to gain compatriots in their complaints
- often disrupts intimacy, drives people away, or contagiously infects others
- incites the anger and displeasure of God

Groaning

- expresses our inward weariness, sadness, brokenness, or pain in light of our situation
- accompanies itself with attitudes of humility, contrition, request, and dependence
- most frequently is expressed privately, in the lonely night seasons
- is directed toward God alone and invites His compassionate care and kind help with which He graciously responds

Grumbling is troublesome on many fronts. Groaning can grow our relationship with God as we lean on Him and can then enable us to be a helpful testimony to others. Do you see the difference? God does. You and I have a choice to make, every day. I am personally very thankful for this gracious option.

For Prayer Today

- If you've been doing a lot of grumbling and complaining, confess that to the Lord and enjoy His refreshing cleansing and forgiveness
- Spend time alone with God and share your heartaches and needs with Him, humbly trusting Him to care for you and your family.

Personal Notes and Responses

ETERNAL ENCOURAGEMENTS #45

Hide and Seek – Show and Tell

"We will not hide them from their children, shewing to the gener-
ation to come the praises of the LORD, and his strength, and his
wonderful works that he hath done...he commanded our fathers,
that they should make them known to their children: that the gen-
eration to come might know them, even the children which should
be born; who should arise and declare them to their children:
that they might set their hope in God, and not forget the works of
God, but keep his commandments..." (Psalm 78:4-8) "...And these
words, which I command thee this day, shall be in thine heart: and
thou shalt teach them diligently unto thy children, and shalt talk
of them when..." (Deut. 6:4-9)

"Hide and Seek" was certainly a fun and simple game that most of
us played often as children. But it should not be played in the spiritual realm between adults and children. Do not "try this at home!"

In the Bible, God ordered parents not to hide a knowledge of God
or His wonderful works from their children. You wonder, who
would do that? Why? How?

Some do it deliberately because they have no interest in spiritual
things. But many others do so inadvertently. By filling a family
schedule with everything but teaching the Bible makes it difficult
to fit it in. By demonstrating that entertainment and hobby pursuits are most important daily, our children learn that God and His
Word and not very important at all. By keeping the family home
from church robs them of spiritual input and teaches that church
is just not important also hides truth about God from the next
generation. The philosophy that parents should not direct their
children but should let them grow up and choose for themselves
their own version of life also sadly and dangerously contributes
to ignorance about God.

Let's stop playing "Hide and Seek" about God and His Word. Instead, let's mature quickly into a "Show and Tell" mode. Deut. 6:1-12 gives us clear instruction as to how to do so. Please read this passage thoughtfully.

1. Parents are to love the Lord completely and live by His commands and truths. Doing so will "show" emphatically and daily how important and wonderful God is to our little ones who watch us day and night.

2. Parents are then to teach and talk ("tell"), formally and informally, diligently and continuously, in the house and outside, at bedtimes, and morning times, answering questions, challenging behavior, etc. making the things of God central to and a normal accompaniment to all of life.

I plead with you now, parents and grandparents, the spiritual well-being of your family, the character development of your children, the spiritual effectiveness of our churches, and even the future success of our nation largely depends on what we do with our children as we show and tell them the importance of knowing, trusting, and living for God with our lives.

For Prayer Today
-   Ask God to move families to evaluate their priorities and to build their lives and daily schedules around knowing and serving God and others.

Personal Notes and Responses

ETERNAL ENCOURAGEMENTS #46

The Gloom and the Glory

"My God, my God, why hast thou forsaken me? why art thou so far from helping me, and from the words of my roaring?...But I am a worm, and no man; a reproach of men, and despised of the people...I am poured out like water, and all my bones are out of joint: my heart is like wax; it is melted in the midst of my bowels...thou hast brought me into the dust of death...They pierced my hands and my feet..."(Psalm 22:1-31) "...he humbled himself and became obedient unto death, even the death of the cross. Wherefore God also hath highly exalted him, and given him a name which is above every name: that at the name of Jesus every knee should bow...and that every tongue should confess that Jesus Christ is Lord, to the glory of God the Father." (Phil. 2:5-11)

Psalm 22 is an awesome Psalm that clearly depicts many details of that dark Friday when our Savior, the totally innocent God-man hung on that Roman device of torture, shame, and execution for the sins of all mankind, willingly suffering the punishment that we all deserve. But it was many hundreds of years earlier when David wrote of that event in such excruciating detail! (Please read all of Psalm 22 for the full impact of that passage.)

What should we learn from this Psalm? Several important things, at least.

1. The suffering of our Savior was planned and predicted ahead of time. It had been scheduled by God and took place as planned. (Acts 2:22-24, 29-36)
2. Even as the Father did with the Son, suffering is a necessary ingredient by which God accomplishes His purposes for His people. He did not change plans, cut Christ's suffering short, or lighten the burden, but He allowed all the cruelties to be experienced by Him, even to His painful death and burial.

3. Then the Father did the unexpected and the extraordinary as He raised the Son from the grave and exalted Him to the highest position of power and authority to rule over the universe and the hearts of mankind for eternity.

No one willingly signs up for suffering, except our Savior did do so. But for the believer, any suffering that God allows into his life is indeed purposeful and will accomplish God's perfecting will in his life as he trusts and cooperates with God through it all. Then, at the other end of it will be blessing and fulfillment forever.

For the child of God, suffering is not permanent, but purposeful. "This too shall pass" is a true truth, and in eternity, it will never return! "For I reckon that the sufferings of this present time are not worthy to be compared with the glory which shall be revealed in us..." (Romans 8:18-39)

For Prayer Today

- Ask God not only to help you with any present suffering you are experiencing but also to accomplish His purposes for it.
- Anticipate the future glories and perfections that you will know as a child of God and thank Him ahead of time for all that He has planned and prepared for you.

Personal Notes and Responses

Eternal Encouragements #47

Of Scales and Mirrors

"Know ye not that they which run in a race run all, but one receiveth the prize? So run, that ye may obtain. And every man that striveth for the mastery is temperate in all things...I therefore so run, not as uncertainly...But I keep under my body, and bring it into subjection: lest that by any means, when I have preached to others, I myself should be a castaway." (I Cor. 9:24-27) "When thou sittest to eat with a ruler, consider diligently what is before thee: and put a knife to thy throat, if thou be a man given to appetite..." (Prov. 23:1-3)

I really like my bathroom scale, though it is brutally honest. In contrast to it the scale in my West Virginia doctor's office always put my weight about 12 pounds heavier than my scale does. Even after I remove all things from my pockets, my watch from my wrist, my phone from my grip, and try standing on one leg (my lighter one), I still appear that much heavier. Recently having moved to Ohio, I discovered that my new doctor's scale also adds those 12 pounds to my record.

I ask you, how could two different doctors in two different states both be using totally defective scales? How is that possible? I do like my own scale.

Then there are those mirrors; how revealing they are! I prefer the small ones that clearly show me from my bulging biceps upward. (Actually, the bulge is a bit lower.) I also think those full-length mirrors should be banned from all motel restrooms. Way too much ugliness there!

The Bible actually acts as a means to show us what we really are like and the areas which must change. In it we are warned that allowing our lusts and appetites to control us can lead us into trouble and into a serious defiling of the testimony of God in us and a disqualifying of us for ministry opportunities.

We are told that gluttony is forbidden for the Christian, that sexual desires should be fulfilled in a loving, marital relationship only, that we should be controlled only by the Holy Spirit, not by food or drink or drugs or anger or greed, etc. (Titus 1:12-13; Prov. 28:7; Gal. 5:16-21; Eph. 5:1-7, 15-21; Col. 3:5-11; I Thess. 4:1-7). We are instructed to do all things with moderation (Phil. 4:5) and to allow the Holy Spirit to produce self-control in our lives. (Gal. 5:22-23) We are to drive through each day under the influence of God's Holy Spirit alone.

James 1:21-25 refers to the mirror of God's Word, how we are to gaze into it often, take note of what needs to change and then to obey God in doing so. Are we doing this?

Let's not be like King Belshazzar in the book of Daniel whose lust-driven, drunken party was interrupted by the divine message that his time was about up and his personal spiritual "weight" was announced on the wall and found to be eternally inappropriate (Daniel 5:18-30).

For Prayer Today
-   Pray for the many folks who struggle with their appetites and desires, letting them dictate many of their poor choices and decisions.
-   I humbly admit that too much junk food and too little exercise are dangerous habits of mine; my testimony is so poor in this area so, you can be praying for me, too, please.

Personal Notes and Responses

A Primer on Prayer – Part 1

"After this manner therefore pray ye: Our Father which art in heaven, Hallowed be thy name. Thy kingdom come. Thy will be done in earth, as it is in heaven. Give us this day our daily bread. And forgive us our debts, as we forgive our debtors. And lead us not into temptation, but deliver us from evil: For thine is the kingdom, and the power, and the glory, for ever. Amen." (Matt. 6:9-13)

With this devotional and the next, I want to get somewhat provocative. I want to provoke you to think deeply about what we call "The Lord's Prayer". It is certainly a well-known passage, is read, recited, and sung often in all kinds of places and events by all kinds of people. But in most cases, I believe, it is used in almost total ignorance of its true meaning and though it may impress others, it may invoke little help from God with its use. (Are you provoked yet?)

In teaching His disciples how NOT to pray in the preceding verses (6:5-8), Jesus commanded us not to pray like the hypocrites (pretenders) and the heathen (who don't really know or trust God). They often pray publicly to be seen and heard by others or frequently pray words repeatedly in a vain or empty fashion, not even understanding what they are really saying. And yet that is most often exactly what many do with this very prayer. (How's that for starters?)

Now, let's examine the first part of this "model prayer" our Lord used to teach on this subject. It begins by acknowledging a special relationship with God.

1. **God is addressed as our Father in heaven.** This is a rather personal and paternal relationship but for Him to be our Father, we must then be His children. We are certainly not born that way but must be "born-again" into His family, by repentance of our sin and by placing our

trust in Jesus Christ as our Savior. (John 1:12; 3:16-18; I John 3:1-2) Only then can we address God as "our Father". Note also that He is a holy God and is to be revered and respected by His children. His name is to be kept hallowed or sacred.

2. **God is then acknowledged that He is a sovereign king whose kingdom is real and His will is to be desired.** "Thy kingdom come; Thy will be done in earth as it is in heaven...For thine is the kingdom, and the power, and the glory, for ever." Whoa, wait a minute! I thought prayer was all about asking for my little kingdom, my realm and responsibilities and desires. I want God to do what I desire Him to do for me and mine. Yes, we can bring to God our needs and desires but the bigger picture here is to line up our requests with His sovereign will for us. We share our needs but desire that our Father and King will do what He deems best for the sake of His name and Kingdom. (See another prayer of Jesus in Matt. 26:36-44.)

Ok, I think this is enough for today but please think about these facts and those that follow, should you plan to pray this prayer.

For Prayer Today

- If you are really a child of God, talk to Him with reverence but also as your Father, who resides in heaven. Be real and personal and loving to Him.
- With whatever situations you bring to Him, ask that His will be done, that His purposes will be fulfilled, etc.

Personal Notes and Responses

ETERNAL ENCOURAGEMENTS #49

A Primer on Prayer – Part 2
(We do want to pray effectively, don't we?)

"Give us this day our daily bread. And forgive us our debts, as we forgive our debtors. And lead us not into temptation, but deliver us from evil: For thine is the kingdom, and the power, and the glory for ever. Amen. For if ye forgive men their trespasses, your heavenly Father will also forgive you: but if ye forgive not men their trespasses, neither will your Father forgive your trespasses." (Matthew 6:11-15)

So, in this two-part devotional, am I suggesting that it is wrong to pray what we call "The Lord's Prayer"? First, that title is a misnomer; Jesus would never have prayed that prayer, especially the part we look at today. It is a sample, a model prayer that Christ used to illustrate several important components that we should include when we pray. He wasn't expecting us to repeatedly recite these exact words. But He wanted us to understand their precise meaning, should we indeed use them on occasion. Intelligent, honest, sincere, dependent, respectful praying that reflects these prayer elements is the point. Let's continue.

"Give us this day our daily bread." God wants us to depend on Him and to call on Him *daily* for all our basic needs. He wants to provide for us and often waits for us to call on Him. Amazing and thrilling. But many times we ignore this part because we need very little; we're all on the wealthy side of the world and credit is abundant and Amazon is amazing – and fast! We can get what we want whenever and from wherever we want it.

"And forgive us our debts, as we forgive our debtors. And lead us not into temptation, but deliver us from evil." What? As we pray, we must deal with sin, both ours and others'. And they are connected. We are to ask God to forgive us to the extent and in the same way as we are forgiving of the sins that others have committed against us. Yikes! That's certainly not what I want because I have great difficulty forgiving others some times. Hurts, pains, bitterness, grudges can sometimes find long-term lodging in my heart and mind. But these attitudes can hinder our praying and even our being forgiven ourselves. Withholding forgiveness is sin against God and others and must be dealt with as we pray. Read again the verses above that follow the prayer. Also, "If I regard iniquity in my heart, the Lord will not hear me." (Psalm 66:18) As we thus deal with past sins, we can trust the Lord for victory over future sins and the evil one, "Lead us not into temptation; deliver us from evil."

Will you agree with me that we need to really think through this model prayer seriously, not so that we repeat its words mindlessly but that we evaluate our own prayer habits in light of this sample prayer and make whatever adjustments that may be needed?

For Prayer Today
- As you deal with any sin in your prayer, read again I John 1:8-10 and Eph. 4:31-32 and rejoice in God's abundant forgiving grace and love.
- As you pray, make any "upgrades" to it in light of this sample prayer the Lord used to teach us how to pray.

Personal Notes and Responses

An Identity Crisis

"Therefore, if any man be in Christ, he is a new creature: old things are passed away; behold, all things are become new." (II Cor. 5:17) "But as many as received him, to them gave he power to become the sons of God, even to them that believe on his name:" (John 1:12) "...and ye are complete in him..." (Col. 2:9-10) "... who hath blessed us with all spiritual blessings in heavenly places in Christ..." (Eph. 1:3-14) "...his divine power hath given unto us all things that pertain unto life and godliness...exceeding great and precious promises..." (II Peter 1:1-4)

Do you remember the "Who's Who" book in which many hoped to find their names some day? I think I am listed in "Who's He?"

Many today appear to be struggling with their true identity. Some are questioning their qualifications for fitting into society, their reason for living, their sexual orientation, or even their gender. Some are still meandering through life, looking for themselves; others deem their lives not worth living at all and seek to end it.

All of the above is representative of a serious identity crisis. Not really knowing who we are and why we are here does cripple us from a fully wonderful and purposeful life. Simplistically, I repeat that only in connecting personally with the God of the universe through faith in Christ can one realize in its completeness our true identity and purpose. Unfortunately, even believers in Christ struggle with this; we often do not understand the many ways by which our true identity has dramatically changed – forever. Please read the following statements and their accompanying Scriptures; they describe many truths about your new identity in Christ.

1. You are a re-born child of God in His family. (John 1:12-13; I John 3:1-2)
2. You have been cleansed and forgiven of all your sins. (Eph. 1:7), never to be condemned by them. (Rom. 8:1)

3. You have been chosen by God who loves you. (Eph. 1:4; I John 3:16)
4. Your guaranteed eternal home is heaven, with the Lord (Eph. 1:5: Phil. 3:20-21; John 14:1-6)
5. You will inherit from God eternal blessings (Eph. 1:11; Rom. 8:16-17; I Peter 1:3-5)
6. You have received the Holy Spirit who lives within you to teach, comfort, lead, and to grow you toward Christlikeness. (Eph. 1:13-14; John 16:13-15)
7. You now have the greatest reason for living, the highest purposes in life to fulfill – to represent Jesus in this world, to love, honor, and serve Him every moment, and to talk of Him to others who desperately need to know what life is all about and how to know their Creator and Savior. (II Cor. 5:17-21)

Christian friend, please know that all of the above and much more describes your true identity, and, that it can never be lost or stolen! It is who you really are and will be forever! Think about this, deeply and seriously, then rejoice daily and praise God!

For Prayer Today
- Thank God for making you who and what you are today and for His commitment to stay with you, working with you forever!
- Ask Him every day to guide your steps, your words, your decisions, and your contacts with people so you can fulfill His purposes for you daily.

Personal Notes and Responses

Nobody!

"Who shall separate us from the love of Christ? shall tribulation, or distress, or persecution, or famine, or nakedness, or peril, or sword?...Nay, in all these things we are more than conquerors through him that loved us. For I am persuaded, that neither death, nor life, nor angels, nor principalities, nor powers, nor things present, nor things to come, nor height, nor depth, nor any other creature. shall be able to separate us from the love of God, which is in Christ Jesus our Lord." (Rom. 8:35-39)

Have you ever met anyone who had a case of "the nobodies"? As a former pastor, I often encountered it among people who had chosen to leave their church for whatever reason. When I would contact them about it, they wanted to talk about the "nobodies". Nobody called. Nobody visited. Nobody even sent a card. Nobody even noticed we were absent. Really...nobody cares! Maybe you've succumbed to this condition sometime.

Lonely people are very vulnerable to contracting this condition and in our homes, hospitals, nursing care homes it can be contagiously wide-spread. Repeating to oneself that catchy theme, "Nobody cares, nobody loves me, nobody..." just imbeds that condition more deeply in our soul and even in those nearby. The "cure" is not marshalling lots of visitors or sending lots of gifts, as helpful as that may be, but is found in believing several precious truths about God from Psalm 139.

"Nobody knows how I feel, what I have to put up with around here." "O LORD, thou hast searched me, and known me. Thou knowest my downsitting and mine uprising, thou understandeth my thought afar off. Thou compassest my path and my lying down, and art acquainted with all my ways...Such knowledge is too wonderful for me..." (Psalm 139:1-6) **God knows! He really does!**

Nobody will find me. I'm going into hiding! I'm leaving. Job. Marriage. Church. I've had enough. "Whither shall I go from thy spirit? or whither shall I flee from thy presence? If I ascend up into heaven, thou art there: if I make my bed in hell, behold, thou art there. If I take the wings of the morning, and dwell in the uttermost parts of the sea; even there shall thy hand lead me, and thy right hand shall hold me..." (Psalm 139:7-12) If you belong to the Lord, **God is always with you; you cannot hide from Him. You are not alone. He is with you!**

Nobody cares about me. Nobody loves me. "For thou hast possessed my reins: thou hast covered me in my mother's womb. I will praise thee; for I am fearfully and wonderfully made: marvelous are thy works; and that my soul knoweth right well..." (Psa. 139:13-18) **You are a product of God's unique, creative design and an object of His loving care.**

And from our opening passage (Rom. 8), nothing and "nobody" can ever stop God's eternal love and care for you!

For Prayer Today
-	Read and think through Psalm 139 and then thank God for those special truths about Him and His relationship with you.
-	Pray much for those who are desperately lonely, that God will send them special awareness and reminders of His love and provision for them.

Personal Notes and Responses

Do Not Be A Fooled Fool!

"In the mouth of the foolish is a rod of pride: but the lips of the wise shall preserve them. Go from the presence of a foolish man, when thou perceivest not in him the lips of knowledge...but the folly of fools is deceit...the fool rageth, and is confident...the foolishness of fools is folly...The way of a fool is right in his own eyes..." *(Prov. 14:3, 7, 8, 16, 24, 12:15)*

In the Old Testament, the concept of a "fool" is derived from three Hebrew words. Their definitions range from "one who is thick-headed or mentally sluggish and dull, to one who chooses to reject and refuse truth and knowledge, preferring his own perceived false notions of reality. An obstinate pride drives the fool to always think that he is right and thus he refuses advice or instruction from others. Such mental lockdown continually feeds his own notions and leads to ultimate self-deception, shame, and destruction.

The "fool" is fooled and then goes on fooling himself. By rejecting truth and adopting what is false, the fool is deceived and continues to deceive himself, a very sad state.

The Word of God warns us often that we not become deceived by sin or its proponents and then compound the lies by adopting them as truth and thus, tragically be deceiving ourselves. Notice a few such admonitions.

1. Do not be deceived about yourself. (Gal. 6:3) Do not think too highly of yourself. Don't fool yourself that you are greater than what God made you.
2. Do not be deceived about the coming harvest. (Gal. 6:7-9) If we plant good things into our lives and families, we will reap good things. If we plant sensual, worldly things, we will produce a sinful, corrupted crop.
3. Do not be deceived about the nature of sin. (James 1:13-16) It starts from within our hearts – lust – sin – death (to

lives, relationships, ministries, pleasures, etc.) Let's not play with it, deceiving ourselves that it is harmless.

4. Do not be deceived about the Word of God. (James 1:18-25) Believing that simply hearing it without obeying it is enough is disastrous self-deception. Being obedient doers of God's Word brings growth and blessing.

So, have you been deceived in any of the above areas? Have you been believing some lies and so have been even further deceiving yourself? That's the definition of a fool, in God's eyes, my friend.

For Prayer Today

- Have you foolishly been living out any of the above lies and need to confess that as sin? It is foolish not to do so. Please do so.
- Ask God to reveal His true view of things in your life, then get into His Word to discover His wisdom for your paths.
- Pray for all governmental leaders to have discernment to know the difference between lies and truth, between foolishness and wisdom and then to serve from a position of truthful wisdom. Pray that as well for our voting citizens.

Personal Notes and Responses

"But, I Don't Want To Be a Burden!"

"...And the king said to Barzillai, Come thou over with me, and I will feed thee with me in Jerusalem. And Barzillai said unto the king, How long have I to live, that I should go up with the king unto Jerusalem? I am this day fourscore years old: and can I discern between good and evil? can thy servant taste what I eat or what I drink? can I hear any more the voice of singing men and singing women? wherefore then should thy servant be yet a burden unto my lord the king?...Let thy servant, I pray thee, turn back again, that I may die in mine own city, and be buried by the grave of my father and of my mother..." (II Samuel 19:31-39)

Debra and I were reading this passage the other day and I was stunned by its inclusion of this conversation. Though it was between king David and a gracious foreigner to whom the king was offering some reciprocal hospitality, it is certainly a reflection of many family conversations being held today, though often less cordially.

What do we do with our aging family member who is struggling and will soon be unable to live by themselves? Can any of us take her in? How can we convince her to leave her long-term home? (I've been on the observation deck of many of these "discussions" and have often wondered, how can one mother raise 9 children but 9 grown children can't care for 1 mother?) Anyway, it is quite a complicated and emotional dilemma for many families today.

This passage is not instructive but is a bit illustrative of such a scenario. Take note of a couple of important realities here.

1. It is helpful when one party or the other can admit their age and its accompanying disabilities. Barzillai must have had a written list in his pocket; I suspect he had memory lapses, as well but he came right out with them.

2. It is also helpful when both sides recognize the resources that they have available to them. Verse 32 tells us that Barzillai was a very rich man. As king, David probably had unlimited resources for taking in his friend.
3. Barzillai then stated what he really wanted to do, to die at home and be buried with his parents. With his desires clarified and resources available, David conceded and they bade farewell to each other.

It is important that such conversations take place among honest and humble family members. The loved one's wishes must be heard and considered. Those who can help, to whatever extent, should offer it. Options should be explored. Decisions must be made. Loving, patient care and respect should dominate those conversations, by the grace of God.

For Prayer Today

- Are you presently embroiled in such a situation? Pray much for God's wisdom, courage, timing, extra grace, patience, and love for all the family involved, etc.
- Pray for God's provision of ideas, options, resources, and guidance toward good solutions and for family harmony and support.

Personal Notes and Responses

Plaques and Plagues

*"...If there be in the land famine, if there be pestilence, blasting, mildew, locusts, or if there be caterpillar; if their enemy besiege them in the land of their cities; whatsoever **plague**, whatsoever sickness there be; what prayer and supplication soever be made by any man, or by all thy people Israel, which shall know every man **the plague of his own heart**, and spread forth his hands toward this house: then hear thou in heaven thy dwelling place, and forgive and do..." (I Kings 8:22, 37-39)*

I still chuckle at a scribbled note in my files in which I was encouraged to consider honoring a long-time Bible Club Director at an upcoming church event with "a plague".

The verses above were part of a prayer that was prayed at the official dedication of Solomon's Temple, erected for the worship of Almighty God. It was an awesome structure and an awesome prayer of dedication but after two chapters of detailed blueprints and seven years of precise construction, there is no mention of any plaque attached to the building honoring its builders or supervisors. But in this long prayer, "plagues" are mentioned at least twice.

It was well known by the nation of Israel that during their long history whenever they rebelled against God, went their own way, worshipping and serving false gods, diving deeply into every form of immorality, etc. that God often responded with a disciplinary hand of pestilence, disease, famine, enemy attacks, and large numbers of deaths. Such heavy plagues were meant to humble the nation and turn them back to God.

The real key to this, though, was when individuals recognized and repented of their own, personal sinful condition, "the plague of his own heart" and "returned to You with all their heart and soul..." (I Kings 8:38-52) that that person was then forgiven and could come to know the full blessings of God.

The extent of our present crisis is not simply national; it is international. It is worldwide. And, our personal plague of sinfulness has touched every single person alive. What may God be saying to our world through this? Our response must be personal. Have you ever recognized that right from your start, your heart has been plagued by sin? Have you repented and put your trust in Christ to save you? It is the only way to personally know His forgiveness and freedom from sin's power and ultimate eternal punishment.

For Prayer Today
- Has God been tugging at your heart recently, in light of coved-19 and other trials? Talk to Him about your soul's condition and do some real business with Him.
- Pray for revival, a turning to God to take place across our world today that multitudes will turn from their sin and bow humbly before Almighty God.

Personal Notes and Responses

ETERNAL ENCOURAGEMENTS #55

Redeeming the Time

"...walk in love, as Christ also hath loved us, and hath given himself for us...walk as children of light...See then that ye walk circumspectly, not as fools, but as wise, redeeming the time, because the days are evil. Wherefore be ye not unwise, but understanding what the will of the Lord is." (Eph. 5:1-17) "Walk in wisdom toward them that are without, redeeming the time." (Col. 4:5)

As a commodity, we have learned how to tell time, mark time, keep time, make time, waste time, save time, lose time, kill time, and even do time! But how do we "redeem time"?

Actually, the Greek term translated in the verses above for "time" is not the usual word (kronos) noting the "passage of time" as we do with clocks and calendars. It is not in regard to the quantity of time but to its quality. It's "opportunity time" (kairos). It refers to a set time, a specific time in which to invest significantly what is important. The word "redeem" means to buy back or completely, that is, when we discover specific seasons, hours, or moments of time that provide unique opportunity for special use, we are to buy up those opportune times and use them well for things that really matter. When we hear opportunity knocking, we must throw open the door and welcome him in.

In these unique seasons of our lives, I believe that most of us have discovered opportune times that we never had or never recognized before. We ought to be jumping on these opportunities and investing them with valuable efforts toward God and others.

Parents have often defended their limited time with their children as valuing quality time over quantity time. Perhaps now that many of us have more of both, let's not waste these opportunities. Let's creatively use them to walk in love toward our family and neighbors. Let's walk in the light, avoiding the darker exploits and entertainments of our world. Let's walk in wisdom and according to the Spirit of God's control and His will. Let's walk toward the lost with the gospel of love and grace. Let's make these times really count – for eternity!

Let's not yawn our way through each day to the relentless ticking of the passage of time. Let us wake up from our lazy slumber and buy up every special opportunity to love our families and others with God's love and grace. May God's sovereign clock alarm us not to miss the opportunities that He places before us daily! (See also Eph. 5:14 and Romans 13:11-14) Let's redeem these times!

For Prayer Today
-   Ask God to help you evaluate your use of time and make any adjustments you need to make to please Him.
-   Pray for wisdom in discovering special opportune times where you can uniquely bless others and then invest yourself wholeheartedly in them.

Personal Notes and Responses

ETERNAL ENCOURAGEMENTS #56

The Power of Words

"Even so the tongue is a little member, and boasteth great things. Behold, how great a matter a little fire kindleth! And the tongue is a fire, a world of iniquity: so is the tongue among our members, that it defileth the whole body, and setteth on fire the course of nature; and it is set on fire of hell...But the tongue can no man tame; it is an unruly evil, full of deadly poison...Out of the same mouth proceedeth blessing and cursing. My brethren, these things ought not so to be." (James 3:5-10)

I am always a bit stunned by the strength of these words by James on the subject of our speech. But then a brief reflection on many testimonies from others and my own experiences certainly agree with the Scriptures that much damage, defilement, discouragement, and destruction can take place even with the use of a few words.

It doesn't take much to lose control or to deliberately choose to speak ill to or about others. Words spoken in anger can hurt people deeply. With gossipy talk we can damage someone's reputation in the minds of others. Repeated criticism can discourage folks and rob them of hope. People can be deceived and led astray by lies, distortions, and even flattery and valuable trust can be destroyed. Continual complaining and nagging can drive people to despair. Conveying someone's private information to others is a criminal offense today. Coarse, crude speech degrades the preciousness of life and brings defilement and intimidation and fear to others. Friendships and families can splinter and shatter by inappropriate and unguarded speech.

James' strong words make more sense now, don't they? Fortunately, our "gift of gab" has a tremendous upside, though. Good words are powerful, too, and the list of potential great uses of our speech is incredible.

We can speak loving words (Eph. 4:15), pleasant words (Prov. 16:24), soft words (Prov. 15:1), kind words (Eph. 4:31-32), encouraging words that build up others (Eph. 4:29), cheerful words (Prov. 12:25), and words of friendly greeting, etc. With our words we can confess sin, offer apologies, and express forgiveness to others. (Eph. 4:31-32) We can gently admonish and guide some who is straying. (Gal. 6:1) We can lift our voices in praise and worship of our great God and express genuine thanksgiving to Him. (Psalms) We can write and send messages of sympathy, gratitude, or celebration. (Phil. 1:3-11) We can pray and fellowship with God and take His Words to bless others. We can share a word of witness to a lost person and point them to Jesus. (Acts 1:8) We can ask for prayer support and be praying for others. (Romans 15:30-33)

Let's remain aware of the powerful potential of our words, for good or evil, and let's ask God to help us honor Him and bless others with them.

For Prayer Today
- Pray the words of Psalm 19:14, desiring that your words please God at all times.
- Pray for those in need of some loving and kind words, and then deliver them some.

Personal Notes and Responses

Saving and Spending are Spiritual

"There is treasure to be desired and oil in the dwelling of the wise; but a foolish man spendeth it up." (Prov. 21:20) "The thoughts of the diligent tend only to plenteousness; but of every one that is hasty only to want." (Prov. 21:5) "A good man leaveth an inheritance to his children's children..." (Prov. 13:22) "Through wisdom is a house builded; and by understanding it is established: and by knowledge shall the chambers be filled with all precious and pleasant riches." (Prov. 24:3-4)

In a previous "financial" devotional, I made the point that, for the Christian, priority # 1 for "our" income is giving; that we should give a portion of what God has provided for us back to Him in worship of Him. But what about the rest of the money? That is mine to do with what I want, right? Not exactly.

The glitch in thinking that way is that we forget that actually, we own nothing. It all belongs to God and thus, He can give direction about its use. (Psalm 24:1; 50:10-12; I Cor. 4:1-5) Saving or spending then, is also a spiritual activity since we are handling God's money. And, as always, His wisdom is best, on any subject. Below are several wise encouragements for our use of His resources.

1. From what is provided and earned, some of that should be set aside for future needs and plans. This is wise. Spending or wasting everything is foolish. (Prov. 21:5, 20; 13:22)
2. Wisdom involves looking ahead, anticipating future problems and saving regularly for them. (Prov.27:12) Not to do so is foolish.
3. Counting the cost of an object or project, then evaluating whether it is affordable or worth it, before embarking on it, is wise. (Luke 14:28-32)

4. Foolishness, ignorance, or misunderstanding are not the ways to build a house or accumulate wealth. Wisdom, knowledge, and understanding are. (Prov.24:3-4)

5. Contentment should guide our spending, not greed, covetousness, or a love of money. (I Tim. 6:6-12, 17-19; I John 2:15-17; Heb. 13:5-6) We also should avoid selfish hoarding (Luke 12:15-21; Matt. 6:19-21, 24) and trusting in our riches, instead of the Lord who provided them. (I Tim. 6:17-19)

So, generous giving to the Lord and to others is priority # 1. You can afford to give if you do it first, then live on what is left. Saving some of your income is a very wise second step with the money. You can save if you do it second, then live on what is left. You can't afford then to pay your bills, buy food, etc.? Yes you can, if you are walking with God, His wisdom and provision will enable you to have what you need daily. Wise planning, careful shopping, avoidance of debt, and lots of helpful advice by authors, Larry Burkett, Dave Ramsey, Ron Blue, Mary Hunt, and others are highly recommended.

For Prayer Today

- Ask God to help you avoid following foolish advice and bad habits that have contributed to financial troubles for you and your family
- Plead with God for His provisions and wisdom and for the discipline to follow His ways of managing His money.
- Pray for others who are seriously struggling financially.

Personal Notes and Responses

ETERNAL ENCOURAGEMENTS #58

Humble Pie

"Likewise, ye younger, submit yourselves unto the elder. Yea, all of you be subject one to another, and be clothed with humility: for 'God resisteth the proud, and giveth grace to the humble.' Humble yourselves therefore under the mighty hand of God, that he may exalt you in due time: casting all your care upon Him; for He careth for you." (I Peter 5:5-7)

John Rosemond, in his terrific book, "Parenting by the Book", reminds us that our grandmas never thought pride and high self-esteem were good and healthy in our children. They valued humility and modesty and sought to pass on those virtues to the younger generation. Expressions of pride indicated that the child was acting too big for his britches or was on his high horse and that those attitudes had better change quickly, or else! Grandma was actually espousing God's viewpoint on the subject.

God hates pride, resists and fights it as He encounters it but promises to give His grace, His help to those who are humble and even exalt them. So, what is this thing called humility?

Some clever sage said that humility is not thinking less of yourself but is thinking of yourself less. It is the opposite of pride which is always thinking too highly of oneself, is boasting, demanding one's own way, putting others down, and being unwilling to serve others. Pride is an attitude of entitlement and ingratitude. But humility recognizes that all we are and have is because of God and thus continues gratefully to depend on Him daily.

From our passage above, as well as in James 4:6-17, humility can also be described as an attitude of submission to God and to human authorities, an eagerness to help and serve others, a willingness to suffer inconvenience and pain, and a casting of all our cares and problems in prayer to God daily. It is a denial of self and an esteeming of others better and more important than ourselves. (Phil. 2:1-8)

Both James and Peter command us to "humble yourselves", in other words, take the initiative to choose an attitude and a lifestyle of humility and service. If you don't humble yourself, God or others may have to humble you. That's where the "humble pie" comes in. You may be forced to swallow a large piece of it. When God has to knock the props out from under us as He fights our sinful pride, there is no pleasure in it. The ingredients of humble pie are hefty measures of guilt, shame, regret, embarrassment, humiliation and often, great loss. And it tastes just horrible! Let's humble ourselves and really enjoy God's grace each day!

For Prayer Today
- Ask the Lord to help you humble yourself and then to keep you humble.
- Ask Him to show you ways to put aside your own personal desires in order to serve someone else.

Personal Notes and Responses

Is It Well With Your Soul?

"He that dwelleth in the secret place of the most High shall abide under the shadow of the Almighty. I will say of the LORD, 'He is my refuge and my fortress: my God; in him will I trust. Surely, he shall deliver thee from the snare of the fowler, and from the noisome pestilence. He shall cover thee with his feathers, and under his wings shalt thou trust: his truth shall be thy shield and buckler. Thou shalt not be afraid for the terror by night; nor for the arrow that flieth by day; nor for the pestilence that walketh in darkness; nor for the destruction that wasteth at noonday." (Psalm 91:1-6)

The story behind the well-loved hymn, "It is Well with My Soul" has been oft-told. Horatio Spafford, a Christian lawyer and supporter of D.L. Moody's in Chicago saw his vast real estate holdings destroyed by the Chicago fire in 1871. Two years later he sent his wife and four daughters ahead on a ship to England to investigate educational possibilities there for the children, but a mid-ocean collision with an English vessel sunk their ship. Among the 226 passengers who drowned were the Spaffords' four girls.

One dramatic version of the story has Horatio penning the words to this hymn on board another ship as it passed over the place where his daughters were lost. Whenever he wrote it, it was the result of God's incredible peace comforting and guarding his soul in spite of his overwhelming losses. He wrote...

"When peace like a river attendeth my way; when sorrows like sea billows roll, whatever my lot, thou hast taught me to say, 'It is well, it is well with my soul.' Though Satan should buffet, though trials should come, let this blessed assurance control, that Christ hath regarded my helpless estate and hath shed His own blood for my soul. 'It is well with my soul...'"

How is it possible to survive life's hardest storms and attacks with an ability to carry on trusting God and doing His will? Only this.

When you realize God's great love for you and all the suffering that Christ went through in order to provide eternal salvation for you, and you then admit your sinful condition and place your trust in Him to forgive and to save you forever – then He gives the strength and capacity to weather the storms of life. If you have trusted Him for your "forever", then you learn you can trust Him for today or tomorrow or with whatever. It can then be so very well with your soul.

"My sin – O the bliss of this glorious thought, my sin, not in part but the whole is nailed to the cross and I bear it no more! Praise the Lord, praise the Lord, O my soul! It is well… It is well… It is well, it is well with my soul."

For Prayer Today
- If you have not yet done so, please turn from your sin and place your trust in the Savior who died in your place and wants to save you.
- Talk to God often about the deep waters of your life and ask for His peace and guidance through those storms.

Personal Notes and Responses

Fear vs. Faith

"And the same day, when the even was come, He saith unto them, 'Let us pass over unto the other side.' And when they had sent away the multitude, they took him even as he was in the ship...And there arose a great storm of wind, and the waves beat into the ship, so that it was now full. And he was in the hinder part of the ship, asleep on a pillow: and they awoke him, and say unto him, 'Master, carest thou not that we perish?' And he arose, and rebuked the wind, and said unto the sea, 'Peace, be still.' And the wind ceased, and there was a great calm. And he said unto them, 'Why are ye so fearful? How is it that ye have no faith?...' (Mark 4:35-41)

Ah, yes...fears! We all have them, don't we? The human experience includes very natural fearful responses to things that frighten, intimidate, confuse, or overwhelm us. Some fears helpfully provide caution or hesitancy toward some real or perceived threat. Some enable time to think through options rather than just plunging ahead. But many fears simply torment us and paralyze us from doing what God wants us to do.

My parents enjoyed telling folks that when I was a toddler I was afraid of going outside, because the grass tickled my ankles. (That might explain my reputation of simply "loving the great indoors" as well as my penchant for wearing socks. Hmm.) My fear of water kept me from learning to swim. Official ministry years as a pastor had me trembling before entering difficult confrontational or counseling situations.

In the Bible, for the believer, there is a special response recommended for our fears. It is to "faith it", to trust God and to call on Him when fears are assailing us. In the account above, the disciples were facing real danger; the Lord rescued them and then confronted them about their lack of faith – in Him. Faith in the Lord can conquer our fears.

Someone said that there are 365 "Fear nots" in the Bible, one for each day. I've not counted them but I've listed a few of them below for your consideration.

1. Fear not but trust God to do even the impossible in His will. (Luke 1:30-38)
2. Fear not but trust God when physical elements threaten your safety. (Mark 4:35-41)
3. Fear not but trust God even when you suspect He does not care. (Mark 4:35-41)
4. Fear not but trust God's presence when in a season of loss (Psalm 23:4)
5. Fear not but trust God when wickedness appears over-whelming (Ps. 27:1-3)
6. Fear not but trust God when you doubt His love for you. (I John 4:17-19)

Members of the family of God need not live in fear, not with the God we have. Instead of being gripped by fear, let's be gripped by our God as we "faith it".

For Prayer Today
- Make a list of the fears that haunt you and talk to God about them.

Personal Notes and Responses

_____

Where the Birds Don't Sing (Apparently)

"By the rivers of Babylon, there we sat down, yea, we wept, when we remembered Zion. We hanged our harps upon the willows in the midst thereof. For there they that carried us away captive required of us a song; and they that wasted us required of us mirth, saying, 'Sing us one of the songs of Zion.' How shall we sing the LORD's song in a strange land'"? (Psalm 137:1-4)

In the 1970's or so, the Audobon Society began advertising a "bird clock". The face of it featured beautiful paintings of twelve beloved birds and on each hour you could enjoy each distinctive song of that bird. Wow! With our love of the birds, we just had to have one but then I saw the price tag. I believe it was something like $39.95 plus tax and shipping. No thanks; I can do without that.

Maybe a year later in a discount store I suddenly came upon a pile of bird clocks for the ridiculous low price of around $7.95! I sensed heaven smiling on me as I grabbed one and strutted happily home. Debra was so pleased. We quickly installed the batteries, hung it up and looked forward to its first musical offering.

I remember almost leaping out of my chair as it wound up and emitted several loud screeches. After an hour-long intermission, the second selection was different but was comprised of distinct howls and groans. It was awful. We pulled the clock off the wall for a closer look and discovered that the face of the clock pictured hardly one bird that we could identify and the makers of this clock hailed from the far east. I do hope they have birds over there that know how to sing but not one of the selections we heard could have made the top twelve list on any music chart. Even Disney could not have gotten any four of those birds to harmonize together.

After some days of enduring (and laughing at) a punctual succession of other-worldly shrieks and screeches that jarred us and started chills down our spines, we took the clock down. I exorcised its batteries and stashed it somewhere (till we sold it at a yard sale to a happy customer. We were smiling also.)

The passage above reminds us that sometimes we believers can find it hard to sing. Disastrous circumstances, political upheavals, personal losses can often rob us of our ability or motivation to lift our voices in song to God.

It is interesting to realize that even this passage of lamenting is found in Israel's songbook, the Psalms, and was probably sung often in timely situations. I am amazed how frequently in that book that singing is emphasized and commanded. God does understand our difficulties and our emotions and He wants us to cry out to Him, even in song. Let's not ignore music in our relationship with God; it can make a great difference in our outlook and attitudes.

For Prayer Today

- Sing to the Lord your praise and prayer to Him today; even use a few of the songs in Psalms to express your thoughts to God.

Personal Notes and Responses

Caring for the Crushed

"...and there came a messenger unto Job, and said, 'the oxen were plowing, and the asses feeding beside them: and the Sabeans fell upon them, and took them away;...slain the servants with the edge of the sword...the fire of God is fallen from heaven, and hath burned up the sheep, and the servants, and consumed them;...the Chaldeans made out three bands, and fell upon the camels and have carried them away, yea, and slain the servants...thy sons and thy daughters were eating and drinking wine in their eldest brother's house: and, behold, there came a great wind came from the wilderness, and smote the four corners of the house, and it fell upon the young men, and they are dead;...' Then Job arose, and rent his mantle, and shaved his head, and fell down upon the ground and..."(Job 1:13-22)

We will get back to Job regarding his day full of catastrophes real soon. For now, I want us to remember that many people around us have been dealing with overwhelming hardships and tragedies that have shattered their lives, families, and businesses and robbed so many of all hope. How can we minister to them? How might we help them?

Believe it or not, I want to share some suggestions based on, of all people, Job's "friends". They certainly don't deserve many accolades but their initial visit to Job reveals some wisdom in their approach to him. Please read Job 2:11-13 and notice several things.

1. They saw and sensed the greatness of Job's loss and grief and acknowledged it. Very quickly, they made a visit to mourn and comfort him.
2. They were saddened and shed tears over his plight. They identified with him, joined him on the ground, even shredding their clothes as he had his.
3. They silenced themselves – for an entire week (!), quietly respecting the deep pain of his grief. (Knowing from

the rest of the book how much they had to say, this initial restraint is amazing.) It was when they began to talk that things went downhill fast. These dear people do not need lots of words, advice, promises, etc. They need our care.

4. They sacrificed their own plans and agendas to invest time in him. It wasn't "business as usual". It was inconvenient and unselfish to be there with him.

We know that in our present (covid) situation, personal visits are mostly prohibited but that doesn't erase the need for serious bereavement care. Frequently, "friends" back away from someone caught in these depths, because such care can be costly or "we don't know what to say", etc. Let's not abandon these hurting folks. Let's find ways to identify with them and to express love and care. Little talk and lots of listening. Respectful sensitivity. Over-the-phone compassionate prayer for them. Sincere cards and handwritten notes. Small gift. A special treat. Etc.

For Prayer Today
- Ask the Lord for wisdom to reach out to someone who is deeply grieving right now.
- Pray faithfully by name for the many you hear about who are seriously struggling over losses and tragedies.

Personal Notes and Responses

Lessons from an Extreme Sufferer

"...Then Job arose, and rent his mantle, and shaved his head, and fell down upon the ground, and worshipped. And said, 'Naked came I out of my mother's womb, and naked shall I return thither: the LORD gave, and the LORD hath taken away; blessed be the name of the LORD.' In all this Job sinned not nor charged God foolishly... 'Shall we receive good at the hand of God and shall we not receive evil?" (Job 1:1-2:10)

If you have never read the book of Job, please turn there now and read the first two chapters. It is an incredible story involving shocking tragedies, riveting plot-line, some surprise main characters, a behind-the-scene challenge, and an epic attempt to settle some of the major issues about which Christians wonder and debate today.

Job is introduced to us as a noble, God-fearing man who lived righteously and sought to lead his family to honor God. He had great wealth and 10 children and was recognized as the greatest of all the people of the East. But, unbeknown to him, in a secret meeting between God and Satan (!) a daring challenge is made concerning Job's true character by Satan and God grants him the freedom to attack Job's life and family to test his faithfulness. In one day's time, moments apart, Job receives four messages that his wealth, most of his servants, and all of his children were lost.

When Job passes that test, round two begins with God's permission for Satan to attack Job's health. At his lowest condition of pain and grief, his wife attacks him with anger and demands that he curse God and die. But the verses above reveal Job's attitude at that time. Amazing! Then Job's friends arrive and after a week of compassionate silence, they light into him, charging him, accusing him of some wrongdoing, blaming him for his troubles, and doubting his testimony. This difficult debate is recorded in chapters 3-37, while

God remained totally silent, until He climaxes the book with His powerful words in the remaining chapters.

What do we do with this story? It rattles us somewhat but what are the possible take-aways from it?

1. Difficult adversity can and does happen to good and godly people and it is not always because of personal sin. God may use it for many purposes.
2. God is sovereign over all. Though He allows Satan, even today, to affect our world, He is ultimately in control and Satan's power is very limited.
3. Hardship can bring disunity and disagreement among friends and family members who have strong opinions about one's situation. Expect it.
4. By trusting God, it is possible to endure and survive incredible difficulties, to learn and grow through them, and to benefit others from those experiences. (James 5:10-11)

I have often wondered why in the world God put Job through all of this. I really suspect that one big reason was so that we'd have the Book of Job in our Bibles and could learn many challenging lessons from his story. Are we doing so?

For Prayer Today
- Pray that you will continue to learn the lessons that God wants to teach you through the trials of life. Pray for your faith in God to grow as you walk with Him.

Personal Notes and Responses

Eternal Encouragements #64

Delays and Detours

"A man's heart deviseth his way: but the LORD directeth his steps."
(Prov. 16:9) "The steps of a good man are ordered by the LORD:
and he delighteth in his way." (Psalm 37:23) "Now when they
had gone throughout Phrygia and the region of Galatia, and were
forbidden of the Holy Ghost to preach the word in Asia, after they
were come to Mysia, they assayed to go into Bithynia: but the
Spirit suffered them not." (Acts 16:6-7)

I remember well a very busy season of pastoral ministry in PA when my ministry of care to the sick and shut-ins was being seriously hampered and hindered. It seemed like every road was blocked and congested due to detours and other difficulties. I couldn't get anywhere easily and was often late for important appointments. I was so frustrated, frequently asking "How in the world can every road be blocked up?!?" Then one day I noticed the sign that answered my agonizing question. It said simply, "Men Working". Ohhhh, so that's why…ok.

But the problem was that I rarely saw these men who were supposed to be working. The sign should have declared, "Men Drinking Coffee", "Men Eating Lunch", "Men Leaning on their Shovels", or "Not Sure Where the Men Went". Though I couldn't see hard evidence of the sign's message, I needed to take it by faith.

Sometimes in the midst of another long delay or a frustrating detour away from my hopes and plans, I wish a sign would drop from heaven right before my eyes that would read…"God Working". I might not be able to see what God may be doing or understand His purposes for the delays but I must then trust that He is indeed at work. For the believer, He promises to work in all our circumstances to grow us toward maturity and Christlikeness. (Rom. 8:18-39)

One day I traveled to Philadelphia to visit with a lady who had cancer. I always found that city to be extremely difficult to get around, especially to a hospital that was new to me. On this day, I became so extremely upset with the traffic, the confusing set of directions I had, and my usual poor sense of direction. A trip that usually took an hour was two that day and by the time I entered the hospital my attitude was not good. I rushed to the lady's room only to discover that her door was closed and I was asked to wait in the hallway. More frustration and irritability on my part. About fifteen minutes later, a gentleman slipped out, and I rushed in, only to be met with the tears of the 40-year-old daughter in bed and her mother at her side who said, "Pastor Jones, you could not have come at a better time!" The doctor had just informed them that the daughter's condition would be terminal and that she had very little time left.

My plans and timing were not God's. He did not want me there earlier. The delays were His doing and for His purposes. O Lord, may I better trust you in these situations!

For Prayer Today
-   Ask the Lord to help you trust Him during the delays and detours of life and to guide your steps day by day.

Personal Notes and Responses

Paul's Bucket List

"Now, I would not have you ignorant, brethren, that oftentimes I proposed to come unto you, (but was let hitherto, that I might have some fruit among you also, even as among other Gentiles." (Rom. 1:13) "...according to my earnest expectation and my hope, that in nothing I shall be ashamed, but that with all boldness, as always, so now also Christ shall be magnified in my body, whether it be by life, or by death. For to me to live is Christ, and to die is gain." (Phil. 1:19-21)

The term "bucket list" was apparently coined by a filmmaker for a 2007 movie by that name. It refers to a person's collection of goals, aspirations, or achievements that one hopes to accomplish in his lifetime or, before he kicks that proverbial bucket.

The Apostle Paul referred to several of his goals in his writings such as preaching the gospel in places where Christ was unknown (Rom. 15:20-21), collecting and delivering funds to needy Jerusalem saints (15:25-28), and to finally get to Rome, after many failed attempts to do so, to minister to the folks there (15:22-24).

But when he wrote to the Philippians, Paul was a Roman prisoner and was possibly facing execution at any time. Realizing that his remaining time in life could be very short, he pens his remaining "bucket list" desires and aims. (I re-study this passage annually around New Year's to re-evaluate my own goals and plans.)

In brief, he says, whether I am living or dying, I want to so live that I magnify Jesus Christ to others. He earnestly desired that when someone looked at his life, they would clearly see the very character, attitude, and mission of Jesus Christ. He didn't want his life to portray a blurry, darkened, or frenzied view of striving for this world's values and pleasures. In his busy life or on his deathbed, he wanted his living or dying to point to Jesus Christ. Why? Because of what he said next.

He knew the real purpose of life, what life was all about. "For me to live is Christ and to die is gain." Life is all about knowing, trusting, and living for Christ and as a result, death, then, is all gain, all profit.

Is Paul's main bucket-list item somewhere on your list? For what are you living?

For Prayer Today

-   As you set up daily to-do lists or annual goals and projects, ask God for wisdom and direction, especially for the most important areas of life.
-   Ask the Lord to use your life to point others to knowing the Savior.
-   Pray for others who appear lost or wandering through life without meaning or purpose and for those who may have little time left – that they will come to know Jesus Christ as their Savior.

Personal Notes and Responses

Smokey the Bear Club

"...But now hath God set the members, every one of them in the body, as it hath pleased him...that there should be no schism in the body; but that the members should have the same care one for another..." (I Cor. 12:18-26) "And let us consider one another to provoke unto love and to good works: not forsaking the assembling of ourselves together, as the manner of some is; but exhorting one another..." (Heb. 10:24-25)

When I was a young child I sent away for a membership in the Smokey the Bear Club. How excited I was when I received my certificate, a song sheet of the club theme song, and my membership card which I proudly carried in my otherwise empty wallet. The neat thing was that it carried no real responsibilities except to watch out for forest fires and to be careful to prevent them. (With my early-on love for the great indoors, I had little opportunity to follow through on these instructions.) I still remember the words to the song, though!

It instructed us kids to recognize the dangers of a forest fire for all the animals and birds, and plants and trees and to be alert to any sign of a fire. It assured us that Smokey was on duty, growlin' and howlin' and sniffin' the air. We were urged to do the same, probably not the growlin' and howlin' though.

Some people think that joining a church is similar; they choose to belong but believe that there are no real responsibilities except to be careful not to start any fires. But the New Testament records quite a list of activities that members of the body of Christ should involve themselves with each other. Let me list some of them.

We are to gather together often (Heb. 10:25), encourage one another (10:25; I Thess. 5:11), admonish one another (Rom. 15:14), receive (welcome) one another (Rom. 15:7), build up one another (Rom. 14:9), bear (maybe that's Smokey!) one another's burdens and restore one another (Gal. 6:1-2), comfort one another (I Thess. 4:18; 5:11), forgive one another (Col. 3:13), love one another (I Peter 1:22-23), pray for one another (James 5:16), serve one another (Gal. 5:13), etc. Then there are the wonders of worshipping our God together and the adventure of rescuing lost and hurting people with God's love and saving grace. (Acts 2:41-42; Matt. 28:18-20) Wow!

Trusting Christ as your Savior and then joining a like-minded local church is the thing to do. But do not think of church as another Smokey the Bear Club. Do not be content just to sing the songs and avoid starting fires. Join in and enjoy the blessings of giving and receiving God's grace and love with others!

For Prayer Today

- If you are not a member of a good local church, ask God to guide you to one where you can grow spiritually and can serve God and His family
- Pray for churches today that are struggling with difficult situations, that they will remain faithful to their purposes and will be caring for others and reaching the lost.

Personal Notes and Responses

How Big is God?

"...for the glory of the LORD had filled the house of the LORD. Then spake Solomon, the LORD said that he would dwell in the thick darkness. I have surely built thee an house to dwell in, a settled place for thee to abide in forever...But will God indeed dwell on the earth? behold, the heaven and heaven of heavens cannot contain thee; how much less this house that I have builded?" (I Kings 8:10-27)

I think Solomon got it right. On the occasion of the dedication of the newly constructed majestic temple, Solomon uttered those words. He knew that the God whom Israel worshipped is far greater than could be effectively housed in an earthly structure. In his prayer repeatedly he admitted that heaven was God's dwelling place. The temple's glorious construction was for the name of the LORD to be planted among His people and so that all other people could come to know the God of Israel (8:22-61).

But what about God's actual size? Can He be weighed and measured? No, first of all, God is a spirit, which makes Him unmeasurable in the physical sense. Theologians, though, have attempted to describe the very nature of God and below are some of His basic "spiritual dimensions".

God is infinite, eternal, and boundless. He is not limited by time or space. He created time and space but exists beyond it all. (Psa. 90:1-2; Isaiah 40:12-31; Rev. 4:8-11)

God created all things including mankind. (Gen. 1-2; John 1:1-3; Col. 1:15-17)

God is sovereign, the ultimate and absolute authority over all. (Acts 17:24-31; I Chron. 29:10-12; Dan. 6:25-27)

God is all-knowing. (Psalm 139:1-6, 13-18; Acts 15:18)

God is all-powerful. (Eph. 3:14-21; Luke 1:37; Rev. 19:6)

God is everywhere present. (Psalm 139:7-12; Jer.23:23-24)

God is holy, separate from all else, the standard of righteousness and justice by which He will judge mankind one day. (Psalm 45:6-7; 97:1-2; Isaiah 6:1-5; 57:15; Hebrews 9:27)

We are just scratching the surface with these truths but please think on them. If you have a personal relationship with God through Christ, ask yourself, "Why do I ever fear, worry, or live with dread about the future?" Paul asks, if this kind of "...God be for us, who can be against us?" (Rom. 8:31)

When we forget all that our God really is, that's when our faith weakens and our doubts and fears grow strong. Think through the above points and rejoice with confidence in our great God and be eternally encouraged!

For Prayer Today
- Spend time just worshipping God today for all that He is and has done for you.

Personal Notes and Responses
_____

Shepherding Our Children's Hearts

"...thou shalt love the LORD thy God with all thine heart, and with all thy soul, and with all thy might. And these words, which I command the this day, shall be in thine heart: and thou shalt teach them diligently unto thy children, and shaltl talk of them when thou sittest in thine house, and when thou walkest by the way, and when thou liest down, and when thou risest up..." (Deut. 6:4-12)

It is vitally important that we raise our children to know, trust, and live for the Lord. This alone can provide a stable foundation for their lives and an exciting personal relationship with their Creator God. Many parents respond that they have no real time to do so. I respond that certainly none of us have extra time for this cause but, the Scriptures above indicate that we should do this *while we are doing our normal activities,* when sitting, traveling, lying down, rising up, etc. We are to both teach and talk of the things of God naturally and weave them into all we do. In addition to a brief devotional time after dinner there were two main ways I attempted to do this.

During our son's pre-school and elementary years I would put him to bed most nights with "David and Daddy Time". He'd climb into bed and I'd sit on it and we'd talk. I'd either tell him a brief story, read to him, sing with him, share a verse with him, laugh with him (some tickling required at times), etc. Usually only about 10 minutes, with his undivided attention, I could also share experiences from my life and how God worked with me, how He miraculously provided for me, etc. Sometimes, I'd ask him for a question or about how school was, etc. Then I'd pray with him, often very specifically about that next-day test or special need and then I'd slip out.

Also during those years over two summers, once a week I took him with me on my early morning walk. One summer over ten outings we discussed the Ten Commandments, explaining them and even memorizing them together on our walk. The following summer I took ten concepts from the book of Proverbs to discuss as we walked. I called them "Wisdom Walks" and they were so special to us both.

In David's junior and senior high school years, often I'd ask if I could lie on his bed to read while he did his homework at his desk. He welcomed my presence and often good conversations would break out. During his last couple years of school whenever we really needed to talk, we slipped away to "Talko Bell" for a snack (and conversed with our mouths full!) Actually, our hearts were full as well.

In these challenging times, do not miss the opportunities to impact your children spiritually. Treasure the Lord and His Word in your heart; let your children see and hear that often, not in a heavy-handed way but naturally and genuinely make it a way of life for your family.

For Prayer Today
- Pray often for your own children and grandchildren and for parents who know the Lord to prioritize investing spiritually into those younger lives.

Personal Notes and Responses

ETERNAL ENCOURAGEMENTS #69

Wilderness Wanderings

"And all the congregation lifted up their voice, and cried; and the people wept that night...and all the children of Israel murmured against Moses and against Aaron... Would God that we had died in the land of Egypt! Or would God we had died in this wilderness! ...The LORD spake unto Moses and unto Aaron, saying, ...I have heard the murmurings... as ye have spoken in mine ears, so will I do to you..." (Numbers 14:1-35)

For me, this is one of the saddest stories in all of Scripture. God had chosen Abraham's family for special blessings and purposes but they continued to reject and rebel against God's plan for them. After 430 years of bondage and slavery in Egypt, He delivered them with mighty power and brought them into the desert with Moses for a rather brief trip to the "Promised Land". After several months they arrived at its border, sent spies in to discover its nature, and then decided that they would not trust God to take them in; they would remain where they were – in the wilderness.

In a disciplinary way, God complied with their request and they ended up wandering in the wilderness of their choice for about 40 years until all that adult generation died off (except for several who trusted God). Deuteronomy and Joshua tell the story of the next generation's trust in God to take them into that land under Joshua's leadership.

Sadly, Moses also lost his "ticket" into the land when he allowed his emotions to get the best of him and disobeyed God in a fit of anger due to the complaints and threats of the mob. He also died in that wilderness, after 40 years of service for God there (Numbers 20:1-13).

Let's note several things for our own lives today.
1. Sometimes we make rash decisions due to our frustrations, fears, anger, and pride which we probably wouldn't make

when we are calm, cool, and collected and trusting God's will and wisdom.

2. All decisions and choices that we make carry consequences with them that may affect our immediate families and their futures. (This may be dietary, entertainment, where we live, career choices, how we parent, our attitude toward or relationship with God, etc.)

3. God's methods of working with us are sometimes not interventions and rescues, wiping out consequences, but may be allowing the sowing and reaping principle to have its impact. When man rejects God's ways, he is left with his own ways and resources which may enslave him and his family to a tiring existence of struggle and defeat. (See Psalm 106:8-15 on this.)

So many today seem to be wandering aimlessly in their own wilderness, without clear wisdom or worthwhile pursuits. Some are choosing to give up, seeing no hope for the future, they wander in routine circles without the joy, peace, and purposes for which God created them. Let's not allow difficult times to confine us to our own style of desert-living. Let's trust God's promises and follow Him daily.

For Prayer Today
- In prayer, trust God to lead you onward in His way each day. Then follow Him.

Personal Notes and Responses

ETERNAL ENCOURAGEMENTS #70

Practical Points on Prayer

"...praying always with all prayer and supplication in the Spirit, and watching thereunto with all perseverance and supplication for all saints; and for me, that utterance may be given unto me, that I may open my mouth boldly, to make known the mystery of the gospel, for which I am an ambassador in bonds: that therein I may speak boldly, as I ought to speak." (Eph.6:18-20)

Many followers of Christ still seem to have problems or questions about praying. In past devotionals we have seen some instruction on the subject and now from Paul's instructions to the Ephesian believers, we can clarify a few more thoughts on it. Please note the following truths.

1. **The Many Times for Prayer** – "praying always" We don't have to wait for a special call to prayer, a scheduled prayer meeting, or a controlled ritualized prayer. We can pray at any time and continuously about anything and everything. (I Thess. 5:17; Col. 4:2)
2. **The Manifold Types of Prayer** – "with all prayer and supplication in the Spirit..." We can pray prayers of worship and love for God, of confession, thanksgiving, personal petition, specific supplication, intercession for others, etc. while always desiring the Spirit's will and power in prayer (Romans 8:26-27)
3. **The Mighty Tenacity of Prayer** – "...and watching thereunto with all perseverance..." We are to pray by faith, really trusting God to hear and respond, and expectedly looking for His answers with patience and hope. (Luke 18:1-8; Heb. 4:14-16)
4. **The Mentioned Targets of Prayer** – "...for all saints and for me..." We can pray for all believers everywhere and then for those we know specifically by name for their

requested needs and hopes. Paul asks for boldness in preaching the gospel that others can believe and be saved.

5. **The Main Truth about Prayer** – in this passage is that prayer is part of "spiritual warfare". (I Peter 5:7-8; Luke 22:31-34) Paul describes that real and ongoing warfare and lists the pieces of spiritual armor we should be "wearing", but concludes it all with this emphasis on prayer. (Eph. 6:10-20)

For the believer, prayer is not some formal, polished prayer of recited ritual but is a real conversation with God, at any time about anything, while trusting God's will to be done in response. It is the means by which our enemy can be defeated and evil can be conquered in the lives of people for whom we pray. It demonstrates our moment-by-moment dependence on God and can express our continual praise and thanksgiving to Him.

Don't ignore this awesome privilege and resource in your daily life. I recommend that you keep this "conversation with God" going often throughout every day. It will make a great difference in all you do!

For Prayer Today
-    Thank the Lord for this access to Him during the spiritual battles of life.

Personal Notes and Responses

ETERNAL ENCOURAGEMENTS #71

Keep Looking Up

"Lift up your eyes on high, and behold who hath created these things, that bringeth out their host by number: he calleth them all by names, by the greatness of his might, for that he is strong in power; not one faileth...that the everlasting God, the LORD, the Creator of the ends of the earth, fainteth not, neither is weary... He giveth power to the faint; and to them that have no might he increaseth strength..." (Isaiah 40:26-31)

Multiple and varied trials that have overwhelmed our communities have created a populace that is struggling with discouragement and despair. Our eyes are darkened and downcast and our hope for the future is waning. Personal strength and stamina are degenerating into a growing weariness and weakness. Such was also the case for the nation of Israel in the days of Isaiah.

The first 39 chapters of Isaiah revealed to the nation their present and pending judgment of God, not good news at all. They were scattered among the nations and living in subjection to them. But with chapter 40 the message changes its theme to one of comfort, encouragement, and hope. And it begins by challenging the citizens to "Lift up your eyes on high and see..."your mighty God!

Chapter 40:9-31 describes the greatness of God in that He is sovereignly over and involved in all His creation. This includes the dimensions of the earth and the universe (40:12), His eternal wisdom and understanding (40:13-14, 27-28), His acknowledgement of all the nations as "a drop in a bucket, mere dust, and less than nothing"! (40:15-17) He is the true and living God, compared to the worthlessness of man-made false gods (40:18-20) and sits above the earth in heavens that He has created among the stars that He has named (40:21-22, 25-26). Wow! What a God!

The people of God are then admonished not to doubt God's knowledge or His care even during times of weakness and weariness

(40:27-30 and 10-11). Then they are encouraged with this reassurance, "But they that wait upon the LORD shall renew their strength; they shall mount up with wings as eagles; they shall run, and not be weary; and they shall walk, and not faint" (40:31).

Similarly in the New Testament we find these words of encouragement, "...let us run with patience the race that is set before us, looking unto Jesus the author and finisher of our faith; who for the joy that was set before him endured the cross...For consider him that endured such contradiction of sinners against himself, lest ye be wearied and faint in your minds." (Heb. 12:1-3)

Are you weary and discouraged today? Please, in a fresh way, look up to this awesome God and trust your situation to Him. Be eternally encouraged as you do so.

For Prayer Today
- As you pray, think about this incredible God to whom you pray and be encouraged that He loves and cares for you and has the ability to make a difference in your situation.

Personal Notes and Responses

Keep Looking Around

"Say not ye, There are yet four months, and then cometh harvest? behold, I say unto you, Lift up your eyes, and look on the fields; for they are white already to harvest." (John 4:35)

We have admitted that difficult circumstances can cast our eyesight downward or inward, focusing on our problems or feelings. But there are two other directions for us to gaze instead. First, we need to lift up our eyes to our powerful and gracious God and secondly, we need to glance around us and take note of the needs of others.

John 4 is the very special story of how Jesus crossed cultural barriers to speak to a broken, foreign woman (the "bad Samaritan" as I call her) in a deserted place as she sought for water. As He revealed His true identity to her, she received His living water and became a follower of His. She then raced home to tell others of her life-giving discovery and to invite them to meet the Savior also.

Jesus' disciples returned with food at the tail end of this conversation and wondered why He was talking with such a woman and when He refused the food they brought Him, they questioned the reason for that, too. His reply? "My meat is to do the will of him that sent me, and to finish his work…Behold, I say unto you, Lift up your eyes, and look on the fields; for they are white already to harvest." (John 4:27-35) I believe His command to raise their sights to the harvest fields actually called their attention to the approaching crowd of friends this woman was bringing to Jesus. There was important and eternal work yet to be done to reach and care for these inquiring, lost people. Having lunch was suddenly not top priority.

I believe the eyes of the disciples could have been blinded by prejudice against Samaritans or women in general, their physical hunger was in the way of seeing spiritual hunger in others, and a common practice of postponing important things till later may have factored in this scenario. At least they did not expect this to be harvest time in the lives of people nearby.

I have been guilty of similar limited sight. I've been near-sighted about myself and my agendas or my comfort zone at times and have missed some opportunities to help someone nearby in need. With shame I admit to avoiding a man I considered difficult for several years until God changed my heart and then eventually his as I finally saw his spiritual needs as far more important than my own. But that is a story for another day, Lord willing.

I do suspect that God places some difficult or broken people around us for us to notice them and to step into their world with God's grace and love. But if we continue to walk around with our heads down, focused only on our own needs, we will miss incredible opportunities to see the miracles that God can do in lives around us. (Read John 4:27-42 to catch the incredible ending of that story.)

For Prayer Today

- Ask the Lord to help you to "look around" today to find someone who needs some help, physically or spiritually, and for wisdom in how to get involved. You might be surprised at the effect this may have on you!

Personal Notes and Responses

International Rage

"Why do the heathen rage, and the people imagine a vain thing? The kings of the earth set themselves, and the rulers take counsel together, against the LORD and against his anointed, saying, Let us break their bands asunder, and cast away their cords from us.'" *(Psalm 2:1-3)*

There is certainly no worldwide "peace on earth" today; the extreme opposite is what is true. Global conflict, physical catastrophes, dangerous pandemics, senseless crimes and killings, ethnic animosity and violence continues to shred the very fabric of societies and threatens to destroy all that is good in life itself. From where do all these evils come? The Bible answer is that such conditions start in the sinful hearts of mankind and contagiously affects our whole world (James 4:1-3; 1:13-16; Jer. 17:9).

Our text above indicates that its evil has spread and is evident among the rulers and leaders of governments and nations. Notice three general characteristics of nations and their leaders who do not submit to God. They display an...

1. Arrogance of Leadership–"rulers set themselves" taking a defiant position and are prepared for war. Pride, even national pride can carry with it an arrogant stance and a disparaging view of all others.
2. Antagonism to Lordship–"take counsel together against the LORD and His Anointed (Christ)" Powerful leaders are prone not to submit to the sovereign reign of God; instead they tend to ignore or resist Him.
3. Attraction to Liberty – "Let us break their bands asunder and cast away their cords from us." We hear so much today about people's freedoms and their alleged "rights". People do not want any restrictions or laws placed on them and entire governments are bending over backwards to provide for such a lawless society.

What is God's view of all of this? He laughs! "He that sitteth in the heavens shall laugh: the LORD shall have them in derision." He laughs, not because the situation is funny but because it is so foolish and hopeless. God's wrath and justice-driven judgment is coming on all nations (2:5-9) and Christ will ultimately rule over this whole earth in peace. But notice how this Psalm ends.

Before it is too late and judgment comes, the leaders of the nations are invited to come humbly and repentantly before God and to put their trust in Him. (2:10-12) This is the "good tidings of great joy that shall be for all people", the "peace on earth, good will toward men" (Luke 2:10-14). This is the gospel being offered worldwide to all, including the leaders of the nations! God is so gracious!

For Prayer Today
-   Pray for our country's governmental leaders at every level, that they will recognize their need to turn to God and to govern under His leadership.
-   Pray also for all global governments in light of our passage today.

Personal Notes and Responses

ETERNAL ENCOURAGEMENTS #74

This One's Rated "R"!

"For this is the will of God...that ye should abstain from fornication: that every one of you should know how to possess his vessel in sanctification and honor; not in the lust of concupiscence...For God hath not called us unto uncleanness, but unto holiness." (I Thess. 4:3-7) "...Flee fornication..." (I Cor. 6:13-20)

Rated "R" for *"Really?"* You actually are writing on this subject in a devotional? *Really?*

YES, REALLY!

We live in a sexually saturated and sickened world today where moral norms and standards have almost disappeared and no restrictions or guidelines are expected of the populace at large. Every form of sexual expression is permitted and provided for as selfish lusts are inflamed, sexual addictions are destroying lives and marriages, women and children are used and abused, diseases abound, crimes are committed, and lives are ruined or destroyed. Billions of dollars are made as the entertainment industry and the worldwide, gut-wrenching human trafficking epidemic daily cheapens, degrades, and corrupts what God intended to be uniquely pure and precious.

God's Word is certainly not silent on this subject. God is the gracious creator of our sexuality and wrote the Book on the subject. He wants us to enjoy this aspect of His grace and thus He strongly warns us for our protection even as He grants us this wonderful provision.

PROTECTION – God warns us of the powerful lusts within us and the enticing temptations around us. He acknowledges the pleasures inherent in this area of life but provides strong boundaries to keep us from the sinful entanglements and addictions, from the costly expense of sin's consequences, and the explosive and extensive damage and destruction it brings to individuals, families, and to life itself (as in David's and Solomon's lives). Please read these very clear warnings in these passages; they are meant for our safety and blessing: Prov. 2:10-20; 5:1-14, 20-23; 6:20-35; 7:1-27; 23:24-28; 29:3; I Cor. 6:15-20; I Thess. 4:1-8; II Tim. 2:22; Matt. 5:27-28) Take heed! REALLY!

PROVISION – God's original intention for sexuality was to bless married couples with an exciting and satisfying continual bonding experience that is exclusively their own. This pure and holy union would enhance the totally unselfish giving and receiving of life-long committed love and provide for the multiplication of the family raised in a loving environment for the good and godly impact on our world. It was to be enjoyed freely, without shame or guilt and to be treasured by both parties as a special gift from God. See Gen. 2:18-25; Prov. 5:15-20; Psalm 78:1-8; 127 and 128; all of Song of Solomon, I Cor. 7:1-5; I Thess. 4:1-8; Heb. 13:4.

Some would argue that we are just being "old-fashioned" to think this way. No, this is being "eternally fashioned"; it is the eternal God's perspective and plan. Thus, it is an "eternal encouragement" to enjoy these intimate gifts His way, and with His blessing.

"REALLY!"

For Prayer Today
- If you struggle in this area, as so many do, talk honestly to the Lord, gain any forgiveness or help needed, and begin to adopt His way of life in this area.
- Pray for the many people who are working to help rescue people who have been damaged by sexual bondage and abuse and for lasting help and victory to be gained.

Personal Notes and Responses

The Gratitude Attitude

"In every thing give thanks: for this is the will of God in Christ Jesus concerning you." (I Thess. 5:18) "Be careful for nothing; but in every thing by prayer and supplication with thanksgiving let your requests be made known unto God…" (Phil. 4:6) "By him therefore let us offer the sacrifice of praise to God continually, that is, the fruit of our lips giving thanks to his name." (Heb. 13:15) "Enter into his gates with thanksgiving, and into his courts with praise: be thankful unto him, and bless his name." (Psalm 100:4)

Do you remember how hard it was to teach your children to say "Thank you" to anyone who showed a kindness to them? Just two little words, how hard could it be to remember them and use them without any prompting? Usually with some embarrassment, we'd whisper, "What do you say, Jimmie? Sallie, what should you say now?" Finally the right response came out but mumbled and rather unconvincing. Lessons that needed repetition so very frequently.

One day in an effort to show our young son how often people do things for us that should deserve a grateful response, we visited a favorite Chinese restaurant. We prepped him to notice the opportunities that would surface and, it was a bit overwhelming for all of us, the frequency of them. First was the man who opened the front door and greeted us and the lady who showed us to our seat, handing us our menus. Then came the water glasses, taking our order, bringing more beverages, more napkins, and then the leaving of a generous tip for all the service. It was a fun exercise in addition to a great meal.

God seems to be expecting us to be grateful and to express it rather continually, even for all things! Imagine that! Is this reasonable; is it even possible? It is when we honestly recognize how needy and dependent we are on God and on others.

The very air we breathe and depend on comes regularly from God. The amazing bodies in which we live with all their abilities and capacities were from His design. The ability to work, maintain a job, earn a salary is of His enabling. The many blessings we enjoy as family members, the freedoms and opportunities we have in this country, all are gifts of His grace. And, above all else is the eternal salvation we have through the sacrifice of Jesus Christ, forgiveness and deliverance from sin and membership in the family of God forever.

But we live in a world that is consumed by an attitude of entitlement and an arrogance of pride and self-sufficiency that expects and sometimes demands certain treatment and provisions. Among such people, genuine, humble gratitude is practically nonexistent. So very sad and another trip to that restaurant probably won't help that much.

Let's make sure we are not guilty of ingratitude. Do you want to make someone's day? Write a special thank-you note (not an email or text) to someone who did something lately for which you are grateful. You may be amazed at its impact!

For Prayer Today
- Fill your prayers today with expressions of sincere gratitude and begin including some in every conversation you have with God daily.

Personal Notes and Responses

ETERNAL ENCOURAGEMENTS #76

Suffering Wrongfully

"...but if, when ye do well, and suffer for it, ye take it patiently, this is acceptable with God. For even hereunto were ye called: because Christ also suffered for us, leaving us an example, that ye should follow his steps: who did no sin, neither was guile found in His mouth: who, when He was reviled, reviled not again; when he suffered, he threatened not; but committed himself to him that judgeth righteously: who his own self bare our sins in his own body on the tree, that we, being dead to sins, should live unto righteousness..." (I Peter 2:18-25)

As believers in Christ, we have marveled and rejoiced at God's mercy for us – His withholding from us the punishment which we deserve. We are so blessed by His daily grace – His abundant and continuous goodness to us, which we certainly do not deserve. But in our passage for today, Peter writes about a similar paradoxical condition that is expected of us. (Fasten your seatbelts.)

Have you ever been punished, as a child, for something you did not do? Has your employer ever blamed you, maybe docked you some pay, for something about which you were totally innocent? Have you stood firm on a right and godly position and suffered loss because of those who opposed you? Peter addresses that situation here and in I Peter 2:18-20, he even refers to a workplace relationship where this might happen.

A bit stunning is his next statement, *"For even hereunto were ye called: because Christ also suffered for us, leaving us an example, that ye should follow His steps..."* – in suffering for doing right! Jesus Christ, the perfectly righteous One was charged for all our sin and He willingly suffered in our place. Wow! So, how did He handle this "injustice" in real time here on earth? Peter describes how He did so, expecting us to follow His example when we suffer for doing right. Note the following pattern.

1. He did no sin. Being treated wrongly is no excuse for us to sin against others. He suffered for our sins so we could live righteously. Unfair treatment is an opportunity to respond righteously, not sinfully.
2. He suffered in silence. He did not threaten or revile His tormentors. He didn't shout to the crowd how unfair it all was.
3. He suffered by faith. He trusted His situation to God the Father, the Righteous Judge in heaven. Often, we can't right every wrong or fix every injustice, and we shouldn't seek revenge, but we can trust God with it all; He can right things in the end. (Rom. 12:17-21)
4. He even prayed for God to forgive His tormentors! (Luke 23:34)

You say, "This makes no sense at all. It's not fair. I can't accept this! This isn't justice!" You are right. But neither is God's mercy or grace which He provides for us. They make no sense either except when we realize that they are a genuine expression of God's amazing love for us. Can we not treat others the same way? Can we not follow Jesus' example on how to suffer wrongfully? It's our calling!

For Prayer Today

- If you are angry or bitter because of unfair treatment, review the above verses and ask God to help you to follow Jesus' example.

Personal Notes and Responses

Selective Memory

"Remember, O LORD, thy tender mercies and thy lovingkindnesses; for they have been ever of old. Remember not the sins of my youth, nor my transgressions: according to thy mercy remember thou me for thy goodness' sake..." (Psalm 25:6-7) "...for they shall all know me... saith the LORD: for I will forgive their iniquity, I will remember their sin no more." (Jer. 31:34) "I, even I, am he that blotteth out thy transgressions...and will not remember thy sins." (Isaiah 43:25)

We all have probably heard of "selective hearing", that developing skill among some of our older family members who decide that they only want to hear what they want to hear and so they "tune out" the voices or noises they desire not to hear. Some spouses suspect that their mates actually turn down their hearing aids to appear unable to hear them. One person said to me recently, "Oh, my husband has good hearing aids; what he really needs is a "listening aid!"

Our opening verses today seem a bit similarly amusing as David pleads with God to remember this and that, but not that other thing. He seemed to be hoping that God has "selective memory." And fortunately for all of us, He does!

This is not divine amnesia or some form of dementia that robs God of His ability to remember. It is in accordance with the very character of God that He chooses to remember some things and not others. He calls to mind, is mindful of some things and refuses to do so with others, especially our sins.

God does not and will not ever forget who He is or His essential character of holiness, mercy, lovingkindness, and gracious love. (Psalm 98:1-3) He will always remember and keep the covenants and promises He has made to His people. (Gen. 9:14-16; Lev. 26:40-45; Psalm 105:8-11, 42-45; Ezek. 16:59-60) He calls to His mind, remembers our own frailty and weakness and cares for us tenderly. (Psalm 103:13-14)

But, praise God, He selectively chooses not to call to mind our sinfulness. Through Christ's sacrifice for our sin and our faith in Him, we have been forgiven and cleansed and have been freed from all guilt and condemnation due to them. (Psalm 103:10-12; Jer. 31:34; Rom. 8:1, 31-34) No need to bring them up!

Sadly, so often we fixate on the failures, faults, and sins of others and refuse to let them go. Our chosen refusal to forgive others further sears their offences more deeply into our memories and robs us of the joys of restored fellowship and friendship. At those times, we really need to remember all that God has forgiven us, and then to selectively choose not to dredge up the sins of others but to forgive them. (Eph. 4:31-32; Matt. 18:21-35)

Notice in the verses above from Jeremiah and Isaiah how God's choosing not to remember Israel's sin is so closely tied to the fact that He had forgiven them. Our sins against Him are buried in the depths of the deepest sea with a God-posted "No Fishing!" sign floating above them. And on shore is posted, "No Hatchet Hunting!"

For Prayer Today
- Thank God, that because of Christ, our forgiven sinfulness does not linger in God's memory or interfere with our relationship with Him.
- Ask God to develop in you a selective memory that frees you to forgive others.

Personal Notes and Responses

Our Good Shepherd

"...But he that entereth in by the door is the shepherd of the sheep. To him the porter openeth; and the sheep hear his voice: and he calleth his own sheep by name, and leadeth them out. And when he putteth forth his own sheep, he goeth before them, and the sheep follow him: for they know his voice...I am the good shepherd: the good shepherd giveth his life for the sheep..." Jesus said, I am the good shepherd, and know my sheep, and am known of mine...My sheep hear my voice and I know them, and they follow me: and I give unto them eternal life; and they shall never perish, neither shall any man pluck them out of my hand..." (John 10:1-30)

In both Old and New Testaments, God has often referred to His followers as His sheep, certainly not a flattering designation, but an appropriately accurate one. In today's passage, Jesus clearly identifies Himself as the good shepherd who provides genuine care for His sheep. Let's focus on this relationship that He has with us.

1. **It is a possessive one**. Notice His repeated use of "*my* sheep". He owns us, possesses us; we belong to Him. He is not a hired hand who does not own or care for the sheep as in 10:12-13. We are His! How special is that? The Lord is *my* shepherd and I am *His* sheep.

2. **It is a personal one**. A good shepherd calls his own sheep by name. Jesus knows His sheep and they know Him and His voice. (10:3, 14, 27) Though His flock is massive and global, He provides a personal touch to each one. We are not a number; we have a name, known by the Shepherd! (John 10:3; Luke 10:20; Phil. 4:3; Rev. 21:27)

3. **It is a protective one**. This passage acknowledges the frequent presence of wolves, thieves, robbers, and phony shepherds but this Shepherd provides security and safety continually. He is the door of the sheep fold. He goes before and leads the sheep safely. He was even willing to die for the sheep!

4. **It is a permanent one**. He provides His sheep with eternal life and guarantees that they will never perish or be snatched away by anyone. "...and I shall dwell in the house of the Lord forever." What a guarantee that is! (Psalm 23:6)

When we truly realize how wonderful and precious is this relationship that Christ has provided for us, we will eagerly "hear His voice and follow Him."

As you move through the pastures where the Shepherd has led you, may you continue to open His Word to hear from Him and then to follow Him securely as you serve Him and so many others.

For Prayer Today
- Ask the Good Shepherd to guide you throughout the details of your every day.
- Many of you are literally shepherding others – in your family, workplace, ministry, etc. Ask God to make you a good shepherd for these folks each day.

Personal Notes and Responses

Thieves and Robbers!

"...He that entereth not by the door into the sheepfold, but climbeth up some other way, the same is a thief and a robber...Verily, verily, I say unto you, I am the door of the sheep. All that ever came before me are thieves and robbers: but the sheep did not hear them. I am the door: by me if any man enter in, he shall be saved, and shall go in and out, and find pasture. The thief cometh not, but for to steal, and to kill, and to destroy: I am come that they might have life, and that they might have it more abundantly." (John 10:1-10)

While we were in the sheepfold in our previous devotional, I thought we'd linger here a bit longer to consider the dangers that can be present in our relationship with Christ. Christ made it clear in John 10:11, 15, 28-30 that He died for us and paid the full price of our salvation. Our salvation is secure once we trust in Him and no one can remove us from His eternal grasp. But in the same passage, He alerts us to others who may be climbing into our lives in some other way, not to join us in the family but to steal, kill, and destroy.

These intruders move among us to steal – to take things from us for their own benefit. Others, the robbers often use violent means, emotionally plundering and harming their victims. (Judas was described as a thief; Barabbas, a robber.) But what impact might they have on us? What might they desire to take from us?

We might be robbed of our virtue. Believers, even pastors are seen often to fall into sin that destroys their testimony and their ministries. Our spiritual vision can diminish as we yield to the temptation to focus our time and efforts on earthly things that ultimately do not matter. Our careful vigilance can weaken as we become careless about our lifestyle choices and pursuits. Our valor or courage can disappear as we wimp-out to life's challenges with fear and anxiety. We can even lose our voice, finding ourselves less willing to speak out about our wonderful Savior, remaining silent instead. Instead of frequent victories, we find ourselves often defeated, discouraged, and even unaware of the loss of some precious, eternal valuables.

Whenever you feel like you are under attack or are losing ground to an enemy, please remember that your good Shepherd is nearby. Your salvation is safe. He is at the door of the fold, on duty night and day. He can drive away the intruders and help you restore your losses and enjoy a life of victory and service for Him. He has indeed come that we might "have life... more abundantly"! Let's not allow anyone or anything rob us of those blessings.

For Prayer Today
-   In spite of the steady onslaught of national and personal crises, pray that believers in Jesus will lean hard on Him for help that is needed.
-   Pray for those who are embattled and hurting, that the Lord will grant them refreshment, encouragement, and hope each day, that they will "go in and out and find pasture".

Personal Notes and Responses

The Problems with Prosperity

"He that loveth silver shall not be satisfied with silver; nor he that loveth abundance with increase: this is also vanity. When goods increase, they are increased that eat them: and what good is there to the owners thereof, saving the beholding of them with their eyes? The sleep of a labouring man is sweet, whether he eat little or much: but the abundance of the rich will not suffer him to sleep. There is a sore evil which I have seen under the sun, namely, riches kept for the owners thereof to their hurt. But those riches perish by evil travail: and he begetteth a son, and there is nothing in his hand. As he came forth of his mother's womb, naked shall he return to go as he came, and shall take nothing of his labour..." (*Eccl.5:10- 6:9*)

Many people who struggle with various degrees of poverty often think that having just a bit more money would solve their problems and then all would be well. That is almost never the case. Similarly, those at the opposite end of the economic spectrum trust that their greater resources would provide them security from all the troubles and dangers of life. Often, not true. In fact, wealth can bring on a whole new set of temptations and trials.

In the Book of Ecclesiastes Solomon mentions some of those challenges. First of all, money does not satisfy; the more you have, the more you want. Plus, the more you have, the more people seek to benefit from it. Then, the more you have, the more worries and fears you might have, accompanied by less peaceful sleep. (Remember Christ's words in Matt. 6:19-21 about the moths, rust, and thieves?) Also, the more you hoard selfishly, the more you'll leave behind when you go.

So, why does God bless so many with so much? God does intend to provide for the needs of His people and the enjoyment of such blessings is not wrong. Solomon admitted that in Eccl.

5:18-20. But there is more to it than that. Note what Paul says in I Timothy 6:17-18.

"Charge them that are rich in this world, that they be not high-minded, nor trust in uncertain riches, but in the living God, who giveth us richly all things to enjoy; that they do good, that they be rich in good works, ready to distribute, willing to communicate;..."

God has given us everything we have so that we can continue to give to others who are in need. I want to encourage all of us to look around to discover some opportunity to share what God has given to us with someone else in this difficult time. A grocery, gasoline, or restaurant gift card, a payment of a utility bill, some homemade baked goods, a Visa card to use wherever needed, a fruit basket, a surprise pizza delivery, a Bible, or other helpful books about the Lord, etc.

"It is more blessed to give than to receive." (Acts 20:35) I hope you have discovered that fact.

For Prayer Today
- Ask God to help you to share something from what He has given you with someone else.
- Thank God for all that He has entrusted to you.

Personal Notes and Responses
_____

ETERNAL ENCOURAGEMENTS #81

Secret Sauce

"Take heed that ye do not your alms before men, to be seen of them...But when thou doest alms, let not thy left hand know what thy right hand doeth: that thine alms may be in secret: and thy Father which seeth in secret himself shall reward thee openly... But thou, when thou prayest, enter into thy closet, and when thou hast shut thy door, pray to thy Father which is in secret; and thy Father which seeth in secret shall reward thee openly...when ye fast, be not, as the hypocrites, of a sad countenance: for they disfigure their faces that they may appear unto men to fast...But thou, when thou fasteth, anoint thine head and wash thy face; that thou appear not unto men to fast, but unto thy Father which is in secret: and thy Father, which seeth in secret, shall reward thee openly." (Matt. 6:1-18)

Perhaps we have all eaten something totally delectable and then requested of its maker the recipe only to be stunned when we are told that it includes a secret ingredient of their grandmother's that cannot be revealed. "Secret sauce" is used often to indicate some portion of something that is not made known publicly but happens to be the key to its popularity or success. Have you noticed the emphasis on secrecy from Jesus in this passage from His "sermon on the mount"? Apparently, His followers are to have some secrets, as well.

Jesus instructed that when we give to the needy, when we pray, and when we fast, we should do those things in secret. We should not announce it publicly or dramatically perform it to be seen or noticed by others. We are not to call attention to these habits or activities; they are to be carried on privately and anonymously. The promised result will be that God will bless and reward those obedient activities publicly. The same benefits are guaranteed to those who meditate in the Word of God, day and night. (Psalm 1; Joshua 1:8)

So, do we want God's blessing in all we do in our daily lives? Do we want people to "taste and see that the Lord is good" through us? Do we want to sense the pleasure of God and the amazing things He can accomplish in us and through us frequently? Do we want to enjoy our public activities and interactions with others, knowing that we are making a positive difference in people's lives? Do we really want to bring attention and glory to God in everything we do? Then our "secret sauce" will be what we do privately.

These privately blended necessary ingredients of our lives, our praying, fasting, giving, and study of God's Word will make all the difference in our effectiveness in the lives of others publicly. They will contribute joyfully to the benefit of others and bring great glory to God. Likewise, such success among people will diminish considerably if we neglect these secret sauces and can produce a bitter or sour taste in the lives of those we wish to help.

For Prayer Today

-   So, how is your private life? Ask God to help you develop the discipline of these private activities in your schedule, to prioritize special times with Him, as you prepare to serve others daily. (Don't leave out the secret ingredients!)

Personal Notes and Responses

Morphing – God's Way

"Therefore if any man be in Christ, he is a new creature: old things are passed away; behold all things are become new." (II Cor. 5:17) "I beseech you therefore, brethren, by the mercies of God, that ye present your bodies a living sacrifice, holy, acceptable unto God, which is your reasonable service. And be not conformed to this world: but be ye transformed by the renewing of your mind, that ye may prove what is that good, and acceptable, and perfect, will of God." (Rom. 12:1-2) "But we all, with open face beholding as in a glass the glory of the Lord, are changed into the same image from glory to glory, even as by the Spirit of the Lord." (II Cor. 3:18)

In my growing up years I was never introduced to the more exotic (strange) vegetables like squash (I call it squish) and zucchini. (Thanks, mom and dad!) When I first encountered them, I decided they were repulsive enough to avoid at all costs. I understood why some had humorously advised that at certain times of the summer it was recommended to keep your car and house doors locked tightly to discourage people from leaving zucchinis on your property.

Then my wife got ahold of some zucchinis and worked miracles with them! She changed their very form and I am now delightedly enjoying as much zucchini bread and pancakes that she can produce. Those horrid veggies had been "morphed" – their form had been totally transformed into something incredibly wonderful! It's like they have been converted!

Incredibly, God is into transforming (morphing) people from lost sinners into forgiven members of His family. In our sinful condition, we could be pretty repulsive and selfish, but as God works His miracle of transformation in our lives, we can take on the very character of Christ. (Rom.8:28-30) That is only possible because Christ took on the form of a human man; God became man in order to die in our place for our salvation. He morphed into humanity so we sinful humans could be transformed (morphed) into children of God!

God originally formed man in His own image; the devil deformed man by sin; this world tries to conform us into its worldview; educators try to inform man with knowledge; society tries to reform man of his problems but only Jesus Christ can transform us – to morph us, to change our very form from the inside outward by His saving grace and love.

Review the verses above and rejoice in God's miraculous process of morphing us more and more to be like Him.

For Prayer Today
- Ask the Lord to reveal to you areas of your life on which He is working to change and then cooperate with Him in it.
- Thank God that He can change anyone from a sinner to a saint, a child of God. Pray that others will call on Him to do just that.

Personal Notes and Responses

"Cymbalic" Despair and Delight

"...I remembered God, and was troubled: I complained, and my spirit was overwhelmed. Selah. Thou holdest mine eyes waking: I am so troubled that I cannot speak...Will the Lord cast off forever? And will he be favorable no more? Is his mercy clean gone for ever? doth his promise fail forevermore? Hath God forgotten to be gracious? Hath he in anger shut up His tender mercies? Selah. And I said, This is my infirmity..." (Psalm 77:1-10)

David was not the only human writer of the Psalms who was very honest and direct in challenging God's sense of justice or compassion. Asaph was another one who, in a sense, took His anger and despair to God poetically to another level. Reading most of his Psalms (50, 73-83) will reveal this clearly.

This eminent prophet and musician whom David set up as a chief choirmaster, with David wrote songs of praise and played instruments. Several times it is made clear that Asaph and his sons played on the cymbals of bronze. (I Chron. 15:19; 16:5; 25:1-2, 6; II Chron. 5:12; 29:30; Ezra 3:10) I can well imagine times when the percussion section upped the decibels for the Psalms of Asaph to communicate his angst and anger to God.

But also, like David who began many Psalms in emotional turmoil and frustration, Asaph also ended his pieces with clear direction and determination. Notice in this Psalm what he determined to do in light of his heavy, despairing heart, in verses 10-12.

1. "I will remember the years of the right hand of the most High."
2. "I will remember the works of the LORD...thy wonders of old."
3. "I will meditate also of all thy work."
4. "I will talk of thy doings."

He determined to think back to those times when the strong hand of God responded in deliverance and provision. He recalled those episodes when God powerfully did works of wonder. He focused on those incredible memories, meditating on them and then went about talking and testifying to others about them, reciting how God had intervened on behalf of him and his nation. His excitement over God returned and rejuvenated his hope in the Lord.

His piece of music grew louder into a great crescendo of crashing cymbals as his choir exploded with *"who is so great a God as our God? Thou art the God that doeth wonders...!"* Can't you hear it? I think I can! (77:13-14)

For Prayer Today
- As you talk to the Lord, remind yourself of past times in which you saw God work in special ways and thank Him again for them. Relish those memories in worship of your great God.
- Ask Him for opportunities to talk about Him to others and to share some of those special stories about Him. Ask Him to help you lift your eyes above your circumstances in order to joyously serve Him.

Personal Notes and Responses

One Grand Picnic

"...And when the day began to wear away, then came the twelve, and said unto him, Send the multitude away, that they may go into the towns and country round about, and lodge, and get victuals: for we are here in a desert place. But he said unto them, Give ye them to eat. And they said, We have no more but five loaves and two fishes; except we should go and buy meat for all this people. For they were about five thousand men. And he said to his disciples, Make them sit down by fifties in a company. And they did so..." (Luke 9:10-17)

Ever since I first heard this story as a child, I think it has been my favorite of Christ's earthly miracles. It also may be among God's favorites (beside the miraculous works in the crucifixion and resurrection) because it is one of very few that are recorded by all four gospel writers. (Matt. 14, Mark 6, Luke 9, John 6)

After a long, busy, and exhausting day, the multitudes that remained around Jesus probably numbered around 10,000-12,000 weary and hungry folks, if you assume many women and children were also present. Jesus shocks His disciples with His order to them that they provide food for all these people, a truly overwhelming and probably unnecessary expectation.

Have you ever realized that God sometimes sends or allows us to be confronted with circumstances far beyond what we believe that we can handle. Why does He do this? There are many reasons, but one of them is to provide for us a real life test.

These situations can be times of testing from God. John says in his record, "And this he said to prove him: for he himself knew what He would do." (John 6:6) Gen. 22:1 tells us that God tested Abram about offering up his only son. Deut.8:1-3 says that God used hard times in the wilderness to humble and test Israel to discover and reveal the condition of their hearts in those times.

These situations should be times of trusting God. The disciples' initial reaction was to explain that their very small resources were far from sufficient for the job. They suggested an alternative activity to bypass what Jesus commanded, that they should just send the people away to find their own food. What Jesus said in response was to bring the few food items to Him, to place them in His hands. Instead of looking within for the answers, we also need to place every such situation in God's hands and see what He may do with them.

These situations should be times of thanking God. As Jesus received the meager fare, He looked up to heaven and gave thanks for them. Then He began distributing the food that God multiplied in His hands. Everyone ate all they needed and twelve baskets of left-overs were gathered!

Such challenges need not terrify or discourage us. We can pass the tests as we trust the Lord with them, with gratitude. Don't dismiss this story as just a simple children's Bible story. God wants us adults to get its message as well.

For Prayer Today
- Pray for all those you know who are facing overwhelming circumstances presently with evaporating resources, in light of this story.

Personal Notes and Responses

ETERNAL ENCOURAGEMENTS #85

Strength and Courage

*"...Be strong and of a good courage: for unto this people shalt...
Only be thou strong and very courageous, that thou mayest...Have
not I commanded thee? Be strong and of a good courage; be not
afraid, neither be thou dismayed:..." "This book of the Law shall
not depart out of thy mouth; but thou shalt meditate therein day
and night, that thou mayest observe to do according to all that is
written therein: for then thou shalt make thy way prosperous, and
then thou shalt have good success." (Joshua 1:1-9)*

Joshua had heard those words spoken to him by God, and later
recorded them. About forty years earlier, Joshua and Caleb had
sought unsuccessfully to convince the Israelites that by trusting
and obeying God, they could indeed and must enter and conquer
the "Promised Land". (Num. 13-14) During those four following
decades of wilderness wanderings, Joshua stayed close to Moses
and was being mentored by him. Now, with Moses deceased, God
spoke to Joshua to prepare him to step into Moses' sandals to lead
Israel into the land. But why would he need all this strength and
courage? Several reasons.

1. He would need it to take on something entirely new. He
    would have a new position – as leader of this large, previ-
    ously nomadic nation, in a brand new place on the other
    side of the Jordan River. The "program" would be dif-
    ferent, little traveling but settling into houses and lands
    prepared for them. God's methods of provision would no
    longer be daily "wonder bread" delivered to their tent door.
    Practically everything would be different. People usually
    resist change. (Josh. 1:1-5)

2. He would need it as he took on the military challenges of
    his task, to conquer and defeat the residents of the land.
    There were morally despicable and corrupted peoples to
    be confronted and removed. They would meet with serious

resistance from dangerous enemies. The job would be challenging, indeed. (Josh. 1:1-5)

3. After conquering the land, it would also fall to Joshua to divide up the land and to give to each tribe their allotment of the real estate. What a nightmare doling out any inheritance to a group of heirs can be. This task involved all the land to all the tribes. (1:6)

4. And, throughout it all, God commanded him personally to be obedient to all the laws of God and by conquering his fears and doubts, develop within him God's very character. (1:7-9)

Do you find yourself lately having to do new things in new ways and in new places? Are you overwhelmed with the task of leading and caring for a group of people who are fearful and despondent? Are you struggling to maintain your own personal walk with the Lord?

The key to the strength and courage you may need is to trust the very presence of God with you, His promises to you, and to meditate in God's Word daily. Please read all of Joshua 1:1-9 to see all God's encouragement to Joshua.

For Prayer Today

- For whatever challenges you are facing, ask God for the same strength and courage that Joshua received from Him for your specific tasks and needs.
- In times of dis-couragement, let God's eternal truth en-courage you daily.

Personal Notes and Responses

ETERNAL ENCOURAGEMENTS #86

God Notices and Remembers

"...But to do good and to communicate forget not; for with such sacrifices God is well pleased." (Heb. 13:15-16) "...For God is not unrighteous to forget your work and labor of love, which ye have shewed toward his name, in that ye have ministered to the saints, and do minister." (Heb. 6:9-10) "...Then shall the righteous answer him, saying, Lord, when saw we thee an hungred, and fed thee? or thirsty, and gavew thee drink...? And the king shall answer, Verily I say unto you, Inasmuch as ye have done it unto one of the least of these my brethren, ye have done it unto me." (Matt. 25:34-40)

In three separate and different passages above, God takes note of and gives encouragement to those who are serving others. The first acknowledges the pleasure that God receives as He observes such action. The second emphasizes that God remembers such activity and regards it as indicative of true salvation ("things that accompany salvation" Heb. 6:9-10). And in the third setting which will take place at the beginning of His future earthly kingdom, He indicates that when a child of God served one who is needy during the time of tribulation on earth, that Christ will regard that service as done directly to and for Him. That certainly elevates such ministry to a higher level of value!

Probably most of you who are reading these words find yourself, either by occupational or career choice or by other circumstances, deeply engaged in caring for others who are in difficult straits. Over time you may find yourself growing very weary and drained. You may wonder why others cannot help with the task or why even those whom you are serving keep turning on you and making things even more difficult. You may feel unnoticed and unappreciated. Yet you labor on, sacrificing precious time, money, energy, and even your own health in this effort to care for someone or many in need.

Please know that God notices and regards your service as highly valuable and helpful and very pleasing to Him. It is by His grace that you are able to serve, and the help you provide allows others to see His love and care for them, through you. James 1:27 expresses that the true essence of pure religion is seen when people visit and care for people who are in any trouble, like widows and orphans in their times of brokenness and stress.

As a pastor and one who has served as a chaplain in nursing homes, I have seen how great an impact can be had by even a small amount of tender care. A genuine smile, a listening ear, a cup of water, a moment of laughter, a small card or gift, a light touch… can bring great joy and blessing to the recipient.

For those of you who do this all day long on most days each week, your value and that of all you share with others cannot ever be calculated. Please know that God notices and appreciates it all and that you are making a huge difference in so many lives each day. What a blessed way to live!

For Prayer Today
-   Let's pray much for those who, every day, are serving so many others who need to sense God's loving care for them. Pray for their own health, their stamina, their families, opportunities for rest, etc.

Personal Notes and Responses

180

ETERNAL ENCOURAGEMENTS #87

Order in the...Everywhere!

"Where wast thou when I laid the foundations of the earth?...Who hath laid the measures thereof?...Who hath stretched the line upon it? Whereupon are the foundations thereof fastened? or who laid the cornerstone thereof...? Or who shut up the sea with doors, when it brake forth...when I made the cloud the garment thereof... and brake up for it my decreed place, and set bars and doors...? (Job 38:1-11) "In the beginning God created the heaven and the earth...And God said, Let there be lights in the firmament of the heaven to divide the day from the night; let them be for signs, and for seasons, and for days, and years..." (Gen. 1:1-11) "For God is not the author of confusion, but of peace...Let all things be done decently and in order." (I Cor. 14:33-40)

I have recently become the owner of a brand-new, beautiful, Amish-made desk, complete with two file drawers, four smaller drawers, a special place for a lap-top, cubby-holes to the upper left and right corners and a lengthy bookshelf on top. For over twenty years I have done all my study and writing at a table. I balked repeatedly at spending the money for such a desk until my wife discovered a hidden stash of undesignated cash that we had forgotten about which covered almost the full cost of the desk. I then humbly complied with my wife's desire to bless me with this special gift. I am very thankful.

But the desk came with some serious expectations. For years my work table had been cluttered with piles of papers, magazines, clippings, sermon notes, booklets, opened and unopened mail, etc., like someone's personal landfill (but without the stench)! I repeatedly had to remind her that these were "active piles" and should not be disturbed.

Then this desk arrived. It was obvious that the creators of this desk thought it through thoroughly and meticulously designed it to provide for every need any desk-bound person could have. There is a special place for everything and everything should obviously be kept in its place. I have no excuse for my sloppy chaos any longer.

The Creator of the universe also did the same with this planet for us earth-bound people. He designed it perfectly and placed it in a safely reeling universe. He measured its dimensions, planned limits for its various components and on and on we could go. Please read carefully Gen. 1-2 and Job 38-41 as God describes His orderly work and recognize that He is indeed a God of order. He does not have a sloppy, haphazard approach to life. He is not the source of confusion or chaos; sin has produced that.

In our world of disordered brokenness and where fear and insecurity reign in the hearts of people, please know that our sovereign God is still in control, is holding the elements of our universe together, and is working out the details of His overall plan for His creation. (Col. 1:15-17) He organized this world, ordained that His will be done, and is orchestrating His plan for all of us.

And, as we draw closer to Him through Christ, we can know greater order and peace in our lives.

For Prayer Today
- Is any area of your life in disorder? Commit it to the God Who can help you straighten things out in accordance with His original plan for you.

Personal Notes and Responses

Eternal Encouragements #88

E-Prayers

"...The effectual fervent prayer of a righteous man availeth much. Elias was a man subject to like passions as we are, and he prayed earnestly that it might not rain: and it rained not on the earth by the space of three years and six months. And he prayed again, and the heaven gave rain, and the earth brought forth her fruit." (James 5:13-18) "...And Elijah went up to the top of Carmel; and he cast himself down upon the earth, and put his face between his knees..." (I Kings 18:41-46)

Well, we've all heard of e-mail, e-medicine, e-meals, e-sports, and e-tc. What are "e-prayers"?

I am using that e-lingo to refer to E-lijah's prayers which were both e-xtreme and e-ffective. James uses Elijah as an e-xample of e-ffective praying. And, so shall I.

James refers to Elijah that way as he concludes a section on the subject of prayer that recommended it for all kinds of situations. Among them are for situations of different degrees of suffering, sickness, sinning and even special times of prayer from one's church leaders. (James 5:13-18) Then he mentions the praying prophet, Elijah.

Elijah-Prayers were indeed Extreme in nature. He prayed twice for weather conditions which resulted in an over-three year drought in that country followed by monsoon-like conditions and flooding. He prayed for a widow woman who was impoverished and then bereaved of her only son; both needs were dramatically addressed by God. As he entered an incredible spiritual battle against hundreds of false prophets, this time fire fell from the heavens for the "win" by God and His servant. (All these accounts can be read in I Kings 17-19 Don't miss it.)

Obviously, Elijah's prayers were indeed Effective. Don't you wish you could pray that way? But, why would James use this Old Testament prophet as an example for us if we can't expect God to respond similarly to our prayer efforts? What is there about his praying that we might learn and follow?

First of all, he prayed by faith. He knew or believed what God wanted or would do in each situation and then prayed for God's will to be done each time. Sometimes God's Word (spoken then, written now) make God's intentions very clear indeed.

He also prayed with fervency, a deeply motivated and sincere crying out to God. His praying was not superficial, ritualistic, or hypocritical. It was honest, heart-felt, audible, and desperate. (Often it is only when we reach a level of personal desperation and anguish that we get serious in our praying. And God knows our hearts.) In Bible times, those praying this way were often lying flat on the ground in humility and brokenness. Some fasted from normal life activities to spend concentrated time with the Lord. Fervent prayer is also persistent and patient praying, not giving up if God seems slow to respond. (See Luke 18:1-8.)

Elijah's prayer life exemplifies all of this and illustrates for us what God can do when we seriously cry out to Him for His will to be done.

For Prayer Today
- Bring to God fervently and by faith, your most desperate needs and burdens today. Spend time and energy in crying out to Him. Pray that way also for others who are despairing of life at this time.

Personal Notes and Responses

ETERNAL ENCOURAGEMENTS #89

Ownership or Stewardship?

"Wherefore David blessed the LORD before all the congregation: and David said, Blessed be thou, LORD God of Israel our father, forever and ever. Thine, O LORD, is the greatness, and the power, and the glory, and the victory, and the majesty: for all that is in the heaven and in earth is Thine; Thine is the kingdom, O LORD, and Thou art exalted as head above all. Both riches and honor come of thee, and thou reignest over all...Now therefore, our God, we thank thee, and praise thy glorious name. But who am I, and what is my people, that we should be able to offer so willingly after this sort? for all things come of thee, and of thine own have we given thee...O LORD our God, all this store that we have prepared to build thee an house for thine holy name cometh of thine hand, and is all thine own...". (I Chronicles 29:10-17)

One of the first four-letter words our young toddlers learn to say with sincere expression, perfect diction, and considerable volume is *"M i n e!"* Sometimes it is a declaration of possessive ownership as a favored object is clasped tightly in their arms. Sometimes it comes across as a trumpet call to battle as they spy some other child across the room reaching for some neglected toy, unaware of the skirmish about to begin. And, sometimes, these children become adults who continue to mutter it as an entitlement password to everything within their reach.

Some individuals and even churches actually boast about how much money they raised or how much they give every year. Some people yearn to see their names on some publicly positioned plaque where others can see how much of *their* resources they have donated to some worthy cause. Not so with David. The generous offering simply led Him to praise His Almighty God Who had funded the project from His resources through His people. It was all His all the time.

This amazing mindset is spot-on in truthfulness but we can often forget it and then live like everything is *mine*, at least everything in *my* house, wallet, portfolio, vehicles, etc. When we maintain that attitude toward things we can become protective, selfish, greedy, worried, and easily angered or crushed when *our things* are taken from us, damaged, or diminish in value.

However, if we believe that all we have belongs to God Who has entrusted us with them to manage and use them for His purposes, our attitude can be quite different. We become more careful managers of God's property; we worry less about finances because they are not ours, but His. We become eager givers and sharers of His wealth to others who are in need. And, we rejoice in our incredible God who continues to provide what we need from His generous hand each day.

This prayer was motivated by the super-abundant generosity of people around King David as free-will offerings were given for the building of the first temple. (I Chron. 29:1-20.) But David acknowledged publicly that it was only possible because of what God had earlier granted to them. It was all *HIS*!

For Prayer Today
-   Ask the Lord to examine your attitude toward possessions and to make any adjustments necessary.
-   Thank God for His daily provision of all you and your family need.

Personal Notes and Responses

One Day at a Time

"Give us this day our daily bread." (Matt. 6:11) "Let us therefore come boldly unto the throne of grace, that we may obtain mercy, and find grace to help in time of need." (Heb. 4:16) "My grace is sufficient for thee..." (II Cor. 12:9) "...as thy days, so shall thy strength be." (Deut. 33:25)

The above verses come from different contexts, admittedly. The first from Christ's sample prayer, indicating that we are to trust God for each day's bread (not even day-old bread!). The second one reassures us that at whatever time we need extra gracious help, we can ask and receive it during those very needy times, even in that timely fashion. Paul was told by the Lord that God's grace would be everything he needed at the time of need. The fourth verse is from Moses' final blessing on the tribes of Israel and to the tribe of Asher was said, "As your days, so shall your strength be."

Just as fresh manna arrived 6 days each week punctually for the nation of Israel for 40 years, so every morning, "...his compassions fail not, they are new every morning: great is thy faithfulness." (Lam. 3:22-23)

For most people, life is quite complicated, our calendars fill up, obligations nag at us, and our future seems so confusing. The advice to "take one day at a time" is wise advice, especially in light of God's encouragement to trust Him for each day. Jesus said, "Take therefore no thought for the morrow: for the morrow shall take thought for the things of itself..." (Matt. 6:34) We are told, "Boast not thyself of to morrow; for thou knowest not what a day may bring forth." (Prov. 27:1)

I haven't mastered this discipline but two things I try to do have been very helpful. For major tasks and challenges that stretch over many days, I try to determine all that may need to be done today and get it listed; then I focus on those items only that day. I also try to pray every morning specifically about the details of that day, asking God for each item or resource that may be needed and for His guidance each step through that day.

Lina Sandell Berg wrote hundreds of hymns in the 1800's and has been called the "Fanny Crosby of Sweden". One of my favorites of hers summarizes beautifully our point for today. It is called, "Day by Day".

> "Day by day and with each passing moment
> Strength I find to meet my trials here.
> Trusting in my Father's wise bestowment,
> I've no cause for worry or for fear.
> He whose heart is kind beyond all measure
> Gives unto each day what He deems best.
> Lovingly, it's part of pain and pleasure,
> mingling toil with peace and rest.
> …As thy days, thy strength shall be in measure
> This the pledge to me He made."

For Prayer Today

- Have you made your list for today and determined what your needs might be? Now commit that list to the Lord in prayer, specifically trusting Him with each item. (Repeat process early tomorrow.)

Personal Notes and Responses

Lots of Laughs

*"Then Abraham fell upon his face, and **laughed,** and said in his heart, Shall a child be born unto a man that is an hundred years old? and shall Sarah, that is ninety years old, bear?" (Gen. 17:17) "Therefore Sarah **laughed** within herself, saying, After I am waxed old...? And the LORD said to Abraham, Wherefore did Sarah **laugh?**...' Then Sarah denied, saying, I **laughed not;** for she was afraid. And he said, Nay; but thou didst **laugh**." (Gen. 18:12-15) "And the LORD visited Sarah as he had said...for Sarah conceived, and bare Abraham a son in his old age...and Abraham called the name of his son...Isaac. ('**Laughter**')...and Sarah said, God hath made me to **laugh**, so that all who hear will **laugh** with me..." (Gen. 21:1-7)*

Whenever someone asks me what my growing up days in Phoenixville, PA were like, I frequently say that they were a lot of fun. My dad loved to laugh and to make his family laugh. Almost daily there was some degree of silliness and good humor enjoyed by all. Good-natured teasing, joke telling, silly banter, and goofy fun. We didn't have a car so we went nowhere. We didn't have TV but...we had dad. Friday nights were board game nights playing Uncle Wiggly, Parcheesi, Monopoly, Chinese Checkers, etc. while consuming lots of candy and throwing candy wrappers at each other. Ah, yes; I remember it well.

There is a Bible family whose laughter took divine notice and even recording for our learning. You've met them above. Why so much laughter? It wasn't because things that God said were hilariously funny (though Abe did fall on his face, I'm not certain he rolled around down there), but they certainly seemed so to Abe and Sarah.

1. They laughed because God's repeated promises seemed like complete impossibilities. They both were so old,

having a child seemed inappropriate, implausible, and incredible. But is anything too hard for God? (18:13-14)

2. They laughed because God's promises seemed to take forever to fulfill. It was already too late; she was too old; they were too weak! They doubted God, debated the issue, and denied his ability. (Note God's emphasis on time in 18:10, 14, and in 21:1-2; it was to happen in God's time.)

3. They laughed because God's miraculous fulfillment of His promises to them would not be kept secret. Many others would hear of God's amazing work and would end up laughing with them! (21:6-7) Great joy and fun!

Can you imagine festive gatherings with friends and relatives, "Tell me again why you named your firstborn 'Laughter'? That certainly doesn't sound very spiritual or godly? Why did you do that!?" And their humble testimony of their lack of faith and of God's powerful faithfulness would live on, even till today!

I am so glad that God created us with the ability to laugh and to enjoy life (I Tim. 6:17; Eccl. 3:1, 4). But let's not make light of God's promises and laughingly doubt His character. That's not funny at all.

For Prayer Today

- Are there portions of God's Word that you chuckle at with doubt and disbelief? Ask God to help you to understand and to trust his Word in a life-changing way.

Personal Notes and Responses

ETERNAL ENCOURAGEMENTS #92

A Prayer for a Nation

"In the first year of Darius...which was made king over the realm of the Chaldeans...I set my face unto the Lord God, toseek by prayer and supplications, with fasting, and sackcloth, and ashes; and I prayed unto the LORD my God, and made my confession, and said, O Lord, the great and dreadful God, keeping the covenant and mercy to them that love him, and to them that keep his commandments; we have sinned, and committed iniquity, and have done wickedly, and have rebelled, even by departing from thy precepts and from thy judgments: neither have we hearkened unto thy servants and prophets, which spake in thy name to our kings, and our princes, and our fathers, and to all the people of the land...to the inhabitants of Jerusalem, and unto all Israel, that are near, and that are far off, through all the countries wither thou hast driven them, because of their trespass that they have trespassed against thee...As it is written in the Law of Moses, all this evil has come upon us: yet we made we not our prayer before the LORD our God, that we might turn from our iniquities, and understand thy truth. Therefore hath the LORD watched upon the evil, and brought it upon us: for the LORD our God is righteous in all his works which he doeth: for we obeyed not His voice..." (Daniel 9:1-19)

This is an actual prayer that Daniel the prophet uttered to God on behalf of His nation, the people of Israel. They had been in captivity to Babylon and to the Medes and Persians for about 70 years due to their sinful rebellion against God. Daniel's heartfelt and fervently expressed cries to God reveal several things.

Daniel prayed with an honest humility and contrition. He identified with his country and with their sin. The repeated use of pronouns, "I, we, us" reveals his own admission of shame and guilt before God.

Daniel also knew the cause of the problem and its solution. He did not make excuses and build a defense for the nation's actions. He called it sin, evil, and rebellion, and the solution was not a political change, a more robust economy, or more equity for all. It was genuine repentance before a holy God and undeserved forgiveness and changed lives by His grace.

The Lord God had a unique relationship with Israel including many covenants and promises, which He has not made to any other country, including the United States. Yet our sinful condition as a nation is very similar to Israel's and we find ourselves in bondage to selfish pride, lusts, anger, hatred, materialism, and a lack of reverence for God and His Word. Our nation is sinfully broken and the consequences of it are felt by all. It is time for all of us to humble ourselves and bow before God, asking that He move our people to repentance and to a restoration of reverence to Him. Repentant prayer and changed lives by God's grace are our only hope.

For Prayer Today
- Let's pray for our country, asking God to bring us to our knees in humble repentance, personally and nationally, that He might again bless our land.

Personal Notes and Responses

Learning to Talk...All Over Again!

"Wherefore putting away lying, speak every man truth with his neighbor: for we are members one of another. Be ye angry, and sin not: let not the sun go down upon your wrath: neither give place to the devil...Let no corrupt communication proceed out of your mouth, but that which is good to the use of edifying, that it may minister grace unto the hearers...Let all bitterness, and wrath, and anger, and clamor, and evil speaking, be put away from you, with all malice: and be ye kind one to another, tenderhearted, forgiving one another, even as God for Christ's sake hath forgiven you. (Eph. 4:25-32)

It has been a real joy to be close to our little family here in Ohio and to have a part in loving and training our grandchildren. What a special pleasure it is to listen to their progress in learning to speak. It can be a lot of fun hearing them express themselves for the first time and thereafter. But soon, we are appalled at what can come out of those little mouths and we often may wish they had a whole lot less to say. Their quick lies, their impatient harshness, their anger, their whining...their young sinful nature expresses itself vocally so very often. Some corrective training is needed.

Paul, in Ephesians, teaches that once we come to Christ, as children of God, we may have to learn how to speak all over again, too. He gives several admonitions concerning the direction this speech re-education needs to go.

1. Total honesty must replace lying. At all times we must speak the truth. The reason he gives is that we are members of each other. We belong to each other. Such consistent honesty in our speech always will build strong trust and strengthen our relationships in the body of Christ, especially as we speak that truth in love. (4:15, 25)
2. Birth pangs of anger must not be ignored or put off. Conversations that dispel anger and address problems

constructively must take place earlier rather than later. (4:26-27) Silence isn't always golden; sometimes it's just plain yellow.

3. Our words must be chosen carefully, making sure that they tear no one down but instead provide grace and goodness that will build people up, helping them to grow in the Lord. (4:29)

4. Kind, humble, tenderhearted words that offer forgiveness must replace sinful responses of anger, wrath, evil speaking, malice, etc. Verbally lashing out back and forth must be stilled with words of apology or of forgiveness. (4:31-32)

Is there any area where you may need to learn again how to speak? Like a stroke victim who finds it difficult to speak clearly, sometimes it can be a difficult process. Allow the Word of God to give you instruction and the Spirit of God to control and help you with this. Maybe a good friend can help, as well.

For Prayer Today

- Pray Psalm 19:14 today and often. "Let the words of my mouth and the meditations of my heart be acceptable in Your sight, O LORD, my strength and my Redeemer."

Personal Notes and Responses

How Rich I Am!

*"Or despiseth thou the **riches of his goodness** and forbearance and longsuffering; not knowing that the goodness of God leadeth thee to repentance?" (Rom. 2:4) "But God, who is **rich** in mercy, for his great love wherewith he loved us, even when we were dead in sins, hath quickened us together with Christ, (by grace ye are saved)... that in the ages to come he might shew the exceeding **riches of his grace** in his kindness toward us through Christ Jesus..." (Eph. 2:4-10) "But my God shall supply all your need according to **his riches in glory** by Christ Jesus." (Phil. 4:19) "O the depth of the **riches** both of the wisdom and knowledge of God!..." (Rom. 11:33) "...the unsearchable **riches** of Christ..." (Eph. 3:8)*

As we continue to age, we may come to better recognize those things that are really most important in life and hang on to those things of value which are most precious to us. For many it is material wealth, their savings and investments which they hope will last forever but which seem to fluctuate wildly in value and evaporate quickly.

The most valuable riches do last forever and God is indeed the source and Manager of those. Note three tiers of these "investments", from "entry-level to eternal".

Riches of God's Goodness – To all people everywhere God extends His goodness. God "did not leave Himself without witness, in that He did good, gave us rain from heaven and fruitful seasons, filling our heart with food and gladness..." (Acts 14:17) These riches are a part of His mercy that He extends to all with the desire to lead people to repentance of sin and trust in Christ. Unfortunately, most people reject this mercy and refuse to trust in Him. Eventually the time to invest in Him runs out.

Riches of God's Grace – God's mercy to all is accompanied by the riches of His grace. He withholds judgment for a time while offering His saving grace and goodness to all who will trust in Him. Our eternal salvation is totally paid for and provided to us by this grace, this eternal gracious goodness of God. God loves to give His good gifts to all who trust Him and such giving continues daily for every believer. The returns on our investment in Christ grow daily and can overwhelm us with His love, joy, and peace. This is His free amazing and abounding grace by which we can be saved and then live daily in such generous goodness from Him.

Riches of God's Glory God promises to meet our every need of our earthly and our eternal lives from His unlimited riches in glory, again through Christ! That is quite an amazing guarantee! There's no need to fear or worry in this present life or throughout eternity. God's unlimited resources will be much more than enough to care for us and will enable us to bring Him glory forever (Phil. 4:20).

For Prayer Today
– In spite of any struggles you may be going through, be encouraged by praising God for His abundant eternal riches that He has provided for you. If you are still resisting His goodness and grace, please consider investing (trusting) in Christ for your salvation.

Personal Notes and Responses

Eternal Encouragements #95

A Good and Long Life for our Children

"Honour thy father and thy mother: that thy days may be long upon the land which the LORD thy God giveth thee." (Ex. 20:12) "Honour thy father and thy mother, as the LORD thy God hath commanded thee; that thy days may be prolonged, and that it may go well with thee, in the land which the LORD thy God giveth thee." (Deut. 5:16) "Children, obey your parents in the Lord: for this is right. Honour thy father and mother; which is the first commandment with promise; that it may be well with thee and thou mayest live long on the earth." (Eph. 6:1-3)

You may feel like I am really meddling now but I believe that many parents have drifted very far from the Creator's original design for parenting. And our culture has provided many varied ideas and options to replace what God has said. And the results of doing so are not very good.

Parents used to rejoice when their children learned, "Children obey your parents in the Lord, for this is right." (Eph. 6:1) But then these same parents began believing that the very opposite is true, that "Parents are to obey their children for this is right." Parents began asking children their opinions, wants, or desires about most things and then quickly responding to fulfill those desires. As those exchanges multiply day to day, our little ones learn who it is who is in charge and is making final decisions. "Mommy and daddy exist to serve me and my desires. And, if they resist, I can scream, pout, nag, or become difficult until they do comply." No fun at home.

May I suggest that by putting many questions to our little ones who aren't yet mature enough to make great decisions on their own, we may be abdicating our authority to make such decisions ourselves, and are also neglecting tailor-made opportunities for our children to learn about obedience and respect. (How else will they learn that?) How will they develop the character trait of respectful obedience to their authorities in those early years if we do not give them daily orders or instructions they must obey respectfully? God gave them parents who are supposed to teach and train them to obey and show respect.

Once children become characterized by happily obeying and honoring their parents, those parents can then teach them many things and gradually give them increasing opportunities to handle responsibilities and to make good decisions. But not until they are obedient and respectful.

My concern here is that this command to parents and children is the very first one with a specific promise attached. That promise says that the key for our children to have a good and a long life will be related to the extent that they obey and honor their parents. This adds a level of seriousness to it. There can be sad consequences for ignoring this important command.

Parents, please think much about this and review the following verses seriously. (Proverbs 10:1 13:1; 15:5, 20; 17:21, 23:15-16, 22, 24-25; 27:11; 29:15, 17)

For Prayer Today
-    Pray for parents and grandparents in their courageous efforts to be the loving leaders of their homes and to be training their little ones in obedience and honor.

Personal Notes and Responses

ETERNAL ENCOURAGEMENTS #96

Spiritual Amnesia

"...But he that lacketh these things is blind, and cannot see afar off, and hath forgotten that he was purged from his old sins." (II Peter 1:5-9) "Bless the LORD, O my soul, and forget not all His benefits: who forgiveth all thine iniquities..." (Psalm 103:2-5) "Beware that thou forget not the LORD thy God, in not keeping his commandments...lest when thou hast eaten and art full, and hast built goodly houses, and dwelt therein...then thine heart be lifted up, and thou forget the LORD thy God, which brought thee out of the land of Egypt, from the house of bondage..." (Deut. 8:10-20)

One of the most devastatingly difficult medical challenges that so many families face today is when a dear loved one is diagnosed with some form of dementia or Alzheimer's. They watch with agony as those conditions progress and rob their loved one of their ability to recognize or remember. Awareness of where they are and how to accomplish even simple tasks are gone. Suddenly a spouse, child, or parent cannot be identified and seem to be a threat to them. Fears, unknown before, now harass their mental state frequently. They might lash out in anger to those trying to help them. They cannot communicate with those around them and often can't understand people's words or efforts at kindness. We certainly need to do all we can to aid those who are caring for such family members or patients.

Our passages above reveal that there may be a similar condition among God's family as well. Peter tells us that if we do not keep maturing in our relationship with the Lord; if we fail to see spiritual fruit being produced in our lives, we may develop a spiritual blindness and amnesia. What might that amnesia be like?

We might forget how blessed we are. (Psalm 103) To His children God is overwhelmingly good and generous every day. But when we forget that, we can become complainers and grumblers who focus on our discomforts and unfulfilled desires. We can become pretty miserable people.

We might forget who our family members are. (Eph. 4:25; I Cor. 12:12-27) We might begin avoiding our church family, treating brothers and sisters in Christ as total strangers. We might turn nasty to those who attempt to draw close to us in order to help us.

We might forget how forgiven we are! (Eph. 4:25-32; Matt. 18:21-35) We can easily grow seeds of anger and bitterness in our hearts. We can become very critical and judgmental of others. We can hold on to grudges and hurts, refusing to forgive others as we demand that they get what is coming to them.

Spiritual amnesia among God's people is very serious and devastating, indeed. Let's keep examining our own hearts, or invite others to keep an eye on us to detect any early warning signs. Then humbly, let's confess that sin and enjoy God's forgiveness and wonderful spiritual health once again.

For Prayer Today

-   Ask God to help you remember every day His abundant blessings to you and His incredible forgiveness of all your sins. Thank Him sincerely for all of them daily and for the wonderful brothers and sisters you have in God's local family.

Personal Notes and Responses

The Glory of God and the Dignity of Mankind

"O LORD, our Lord, how excellent is thy name in all the earth! who hast set thy glory above the heavens...When I consider thy heavens, the work of thy fingers, the moon and the stars, which thou hast ordained; what is man, that thou art mindful of him? and the son of man, that thou visitest him? For thou hast made him a little lower than the angels, and hast crowned him with glory and honour. Thou madest him to have dominion over the works of thy hands..." (Psalm 8)

Do you remember in childhood days lying in the yard, looking up into the clouds and imagining seeing all kinds of objects there? When young David as a shepherd on night-shift gazed into the night sky, his thoughts went even deeper.

He meditated on the greatness and glory of God whose presence was recognized all over the earth. His glory and majesty reached far above the heavens and He would deserve and receive praise even from little children that could silence the enemy. (Psalm 8:2; Matt. 21:15-17) David goes on to recognize this incredible creation as the direct result of the hands of God Who again is worthy of awe and worship.

But then David considers humanity and wonders how such a God could concern Himself with such as us. In light of this incredible universe and its Creator, what kind of value do we have as puny humans on this speck of dust called planet earth? Do we matter at all? Does human life have any dignity or worth?

None of us have any angelic status but we were created a little lower than the angels, and do have a degree of glory and honor. We were also placed above all of creation! This Creator God has entrusted His entire creation to us to manage for His glory. We see that in Gen. 1:26-31; 2:15.

Genesis also reveals that not only were we not created as angels, neither were we created as animals. Unlike them, we were created in the image of God! We were made after His likeness! As such, we have the possibility of knowing God and to be in a relationship with Him. David seems to acknowledge that when he inquires, "What is man that You are mindful of him, and the son of man that You visit him?" David knew that God's mind was on him and that He was caring for him and those thoughts amazed him.

Many today are misunderstanding or questioning their own value. Some think way too highly of themselves and may strut around taking advantage of others, while boasting of their accomplishments. Others think too little of themselves and of what God desires them to be or do. They undervalue human life and allow it to be further cheapened and wasted. Both views miss out on this glorious God reaching out to them.

When we understand who this incredible God is and that He can invade our lives and make them fruitful and fulfilling for eternity, we will enjoy life's value and purpose as we serve Him.

For Prayer Today
- Pray for those who may be discouraged that they will recognize the God-given value of their lives and of His awesome care for them as they serve Him.

Personal Notes and Responses

Commitment

"The works of his hands are verity and judgment; all his command-ments are sure. They stand fast forever and ever, and are done in truth and uprightness. He sent redemption unto his people: he hath commanded his covenant for ever..." (Psalm 111:7-9) "I will sing of the mercies of the LORD for ever: with my mouth will I make known thy faithfulness to all generations...thy faithfulness shalt thou establish in the very heavens...O LORD God of hosts, who is a strong LORD like unto thee? or to thy faithfulness round about thee?" (Psa. 89: 1-8) "If we believe not, yet he abideth faithful." (II Tim. 2:13)

I continue to hear it said that people just do not want to commit themselves to anything anymore. People are very slow to sign up to serve on a committee, to bring food to an event, to drive someone somewhere, to serve in the church nursery, etc. Then, among those who have signed up, who have made such commit-ments, quite a number of them fail to keep those arrangements. They just forgot, the dog had to be taken to the vet, they were up too late the night before, etc. Today's employers have difficulty hiring workers who will show up on time or at all for even one full week of work.

I am so thankful that our God is not like that. When He makes a commitment, He keeps it. He is faithful. Several facets of this attribute might be described as follows.

1. God has made **decisions**. As in Gen. 1:26, our Triune God, in eternity past decided to create the world and all its inhab-itants including mankind; He decided to communicate with man, even and especially in writing, and to provide a Savior for man's sin and a salvation that would last for-ever, etc. Decisions and commitments were made by God.

2. God remains **dedicated** to His Word, to His promises. "For ever, O LORD, thy word is settled in heaven. Thy

faithfulness is unto all generations..." (Psalm 119:89-90;
Matt. 5:17-18) God's Word is fixed and established forever. No changes, updates, appendices, annual yearbooks
are needed. God's stated plans, prophecies, and promises remain intact. They will all be faithfully fulfilled.
(Heb. 10:23)

3. God remains **devoted** to His people. For the body of Christ,
the family of God, Rom. 8:18-39 is an amazing passage
underscoring how devoted God is to His people. It is a
total and forever commitment to them. Even in the Old
Testament, God's commitment to the nation of Israel is
also sure and certain; their restored future is guaranteed.
Isaiah, Jeremiah, and Ezekiel repeatedly emphasize God's
devotion to His chosen nation.

4. God also reveals a **determination** to complete what He
has started, to fulfill all His promises, and to carry out all
His plans. (Phil. 1:6; 2:12-13; I Thess. 5:23-24; Heb. 7:25)
Even concerning Israel, He will perform what He promised with "the zeal of the LORD." (Isa. 9:7; 37:32)

Aren't you thankful that our God keeps His commitments, that
His faithfulness is clearly seen through His decisions, dedication
and devotion, and His sovereign determination to accomplish all
that He has planned.

For Prayer Today
- Thank God for His faithfulness and ask Him to help you to
remain faithful to the commitments that you may make.

Personal Notes and Responses

Restfulness

"...And on the seventh day God ended his work which he had made; and he rested on the seventh day from all his work which he had made. And God blessed the seventh day, and sanctified it: because that in it he had rested from all his work which God created and made." (Gen. 2:1-3) "Remember the sabbath day to keep it holy. Six days shalt thou labour, and do all thy work: but the seventh day is the sabbath of the LORD thy God: in it thou shalt not do any work..." (Exodus 20:8-11) "And he said unto them, Come ye yourselves apart into a desert place, and rest awhile: for there were many coming and going, and they had no leisure so much as to eat. And they departed into a desert place by ship privately. And..." (Mark: 6:31-33)

The command to keep the Sabbath day 'holy' or separate from the other six as a day off from all work, as a day of rest, admittedly, is the only command of the 10 that is not clearly repeated in the New Testament. But the original concept of it was embedded in the experience and example of our Creator God as He chose to rest on the seventh day of creation week, not because He was tired, but because His work was completed. Then when that habit was codified into the Law of Moses, the same reason for it was given again. The Jewish people then sought to observe it as a much-revered sabbath tradition, complete with meticulous details and heavy threats about their compliance to it. (Maybe we need a compliance officer to check on us about this discipline.)

Every one of us knows we need regular rest and occasionally some real serious down-time. We cannot keep pushing hard, day and night for long weeks without some needed respite. But those breaks appear so elusive for many of us today. Life is hard and very hectic, workloads are so heavy, and we carry them every-where we go due to the portability of technology today and the whole world's access to us, 24/7. And covid is certainly no friend to this effort to find rest.

Perhaps most of us could cry out defensively, "Well, my work is never done!" which may be true but which doesn't eliminate our need for rest. In fact, it underscores it. The essence of this command is to cease all work for a short time, to allow your resources to replenish and your body to refresh – so that more work could then be accomplished safely. This needs to become a priority in our schedules.

I totally respect the challenge this is to you who are healthcare workers in these days. However please try to get determinedly deliberate to carve out some time, even if it's just a few hours regularly, to step aside, get a babysitter, go on a hike, visit a spa or a gym, sleep in, read a novel, watch a comedy, laugh with some friends over a meal…just put all work on hold for a time – and ask God to refresh you, body, soul, and spirit for your continued work. Remember Christ's words in Matthew 11:28-30.

For Prayer Today
- Continue much in prayer for our nation's exhausted healthcare-related workforce and ask God what you can do to be a help to a few of them near you.

Personal Notes and Responses

Till Debt Do Us Part

"...the borrower is servant to the lender." (Prov. 22:7) "Be not thou one of them that strike hands, or of them that are sureties for debts. If thou hast nothing to pay, why should he take away thy bed from under thee?" (Prov. 22:26-27) "Render therefore to all their dues: tribute to whom tribute is due; custom to whom custom; fear to whom fear; honour to whom honour. Owe no man any thing, but to love one another..." (Rom. 13:7-8) "Go to now, ye that say, To day or to morrow we will...buy and sell and get gain:...For that ye ought to say, If the Lord will, we shall live, and do this, or that." (James 4:13-15)

Our world today can be financially divided into three main groups of people – the haves, the have-nots, and the have-not-paid-for-what-they-haves! In fact, our world seems to be driven by debt and drowning in it. Individuals, families, companies, corporations, local, state, and national governments, are in deep financial trouble related to debt and no one seems to understand the solution. Company closures, housing foreclosures, the destruction of families and, all kinds of criminal conduct find their roots entangled with money problems. Easy and readily available credit is like a trap which a man sets and baits and then catches...himself.

The Bible nowhere recommends debt; in fact, it warns against it. God promises to provide for His children through hard work, through one's family or church family, and through how one manages well the funds that are entrusted to him. God also responds to obedient children who cry out to Him in times of special need with surprising and timely provisions. God wants us to trust and obey Him and to live within the resources that He provides.

When I was very young, the Sears and Roebuck Christmas Toy Catalog arrived at our house in August and, for some reason, my parents turned it over to us three children to begin making our

Christmas lists – with apparently no limitations at all. They then bought us everything we wanted, piles of it every Christmas. Credit was quite new in the early 1950's and my dad took to it like a favored toy – and charged and borrowed for almost everything for the next 40 years, never paying anything totally off. Debt became our chosen lifestyle. The long-range consequences were not pleasant.

I realize that credit is a way of life today and I'm not on some serious critical crusade here. But, there are better ways to live without submitting to worldly ways that are detrimental to our well-being and that of our families. The Christmas season can be quite a temptation to overdo our expenditures well beyond what we can or should afford. Please be careful for your family's sake. Point them in the right direction about handling money with excellent wisdom from God.

Maybe for Christmas, invest in a good book or website on the subject from a biblical viewpoint. I highly recommend the works of Randy Alcorn, Dave Ramsey, or Larry Burkett. Start the next year off differently as a really "new year" financially for your family.

For Prayer Today
- Lots of people are seriously struggling financially today. Pray for them to look to God for His wisdom and help in these areas. Pray for the self-discipline you might need as well.

Personal Notes and Responses

ETERNAL ENCOURAGEMENTS #101

All Things

*"Grace and peace be multiplied unto you through the knowledge of God, and of Jesus our Lord, according as his divine power hath given unto us **all things** that pertain unto life and godliness..." (II Peter 1:2-4) "...And we know that **all things** work together for good to them that love God, to them who are the called according to his purpose..." (Rom. 8:18-30) "...For **all things** are for your sakes, that the abundant grace might through the thanksgiving of many redound to the glory of God." (II Cor. 4:7-15) "...Behold, I make **all things** new..." (Rev. 21:1-5)*

Very few things can be stated as being true about "**all things**". But I have come to deeply appreciate a number of passages that speak of God's intense involvement in the "**all things**" of the lives of His children. Here's just a sampling of my favorites.

The "all things" of our salvation – When we are saved, God powerfully gives to us all that we need for living life in godliness, allowing us to partake of His divine nature and of His great and precious promises as we grow in Him. That's quite a package! (II Peter 1:2-4) "...old things have passed away; behold **all things** have become new." (II Cor. 5:17)

The "all things" of our sanctification (growth toward Christ-likeness) – Romans 8:18-39 is an amazing passage that under-scores the sovereignty of God who controls **all things** in our lives and uses them for our growth toward maturity in Him. That's quite a plan!

The "all things" of our service effectiveness – Paul recognized that all the sufferings that he experienced as he tried to serve the Lord were being used by God to impact other people who would be grateful and glorying to God. (II Cor. 4:7-18) That's quite a purpose for hardship in ministry!

The "all things" of our future – At the end of time as we know it, God says that He is going to create a new heavens and a new earth, making **all things** new. There will be no more sin or death, no more grief and sorrow, no more sickness or pain...**all things** will be made new! What a promise! (Rev. 21:1-5)

So, how do all these things benefit me?

Such benefits include a deeper knowledge of God's incredibly involved love for you, a present joy and hope due to future guarantees of newness, a freedom from discouragement and depression in service, and an evident growth in victory over sin's corruption in your own life. And, there's more!

All of these things are possible because God is deeply involved in the **"all things"** of His children. Not just some things, favorite things, most things, Sunday things, but **ALL things.**

For Prayer Today
-    Ask God to help you believe that He is involved in the **all things** of His children's lives and then trust Him with the **"all things" of your life.**

Personal Notes and Responses

210

A Grand Mission for Grand Parenting

"Except the LORD build the house, they labour in vain that build it: except the LORD keep the city, the watchman waketh but in vain. It is vain for you to rise up early, to sit up late, to eat the bread of sorrows: for so he giveth his beloved sleep. Lo, children are an heritage of the LORD: and the fruit of the womb is his reward. As arrows are in the hand of a mighty man, so are children of the youth. Happy is the man that hath his his quiver full of them: they shall not be ashamed, but they shall speak with the enemies in the gate." (Psalm 127)

Over the last few decades the size of families in the western world has shrunk considerably till today many couples resist the idea of having any children and others look down with dismay or disgust at families with multiplied numbers of little ones. That's a long way from God's original instructions to "Be fruitful and multiply and fill the earth..." Yes, parenting is challenging, competing with other interests, and oftentimes very disheartening. Yet, the opportunity to conceive and raise children toward mature adulthood is intrinsic to the nature and purpose of the family and to the will of God.

Psalm 127 deals with this subject concisely with truths that might help us all.

1. **Parenting is a Spiritual Endeavor.** God is the One who can build the household, guard the city, and parent the children and we should tighten our relationship with Him and ask for His help in this task. He can even provide the sleep we need! (Psalm 127:1-2) We do not have to parent alone. Our Father in heaven will help us!

2. **Parenting is a Stewardship Endeavor.** Children are actually a heritage, a gift, a reward from the Lord. The Lord opens the womb; He allows parents to cooperate with him in the creation of life as He weaves the bodies of these

little ones together within that nurturing place. At birth, a child is placed into the hands of parents as a trust; God is entrusting to mom and dad a little life and He expects them to love and raise that child for Him. (Psa. 127:3; 139:13-16; See also Luke 1:5-17 as an example of this.)

3. **Parenting is a Serious Endeavor.** We are to love, teach, train, and equip our children to deal with life in mature and godly ways. This will include helping them come to Christ and preparing them to deal with sin and to sometimes confront spiritual enemies in the conflicts of life. The Psalmist pictures our children not as trophies to be polished and displayed but as soldiers of character who can go to war and win battles in the areas of life that are most important. (Psa. 127:4-5)

Let's not shy away from this important endeavor. With God's help and direction, it can be a wonderful adventure of preparing our precious little ones for life and service with the blessings of God!

For Prayer Today

Pray for all who have responsibility to care for children today, that they will see their mission as a grand one and call on God for His help daily.

Personal Notes and Responses

Radical Regrets

"...The ground of a certain rich man brought forth plentifully: and he thought within himself, saying, What shall I do, because I have no room where to bestow my fruits?...This will I do: I will pull down my barns, and build greater; and there will I bestow all my fruits and my goods. And I will say to my soul, Soul, thou hast much goods laid up for many years; take thine ease, eat, drink, and be merry. But God said unto him, Thou fool, this night thy soul shall be required of thee..." (Luke 12:13-21) *"...For what is a man profited, if he shall gain the whole world, and lose his own soul?" (Matt. 16:24-27)*

I preached on this parable of the selfish hoarder one day in a nursing facility and a bit later as I entered the room of an elderly gentleman for a visit, I found him at his closet and dresser pulling everything out and tossing it on the floor. When I inquired as to what in the world he was doing, he declared over his shoulder, "I'm cleaning out my barns, preacher. I've got way too much stuff!" We both chuckled at that but I was a bit stunned that someone in a care home would respond that quickly and radically to something I had preached moments before.

Materialism, lusting and striving for riches, covetousness and greed still has a firm grip on many hearts today. Though in most cases there is nothing wrong with striving to be successful in our work and accumulating some things for present needs and future goals, it can often be the case that we sacrifice other valuable things that are worth far more to do so.

It has been said that many crawl over other people as they climb their ladder of success only to find that when they finally reach the top, they discover that their ladder was leaning against the wrong building. What they had attained was not all that important and they had missed out on all kinds of precious relationships and realities of far greater value. How tragic that is.

So, what is your response to the parable above? What is your attitude toward wealth? Where are you spending most of your time and energies? Do you recognize how unpredictable life can be? Are you investing lots of loving time with the family members God has given you? And most important, have you developed a personal relationship with God? Time may be running out!

Your sin is what separates you and keeps you from God. But repentance of sin and placing your faith in the One who took the punishment for your sin to save you and to grant you the gift of eternal life is how one begins that important relationship. You will then be equipped for this life and for eternity.

Please re-read the verses at the beginning of this piece, then read John 3:1-18, 36 and call on the Lord to save you. If I can help you with this decision, please contact me.

For Prayer Today
- Pray for many to turn to God for their salvation in these difficult days.

Personal Notes and Responses

Man's Best Friend

"Iron sharpeneth iron; so a man sharpeneth the countenance of his friend." (Prov. 27:17) "Open rebuke is better than secret love. Faithful are the wounds of a friend; but the kisses of an enemy are deceitful...Ointment and perfume rejoice the heart: so doth the sweetness of a man's friend by hearty counsel. Thine own friend and thy father's friend, forsake not..." (27:5-6, 9-10) "A friend loveth at all times, and a brother is born for adversity." (17:17) "A man that hath friends must shew himself friendly: and there is a friend that sticketh closer than a brother." (18:24)

Contrary to popular opinion that man's best friend is of the canine variety, I believe he can do far better than that. I do understand the allure of "dawgs" (I know that's not how you spell it but it is how I'm pronouncing it for this article! Especially if you draw it out some.) I'm actually quite fond of Snoopy and Garfield myself though they do not jump on me, drool all over me, or demand that I accompany them on frequent trips outside to irrigate some trees and fire hydrants. (What's with the hydrants, anyway? Is their hearing that good that they hear the water running inside and thus they just have to...?) My wife and I tend to be cat people but it would be a real stretch of terminology to call them "friends".

In addition to a close personal relationship with God, man's or woman's best friend should be another adult who is characterized by godliness and wisdom. It may be our spouse or another person but their character must be as described in the book of Proverbs.

True friendship should never be shallow, superficial, or selfish in nature (Prov. 19:4-7). It should not be with those who are disloyal gossipers (16:28; 17:9) or with those who participate in evil or tolerate our own sinful choices or actions (23:20-21; 24:1-2 28:7; 28:19). They should not be those who carry angry or bitter attitudes which can easily contagiously afflict and ensnare us (22:24-25).

Instead, wise and godly friends will be loyal over the long-term and will be a source of joy and peace. They will not tolerate any sinful attitudes or activities that we may be toying with but will graciously rebuke and admonish us whenever necessary to keep us on the right path. True friends really care about the health of our soul and of our relationship with God. They will improve and sharpen our ability to serve God and others.

And we must be the same kind of friends to others, as well. Such mutual friendship and commitment to one another is what should be developing within the family of God continuously for the benefit of everyone and for the glory of God (Rom. 15:13-14; Heb. 3:12-13; 10:23-25).

Do you have such a "best friend"? Are you such a "best friend"?

For Prayer Today
- Ask God to make you the kind of friend that is needed by others around you.
- Pray in these days when isolation and loneliness are so prevalent, that God will provide special friends for those in great need, in spite of difficult restrictions, etc.

Personal Notes and Responses

How "Essential" is "Church"?

"Then they that gladly received his word were baptized: and the same day there were added unto them about three thousand souls. And they continued steadfastly in the apostles' doctrine and fellowship, and in breaking of bread, and in prayers...And all that believed were together, and had all things common; and sold their possessions and goods, and parted them to all men, as every man had need. And they, continuing daily with one accord in the temple, and breaking bread from house to house, did eat their meat with gladness and singleness of heart, praising God, and having favor with all the people..." (Acts 2:41-47)

First of all, let's define the word "church". It is not referring to a building, though buildings are used in most, but not all cases to host meetings of a "church". The New Testament "church" is a group of people who are called out together to trust in Christ as Savior and then to gather in local assemblies as God's family. Church is people; God does not live in buildings but in people who have come to Christ.

Acts 2 records the actual "birth" of this unique group, numbering about 3000 on day one and reveals the nature of this assembly. As we look at the verses above, we recognize what they deemed "essential" right from their start and even during scary and life-threatening times.

They were a learning people, studying the Scriptures and taking them seriously. They were a friendly, hospitable people as they fellowshipped frequently with one another, in houses initially. They ate together frequently as well as celebrated the Lord's Supper in loving response to His sacrifice for them. That kept them mindful of what really brought them together and kept themselves focused on Christ. They were an unselfishly giving people, even to sacrificing their own possessions so that those with financial needs would have enough. And they were a praying people, both praising God often for His goodness and trusting Him with all their needs and concerns.

As you read that paragraph, did anything strike you about it? Didn't it sound like exactly what people need right now, during this pandemic, and during all the crises we face? The church enabled mankind to hear from God through His Word and to be encouraged by Him. The church gathered often in small intimate groups for fellowship, thus addressing the isolation and loneliness of so many. The church hastened to meet one another's physical and financial needs sacrificially. The church stayed grateful for Christ's sacrificial death for their salvation and in prayer trusted Him for all other things.

Don't these elements of a church family sound rather essential to you?

Don't misunderstand; I do believe that it may be wise sometimes not to meet in large groups. We should respect the efforts of our government as they seek to protect the populace from life-threatening conditions and seek to cooperate with sound safety practices even out of love for each other. But we should never stop *being* the church, living like the church, loving like the church, honoring our Savior like the church.

As the church, we are essential to what God wants to accomplish in our world today.

For Prayer Today
- Pray for church families to display true godliness and compassion for others and to bring hope and encouragement to many through Christ.

Personal Notes and Responses

Family Choices and Commitments

"...Now therefore fear the LORD, and serve him in sincerity and in truth: and put away the gods which your fathers served on the other side of the flood, and in Egypt; and serve ye the LORD. And if it seem evil unto you to serve the LORD, choose you this day whom ye will serve;...but as for me and my house, we will serve the LORD..." (Joshua 24:11-15)

Joshua had completed the tasks that God had given him to do; they had taken possession of the Promised Land and divided it up into inheritances for the 12 tribes of Israel. In chapters 23 and 24 he is giving his farewell address to the nation just before he died (23:1-2, 14; 24:29-30) and he urged them to make a life-long commitment to following God.

Were they planning to continue to serve the various false gods from their past or the false gods of their new land? Joshua admonished them to take seriously their need to commit themselves to serving and loving the true God who had delivered them from Egypt, carried them through 40 years in the wilderness, and then had given them freely their new land.

With such a life-long commitment, each family would be setting the course for their future; they would be recalibrating themselves to godly priorities (23:6-8), attaching their affections to the eternal God (23:11), and would be placing their trust in this One who would remain faithful to them (23:3-5, 9, 14). They would be focusing their future on eternal values which would then turn their daily choices in the right direction (23:6-8, 11). Not to do so would bring dire consequences to them (23:12-13).

For about four decades, Israel had wandered in their chosen wilderness, following repeated routines while continuing to reject and rebel against God's will. Packing everything up, trudging through the desert, stopping and setting up camp, staying a while, then repeating the whole process again and again–for forty years! Yes, they were learning from this disciplinary desert quarantine and God was showing them what He could do, etc. But the weariness of life, the repetition of routines, the miseries of wilderness living, was not what God really wanted for them. Then came the conquest of the new land under Joshua and his final challenge to them. For this new generation, it was decision time.

Have you, individually or as a family, ever made such a major course-change in your lives, a determined new direction for your household and its future that is centered around God and His will for you? Apparently, many in Israel made that commitment (24:31) and you can do the same. It can make a huge difference in the nature and future of your family and will carry the blessing of God with it. It may even be something to memorialize, as Joshua did (24:24-28).

For Prayer Today
- Ask God for the courage (23:6) you may need to make such a direction-changing commitment today. If you have already done so, ask Him for the wisdom you need for your daily decisions and your walk with Him.

Personal Notes and Responses

Fainting Spells

*"Wherefore I desire that ye **faint** not at my tribulations for you..."*
(Eph. 3:13) "...let us run with patience the race that is set before
us, looking unto Jesus...For consider him that endured such con-
*tradiction of sinners against himself, lest ye be wearied and **faint***
in your minds...My son, despise not thou the chastening of the
*Lord, nor **faint** when thou art rebuked of him..." (Heb. 12:1-6) "...*
The elders have ceased from the gate, the young men from their
musick. The joy of our heart is ceased; our dance is turned into
*mourning...For this our heart is **faint**..." (Lamentations 5:7-17)*
*"...that men ought always to pray, and not to **faint**..." (Luke 18:1-8)*

The word "faint" in Scripture conveys a condition of "inner weariness, loss of courage, a weakening of energy and resolve, a
yearning to give up or quit", etc. These terms can describe a physical, emotional, or spiritual condition and the experience of them
can be very depressing and debilitating.

1. **Reasons for Fainting** – The Bible acknowledges the reality
   of this condition and reveals some causes of it. Physical or
   spiritual hunger can be responsible when one is not getting the needed nutrition on a frequent basis. (Matt. 15:32;
   Amos 8:11-13) Draining, long hours of extreme labor can
   bring it on. (Heb. 12:1-3) Sometimes we can grow faint-
   hearted when we are rebuked or corrected. (Heb. 12:5-6)
   Hearing and responding to repeated bad or sad news about
   loved ones and folks in our care can drain our batteries and
   lead to depression or despair. (Eph. 3:13) Sometimes it is
   personal sin and guilt that can eat away at us, making us
   miserable and discouraged. (Isaiah 1:1-5; Lam. 5:14-17)
   And, when God doesn't seem to be answering our prayers,
   we can become spiritually weakened and faint. (Luke 18:1)
2. **Resources to Prevent Fainting**
   a. **Our Provisions** – God can supply what we need,
      whether food, (Matt.15:32-39), rest (Matt. 11:28-30),

or spiritual strength and energy. (Isaiah 40:29-31) Get specific and cry out to Him for what you need each day, even when you doubt that He is listening. (Luke 18:1-7)

b. **Our Purpose** – Each of us has a God-given purpose in life that really matters to those around us. We are here to minister to others who need us, using the talents that God has given us. We dare not faint and quit. (II Cor. 4:1, 15-16)

c. **Our Perspective** – Sometimes our work or difficult circumstances fixate our attention totally on earthly and temporary things and we forget the bigger picture. We need to stay focused on the inward over the outward, the eternal over the temporary, and the invisible over the visible. (II Cor. 4:16-18) In this way our spirits can be renewed and refreshed every day.

d. **Our Promise** – In Gal. 6:9-10 we read "And let us not be weary in well doing, for in due season we shall reap, if we faint not..." There will be a harvest time of good fruit over which we have labored long and hard, by God's grace. We will be rejoicing over God's goodness.

For all of you serving in the thick of these difficult times, you are appreciated and we are praying for you. Please reach out to someone if you need help or encouragement.

For Prayer Today

- Pray much for all those who are growing weary and faint in their work, daily. Many are struggling very seriously.

Personal Notes and Responses

The Priority of Prayer

"Continue in prayer, and watch in the same with thanksgiving; withal praying also for us, that God would open unto us a door of utterance, to speak the mystery of Christ, for which I am also in bonds that I may make it manifest, as I ought to speak." (Col. 4:2-4) "...praying always with all prayer and supplication in the Spirit, and watching thereunto with all perseverance and supplication for all saints; and for me, that utterance may be given unto me, that I may open my mouth boldly, to make known the mystery of the gospel...as I ought to speak." (Eph. 6:18-20)

Even as a pastor, I have needed occasional reminders of the importance of spending more time in prayer. For perhaps most of us it is easy to allow the heavy demands of our work and family to leave little time for personally calling on God, fellowshipping with Him, and placing in His hands all that we might have to deal with that day. We have seen in I Thess. 5:17-18 the general admonition to "pray without ceasing..." while we often continue to do everything else... without praying. What might we learn from the above passages on our need to prioritize prayer in our lives?

1. **Be Ceaseless in Prayer.** We are to continue to pray. It ought to be our normal setting for our day. It is not something to put off, to postpone till some more convenient time; it is like keeping God on the line and speaking to Him a bit about everything. Like wearing a "com" in your ear, it involves interacting with Him often. A few suggestions:

   a. Waking time – Begin your day, even while yet in bed, talking to God.

   b. Waiting time – How often are we put on hold, sitting in a waiting room, or in heavy traffic? Do some conversing with God then.

   c.   Worry time – Whenever you catch yourself worrying
        that should be like a phone buzzing in your ear, urging
        you to talk to God about your concerns. (Phil. 4:6-7)
   d.   Wasted time – Are you spending too much time
        watching TV or on the computer recreationally? Set
        aside some of that time to talk to God, then open His
        Word and hear from Him.
2. **Be Conscious in Prayer.** Stay alert and vigilant as you
   pray and throughout the day, be looking eagerly for evidence of God's work in response. Pray with faith, with
   expectancy and even keep a journal of some requests and
   God's answers. This will excite you and keep you praying.
3. **Be Communicating in Prayer.** Don't just "say prayers",
   repeating empty phrases insincerely. (Matt. 6:5-8) Really
   open up and honestly talk with God. Paul emphasizes
   expressing gratitude and praying for others, not only for
   yourself. Our direct conversations with our Heavenly
   Father can make a difference in people's lives, those on
   the front lines of ministry to people's physical and spiritual needs and to everyone moving through life in need of
   God's help.

As we increase in understanding the importance of prayer and discover the great difference it can make in lives, we will be motivated to "put God on hold" far less often, but will keep Him on
the line continually.

For Prayer Today
-   Just start talking to your Heavenly Father about whatever is
    on your heart...

Personal Notes and Responses
_____

Eternal Security or Eternal Insecurity?

"For we ourselves also were sometimes foolish, disobedient, deceived...But after that the kindness and love of God our Savior toward man appeared, not by works of righteousness which we have done, but according to his mercy he saved us...that being justified by his grac,e we should be made heirs according to the hope of eternal life..." (Titus 3:3-7) "For by grace are ye saved through faith; and that not of yourselves: it is the gift of God: not of works, lest any man should boast." (Eph. 2:8-9) "For the wages of sin is death; but the gift of God is eternal life through Jesus Christ our Lord." (Rom. 6:23)

I have been teaching the Book of Romans lately in an adult Sunday School class, now enjoying chapter 8 as I am again amazed and thrilled at how secure our salvation is. That is because it is totally from God who guarantees its eternal duration because of Christ's payment-in-full of our sin debt on the cross.

Our salvation is based on no works or merit of our own. We did not earn it or deserve it; it is a pure and gracious gift from God, received when we repent of our sins and place our faith entirely on Christ and His work on the cross for us. But what about after we are saved; can we lose it? Paul reassures us of its permanence in a number of powerful ways. Once we are saved...

1. There is **No Interruption** to God's continuing work in us. (8:28-30; Phil. 1:6) God promises to complete what He has begun in us by sovereignly using *"all things"* to grow and mature us into Christ-likeness and to glorify us perfectly someday, never losing any of us (John 6:37-40).

2. There is **No Opposition** that can destroy our salvation since God is "for us" to that extent. Notice, God the Father is "for us" (8:31), God the Son is "for us" (8:34), and God the Spirit is "for us" (8:26). "We are more than conquerors

through Him who loved us"! (8:37) Even Satan has been defeated. (Heb. 2:14-15)

3. There is **No Limitation** to what God will provide for us throughout our lives. He will continue to "freely giveth us all things" (8:32) that we need for life and godliness. (II Peter 1:2-4)

4. There is **No Accusation** that will stick to us in God's court since God has already declared us to be righteous. (8:33; I John 2:1-2; Rom. 4:5-8)

5. There is **No Condemnation** for any of our sins, since Christ was already condemned to death for all our sins. (Matt. 20:18; 8:1, 34; John 3:18; 5:24)

6. There is **No Separation** from Christ's love for us. (8:28, 35-39) In spite of how difficult life can get, God is using all things to grow us and Christ continues His loving care of us through it all.

Please read thoughtfully Romans 8:28-39 in light of the above points, then John 3:16-18, 36; 10:28-30; 6:35-40. God does not want you moving through life with insecurity about your salvation. He has made it eternally secure for all who have repented and trusted in Christ.

For Prayer Today
- Thank God for such an incredible salvation and ask His help in sharing this great news with others.

Personal Notes and Responses

The Fellowship of Food

"...Bless the LORD, O my soul, and forget not all his benefits...Who satisfieth thy mouth with good things; so that thy youth is renewed like the eagle's." (Psalm 103:1-5) "Nevertheless he left not himself without witness, in that he did good...filling our hearts with food and gladness." (Acts 14:17) "And they, continuing daily with one accord in the temple, and breaking bread from house to house, did eat their meat with gladness and singleness of heart, praising God, and having favour with all the people. (Acts 2:46-47)

It happened to us again just the other day. After enjoying a nice meal in a restaurant, we were stunned by the news that our bill had been paid by someone else. The after-shock was felt when we learned who our benefactor was, that it again was a younger man, a total stranger to us. Some months earlier, it was three rather loud young men near us who had done the same.

On both occasions we were able to express our profound gratitude for their kindness, then we sat a bit longer and expressed to each other a number of heart-felt emotions. We were so surprised, so blessed, so thankful, so humbled and embarrassed (on my part anyway as I had been harboring some wrong thoughts and attitudes toward that first group). We talked to the Lord again before we left the table, thanking Him for reminding us of His loving-kindness toward us and for urging us to think more about others around us as they had done for us.

The consumption of good food is such a wonderful earthly blessing that we all enjoy. God desires that we freely and fully enjoy these physical delights (Psalm 103:1-5; I Tim. 4:1-5), even promising to provide our basic food needs as we honor Him first. (Matt. 6:25-34) But have we considered lately the special blessings that we can be to others around us as we share with them what God has given to us?

Scripture records mention of Joseph's generosity to his brothers and their families after many years of suffering at their hands. (Gen. 42:10, 25; 44:1; 47:23-27) Then David did similarly as he chose to provide for the descendants of Jonathan, his enemy's son, and insisted that lame Mephibosheth would always eat at the king's table. (II Sam. 9:9-13)

During serious quarantined seasons, we are hindered from having close personal fellowship. But we can still use food as an emissary of love and kindness. Can we make some soup, bake some cookies, or order a pizza, and send them along to surprise a neighbor or someone needing encouragement? Can we send encouraging cards with restaurant or grocery gift cards included? When we shop for groceries, can we think of a few special things we can purchase to surprise someone else? How about a fruit or snack basket someone will enjoy?

When the restrictions are lifted, we can resume closer fellowship and hospitality with others. In the meantime, maybe anonymously, we can surprise someone at a restaurant. That's a favorite of mine!

For Prayer Today
- When you give thanks for your food, ask God with whom you might share His goodness and love.

Personal Notes and Responses

Eternal Encouragements #111

A Smoke Detector on Steroids

"Wherewithal shall a young man cleanse his way? by taking heed thereto according to thy word...Thy word have I hid in mine heart, that I might not sin against thee...I thought on my ways, and turned my feet unto thy testimonies. I made haste, and delayed not to keep thy commandments...Through thy precepts I get understanding: therefore I hate every false way. Thy word is a lamp unto my feet, and a light unto my path...Oder my steps in thy word: and let not any iniquity have dominion over me." (Psalm 119:9, 11, 58-59,104-105, 133)

We had a new smoke detector installed recently in our small cottage. The former one was not working; the new one is wired into the system with a back-up battery. Whereas the old one was mute, this new one has a lot to say.

The "new arrival" let out its first shrill scream rather soon when my wife opened the hot oven one evening to check on the condition of our dinner. Shockingly loud in our tiny place, we jumped in response to its announcement and quickly waved away the heat that it sensed. Lately, we've been jolted by it a couple more times when there's been no smoke, fire, or smog. Maybe a bit of steam. This morning as I passed underneath it on my way to the table it sounded forth again. Maybe I had forgotten my deodorant or my after shave was too strong.

I am thankful that God's Word acts as an alarm system for our spiritual safety. The Psalmist treasured God's Word and emphasized how it helped him maintain victory over sin daily.

Originally, our conscience was designed by God to accuse us when we were heading in a wrong direction (Rom. 2:14-16; John 8:9; I Cor. 8:7; I Tim. 4:2; Titus 1:15; Heb. 9:14). But our sin-prone heart can damage and sear it from its usefulness over time, perhaps like a faulty smoke-detector. But once we trust Christ we receive a two-fold protective alarm system. The Word of God being implanted in our souls and the Holy Spirit living within us working together can alert us to sinful desires or opportunities and warn us away from them. (Gal. 5:16; Col. 3:16-17; Eph. 5:8-21) The power of God can give us the strength to turn away from temptation and obey God even when just a hint of danger is present.

If we are not careful, we can become very comfortable tolerating sinful attitudes and habits, thinking they are really very harmless. However, the smokiness of sin always damages us and endangers our spiritual health and others around us. But if we invest good time each day meditating in and memorizing key Scriptures then this God-provided alarm system will work very well.

For Prayer Today
- Ask God to help you to prioritize His Word in your daily life and then to obey it whenever you "smell" temptation coming your way.

Personal Notes and Responses

How to Meditate on Scripture

"This book of the law shall not depart out of thy mouth; but thou shalt meditate therein day and night, that thou mayest observe to do according to all that is written therein: for then thou shalt make thy way prosperous, and then thou shalt have good success." (Joshua 1:8) "Blessed is the man...But his delight is in the law of the LORD; and in his law doth he meditate day and night..." (Psalm 1:1-3) "I will meditate in thy precepts, and have respect unto thy ways...I will not forget thy word." (Psalm 119:15-16)

Not very long ago I was spending an overnight visit with my elderly mother-in-law in her Pittsburgh apartment. I needed to rise around 4:00 AM to get to my appointment in Beckley WV on time, but I did not want to waken mother that early. So I quickly silenced the alarm, tip-toed into the rest room to wash up and shave. I had left my glasses in the living room and didn't want to risk bothering mother so I did what needed to be done without them.

While my electric razor droned on, I noticed a variety of soaps and lotions on her wash stand. A luminous blue bottle beckoned my attention. I picked it up and through bleary eyes read, "For moistening wet skin." I set the bottle down but a moment later I thought, "What was that again?" Retrieving the bottle and squinting at it, I read the same words. "Oh, ok, that is what it says. I read it right the first time." Seconds later, "Wait a minute, why would anyone want to moisten wet skin? Isn't wet skin already moist?" Up came the bottle again but the print got smaller still. My questions grew larger as I tried to understand more of the script printed on the bottle.

Then I noticed, I think, in bolder print, "To apply..." Aha, maybe these instructions will help me understand this mysterious substance." Then I read something like this. "To apply on arms, use a dime's amount, on legs, a quarter's amount will suffice."

"W....h...a...t...? What does that mean???" Down went the bottle for the final time. Any more handling of it might produce some deep-cleaning genie or something! These crazy thoughts had me chuckling, then almost laughing out loud. Then suddenly I realized what I was actually doing!

I was meditating! On a mysterious message found *on* a bottle from a mother-in-law's private washroom! (Now, there's a plot waiting for development!)

I was trying to read clearly and understand a specific message. I was re-reading it thinking through the message's meaning, paying attention to its specific words. I was mentally asking questions about what I was discovering. If I had time, I might have done a bit of research. But the real key came with those words, "To Apply..."! When we study the Bible, the important thing is that we apply it to ourselves and make use of it. We should take it very personally and then go out in public to obey its instructions.

It won't help us at all if we just leave it in the bottle...I mean... the Bible!

For Prayer Today
-    Ask God to remind you to be thinking through His Word each day and applying it personally.

Personal Notes and Application

_____

The Punctuality of God

"For Sarah conceived, and bare Abraham a son in his old age, at the set time of which God had spoken to him." (Gen. 21:2) "But when the fullness of the time was come, God sent forth his Son, made of a woman, made under the law, to redeem them that were under the law...." (Gal. 4:4-5) "Now Jesus loved Martha, and her sister, and Lazarus. When he had heard therefore that he was sick, he abode two days still in the same place where he was...Then said Jesus unto them plainly, 'Lazarus is dead...' 'Lord, if thou hadst been here, my brother had not died....'" (John 11:1-44)

The Bible teaches that God is eternal, having no beginning or ending. But when He chose to create the universe with its rotating and revolving planet earth, He created the means of marking time with its hours, days, seasons, and years. (Gen. 1:14-19) Then we find God interacting with His creation within this time-bound sphere of life, and later, personally invading earth and living here for over three decades of time, as our Savior, Jesus Christ.

He who is outside of time has committed Himself to mankind in our real-time world. And, the record shows that God is always on time. If He makes time-specific promises, they will take place when and as predicted. He is never early or late, though many times from our limited and human perspective, we question that claim.

God's track record on this includes specific birth notices, even for some elderly and barren (Gen. 21:2; Luke 1:7, 13-25) and pronouncements of coming deaths (Deut. 31:14; 34:1-5; Dan. 5:22-30). They include the precise durations of some of the plagues of Egypt (Gen. 41:25-32; Ex. 5-12:30), the length of years that Israel would be in bondage to Babylon (Dan. 9:1-2), and even an intricate timetable regarding the future of Israel and her Messiah's plans (Dan. 9:24-27). Also, we note the timely and appropriate provision of specific needs in the lives of despairing widows (I Kings 17; II

Kings 4:1-7), etc. Even when His friends thought Jesus was late in not arriving in time to heal Lazarus, Jesus, knowing the right timetable, was appropriately punctual. (John 11:1-44)

Do you think that our record of punctuality is important to God and to those around us? We certainly aren't perfect in this regard but by what reputation are we characterized?

One definition of punctuality that I have always appreciated is – "showing respect for other people and their time". Isn't that good?! Do we make promises that are time-sensitive and then keep them punctually? Or have we made a habit of the opposite, like those in every church who show up late every week, "religiously"? Do we pay our bills on time? Do we arrive, even early, for appointments?

If we claim to be children of God, then His reputation is somewhat at stake in this display of our integrity or lack of it. If we need help with this, let's ask a very punctual God to aid us.

For Prayer Today
-    Thank God for the 24 hours each day He gives us and ask His
     help that we use it wisely.

Personal Notes and Responses

ETERNAL ENCOURAGEMENTS #114

Stormy Weather

"...And there arose a great storm of wind, and the waves beat into the ship, so that it was now full..." (Mark 4:35-41) "And the sea arose by reason of a great wind that blew. So when they had rowed about five and twenty or thirty furlongs, they see Jesus walking on the sea..." (John 6:15-21) "And straightway Jesus constrained his disciples to get into a ship, and to go before him unto the other side, while he sent the multitudes away...he went up into a mountain apart to pray...But the ship was now in the midst of the sea, tossed with waves: for the wind was contrary." (Matt. 14:22-33) "But the LORD sent out a great wind into the sea, and there was a mighty tempest in the sea, so that the ship was liked to be broken...." (Jonah 1:4-16)

After almost three days of snow here in Ohio, things are letting up and brightening today. Perhaps this storm is about over. Most people do not like storms, except perhaps those whose jobs are to track them or to predict their arrivals. Many today seem fixated on the weather channels, finding them rather mesmerizing but often threatening. A pastor friend in PA said Sunday that he does not let all the forecasting bother him. To check the weather, he "looks out the window and if the rock outside is wet, it must be raining, if it's dry, then it's not raining, if he can't see the rock, then he knows it is dark."

Stormy weather is destined to hit us all. Life is not all clear skies and balmy temperatures. Life's storms can be rather intimidating, threatening, and destructive.

Several "storm reports" are found in the gospels and these were not simple weather patterns. But Jesus Himself was involved in them very personally, not announcing them ahead of time or huddling safely inside during them. Notice these observations.

1. **Jesus Controls the Storms and Uses Them**

   Our God doesn't prevent all storms from affecting His children. He may even send us right into their path as He did with his disciples. But He employs them for His purposes. He may be strengthening and increasing our faith. He may be weakening and decreasing our fear. He may be disciplining and rescuing us from sin. (Jonah 1) He may be equipping us and preparing us for future storms. He may be giving us opportunities to help other storm-troubled folks nearby. (Acts 27:9-28:10)

2. **Jesus Calms the Storms and Can Calm Us**

   In each of the storm passages referenced above, God is acknowledged to have calmed the storm and restored His followers to inward peace and serenity. The "Fear not" encouragements are commanded by the Lord and the evidence of His presence and power becomes obvious as we trust Him. He may be viewed at rest within our storm-tossed boat, walking on the stormy waves, or praying for us from shore, but His presence is real and effective in bringing peace as we trust Him. He is with us in every storm of life. That is great news!

For Prayer Today

- Whether life's storms are clearly forecasted or totally unanticipated, let's ask the Lord to deliver us from fear and anxiety at the first sign of any storm, as we trust Him.

Personal Notes and Responses

I Will Not Be Afraid!

"The LORD is my light and my salvation; whom shall I fear? The LORD is the strength of my life; of whom shall I be afraid?... Though an host should encamp against me, my heart shall not fear: though war should rise against me, in this I will be confident." (Psalm 27:1-3) "For whatsoever is born of God overcometh the world: and this is the victory that overcometh the world, even our faith." (I John 5:4-5)

Many of us regard ourselves as members of a community of faith. We believe in a personal God and have trusted Him for our eternal salvation, provided through Jesus Christ. But so many of us today honestly confess to being filled with a nagging fear and dread of each day and of what could happen in the near or distant future. And that fear is driving us into all kinds of panicky thoughts and directions.

O that we could deal with our fears and express David's sentiments as found in the verses above. "No matter what happens, I will not be afraid!" How could he say that? It was because He indeed was trusting everything to God. Such faith can conquer fear every time. So what might that look like? Notice some components of that faith from Psalm 27. (Read thoughtfully the entire Psalm.)

Such faith sets its focus on loving and worshipping our God. (27:4) To seek to develop such close fellowship with God daily, where we can love and talk to Him should be our foremost desire.

Such faith senses a security and safety that God provides. (27:5-6) He knows how and where to hide and harbor us when we are in need of it.

Such faith sings praises and offers sacrifices of joy to God. (27:6) Are we sacrificially and joyfully giving to the Lord in worship or hoarding our resources for the future? Are our days filled with singing praises to Him?

Such faith enters into frequent supplications and prayers to God (27:4, 7) Are we really praying about every detail of every day and committing all to Him?

Such faith struggles at times but then seeks the face of God's forgiveness and blessings, even as others, even family, may forsake us. (27:8-10) Occasional struggles, often due to our sin and unbelief, can complicate things but God forgives and restores.

Such faith studies the ways of God and chooses to follow them. (27:11-12) Are we spending time daily in the Scriptures and learning His ways in order to obey Him?

Such faith strengthens and encourages the believer for the challenges ahead. (27:13-14) Do we boldly move ahead each day in the strength and wisdom that God provides, with continued confidence in Him?

Our God does not want His family living in daily defeat, filled with anxiety and fear. Victory over those enemies can be a daily experience as we truly trust God with everything. May the above verses encourage us to do so.

May we truly be people of faith, not people of fear!

For Prayer Today
- Ask God to drive away your fears and to replace them with a growing faith in Him.

Personal Notes and Responses

Passionate Peter Proudly Proclaimed a Pack of Positions on Podiatry, Prayer, and Personal Pacifism

"Peter saith unto him, Thou shalt never wash my feet. Jesus answered him, If I wash thee not, thou hast no part with me." (John 13:8) "And he cometh, and findeth them sleeping and saith unto Peter, Simon, sleepest thou? Couldest not thou watch one hour? Watch ye and pray, lest ye enter into temptation." (Mark 14:37-38) "Then Simon Peter having a sword drew it, and smote the high priest's servant, and cut off his right ear...." (John 18:10-11)

With apologies to popular Peter Piper who possibly picked a peck of pickled peppers, I call to your attention most people's favorite disciple, Simon Peter. It seems that most of us favor him because we can most easily identify with him. While Peter Piper contributed to us, perhaps a few challenging speech impediments, Peter the apostle provided us some graphically displayed spiritual impediments that we should avoid in our lives. Consider several critical episodes.

"Podiatry" – In the absence of anyone else following a cultural hospitality ritual, Jesus Himself stooped low and began washing the feet of His followers. Peter's pride was assaulted by this and he declared that he would never submit to this personal ministry of Jesus, who then responded by saying, "Peter, if you do not submit to My cleansing you, you cannot partner with me; we cannot continue to fellowship together." I John 1 says the same thing, that unless we often confess our sins to God, He will not cleanse us and our fellowship with God will be interrupted. (I John 1: 5-10)

Prayer- Out into a garden they went for a season of prayer as the betrayer and his mob were approaching. Peter, James, and John were entrusted with this privilege of prayer and watchfulness, but sleep overtook all three, three times! Jesus sympathetically understood their physical weariness but expressed disappointment in their failure. Like Peter again, we often fail to pray fervently and faithfully, as we should be doing.

Personal "Pacifism" – At a critical moment when they should have been alert and prayerful, the enemy arrived and Peter, probably bleary-eyed, decided impulsively that it was time to fight and so, drew his sword...., when actually, it was a time to submit, to surrender. Admonished by Jesus, he watched then as an ear was restored to its proper place.

It got worse as Peter was given three opportunities to testify honestly about knowing the Lord and about His divine greatness. But he, with a sudden and sinfully serious speech impediment, failed miserably at that, too, and left in shame as he caught Jesus eyeing him sadly.

Can you see yourself in any of these scenes? Often when we don't realize our frequent need for confession and cleansing, our toleration of personal sin hinders our prayer life. Then we become too weak to respond correctly to the challenges of life or we miss entirely the opportunities to point others to Jesus.

Read John 21 as Jesus there confronts Peter and restores Him to fruitful ministry. Then see what Jesus did through him in the book of Acts.

For Prayer Today
- Are you discouraged by your failures to follow Jesus? Let Him cleanse you and then begin again to follow Him.

Personal Notes and Responses

Skilled Workers

"Then wrought Bezaleel and Aholiab, and every wise hearted man, in whom the LORD put wisdom and understanding to know how to work all manner of work for the service of the sanctuary, according to all that the LORD had commanded. And Moses called Bezaleel and Aholiab, and every wise hearted man in whose heart the LORD had put wisdom, even every one whose heart stirred him up to come unto the work to do it:" (Exodus 36:1-2)

As the children of Israel headed into the wilderness for their many years of wandering, God planted Himself in their midst and made obvious His presence as a "Resident" in the tabernacle, basically an ornate but very portable "tent". But this fabric-covered and fenced-in structure was not thrown together haphazardly using left-over materials and scraps. No, the place for the Almighty God to dwell deserved the best of materials and the most excellent of workmanship. We find the blueprints and work orders in Exodus 31.

The workmen, artisans, and craftsmen were to "...devise cunning works, to work in gold, and in silver, and in brass, and in cutting of stones, to set them, and in carving of timber, to work in all manner of workmanship... that they may make make... the tabernacle of the congregation...and all the furniture of the tabernacle, and the table and his furniture, and the pure candlestick with all his furniture, and the altar of incense, and the altar of burnt offering with all his furniture, and the laver and his foot, and the cloths of service... and the anointing oil, and sweet incense...." (Ex. 31:1-11) They were also to make the fabric-covered fencing that went around the court of the tabernacle with its supportive pillars, hooks, sockets, etc. They were to design and create the several layers of coverings that became the protective roof of the structure. The priests clothing involved fabric lined with gold and with blue, purple, and scarlet threads and fine woven linen, and breastplate and ephod which encased precious stones representing the twelve tribes of Israel, etc. (Ex.38-39)

I am not a skilled worker in any of those construction and craftmanship areas, nor am I motivated to learn those skills. But I am so encouraged to realize that God does choose and equip specific people for such specific tasks, wiring their DNA, their brains, and their experiences in certain directions. He also develops within them certain passions, interests, and drives into specific fields of work and careers – just as He did with the tabernacle construction project.

"Bezaleel Builders, Inc." came into existence because God put into the craftsmen's hearts His wisdom, understanding, and knowledge in these specific construction areas as well as a stirring in their souls to invest themselves in working on such a project. Excellent skills and passionate hearts were ready and willing to do the job.

Do you see your skill set and heart-felt passions for a specific type of work as a direct equipping and calling from God? Are you trusting Him to enable you to do your work daily? Are you serving others in your work in ways that bless them and honors the God who called, prepared, and hired you to work for Him?

For Prayer Today
-   Thank the Lord for the talents, skills, and interests that He has given you and ask Him to aid you, through them, to serve Him and others daily.

Personal Notes and Responses

Developing Discernment

"Do not drink wine nor strong drink, thou, nor thy sons with thee, when ye go into the tabernacle of the congregation, lest ye die... and that ye may put difference between holy and unholy, and between unclean and clean; and that ye may teach the children of Israel all the statutes which the LORD hath spoken unto them..." (Lev. 10:9-11)

The term "discernment" might be defined as the accurate ability to know truth from falsehood, right from wrong, pure from impure, wise from foolish, and holy from unholy. It can even distinguish the distinctions between what is good, better, and best, between what is just "ok" and what is excellent. This capacity to make sound judgments seems almost to have disappeared from the landscape today.

Our modern world shows no tolerance or respect for this ability. For people today, to discern differences between people, objects, activities, and philosophies is "discriminating", and thus is being determined as almost criminal. How dangerously foolish is that notion.

When my wife pours me a glass of milk, she often sniffs at the open bottle first and, though that habit makes me a bit suspicious, it also makes me feel secure that my spouse has checked it out and judged that the milk is safe and will not bring me harm. Marketers and advertisers often shade the truth about a product which should be examined carefully before an expenditure is made. The entertainment industry throws in our faces all kinds of enticing suggestions and scenes in order to further trap us with sinful and damaging lusts and habits. Abusers of varied substances often pressure their peers into experimenting with things that can destroy lives. Precise discernment and judgment are required!

Yet our world tries to convince us that there are no clear absolutes, no definable categories of right and wrong for everyone. Everything is relative. Ethics are situational. "Morality" is to be decided by each individual based upon their experiences, feelings, or preferences and no one has any right to "judge" or discern any differently. "Political correctness" and individual "rights" rule today with their resulting chaotic confusion.

The Bible makes it very clear that there are eternal absolutes which we must believe and on which we must base all our decisions and they are easily found in God's Word. We must study those pages and build our lives and our decisions on what God says and then we must teach and live them out in front of our children and grandchildren. Notice their benefit in Proverbs 1:2-3 and 4:11-13.

"To know wisdom and instruction; to perceive the words of understanding to receive the instruction of wisdom, justice, and judgment, and equity; to give subtilty to the simple...I have taught thee in the way of wisdom; I have led thee in right paths. When thou goest, thy steps shall not be straitened; and when thou runnest, thou shalt not stumble. Take fast hold of instruction; let her not go: keep her; for she is thy life."

For Prayer Today
- Ask God for heavenly wisdom and discernment about all things; then use them regardless of what is popular or accepted by folks who reject God's standards. (Rom. 12:1-2)

Personal Notes and Responses

ETERNAL ENCOURAGEMENTS #119

The Execution of an Innocent Man

"If ye be reproached for the name of Christ, happy are ye; for the spirit of glory and of God resteth upon you...But let none of you suffer as a murderer, or as a thief, or as an evildoer, or as a busybody in other men's matters. Yet if any man suffer as a Christian, let him not be ashamed; but let him glorify God on this behalf... Wherefore let them that suffer according to the will of God commit the keeping of their souls to him in well doing, as unto a faithful Creator." (I Peter 4:14-19)

The first dubbed "Crime of the Century" took place on the evening of March 1, 1932, my father's 16th birthday when, in New Jersey, the 20-month-old son of the famed aviator, Charles Lindbergh and Anne Morrow Lindbergh was kidnapped. The very intriguing crime totally captivated and mesmerized all levels of American society for several years. It took a year for the authorities to find a suspect, Richard Hauptmann, who denied any involvement in the crime right up to his execution on April 3, 1936.

My father took an avid interest in the case immediately that carried through the rest of his life. He firmly believed in the innocence of the accused and became obsessed with trying to clear his name. Probably thousands of hours of investigating, researching, interviewing, and studying every aspect of the case, then speaking on the subject hundreds of times, further confirmed his beliefs. Getting to know the executed man's widow and son and having them in my parents' home a couple times brought the case very personally to our family. Dad's findings and conclusions are found in his book, "Murder of Justice".

Church history records that people have been persecuting and even killing off followers of Christ in many dozens of countries even to this present day. Christ even predicted such seemingly unjust atrocities. (John 15:18-25; Matt.10:16-31).

It is interesting that in our verses above, Peter instructs that when believers are reproached, accused, or arrested for some alleged violations, and may even suffer for them, that we are to make sure that we are innocent. Make certain that our suffering is unjust and undeserved! We dare not be committing crimes and getting into trouble for doing evil. It is when we do right and still suffer for it, that God is pleased and the testimony of the gospel remains intact. In fact, in the apostles' many cases, the gospel actually spread and multiplied, as believers were made to suffer for simply following Christ. (Acts 4, 5:17-42; Phil. 1:12-18)

Of course, the greatest example of the execution of an innocent Man, was that of our Savior. He was totally innocent of any and all sin, yet willingly submitted to all the indignities and tortures of His execution. He stepped into it willingly in order to suffer and die in our place, taking on our sin and guilt. Our salvation is only possible because our innocent Savior was killed on our behalf. Check out I Peter 2:19-25 to see how He handled it all.

For Prayer Today

- Thank God that Christ, "who knew no sin, became sin for us, so that we might be made the righteousness of God in Him." (II Cor. 5:21)

Personal Notes and Responses

Anguish and Despair

"How long will ye vex my soul, and break me in pieces with words? These ten times have ye reproached me: ye are not ashamed that ye make yourselves strange to me...and plead against me my reproach:, know now that God hath overthrown me, and hath compassed me with his net...He hath fenced up my way that I cannot pass, and he hath set darkness in my paths. He hath stripped me of my glory...he hath destroyed me on every side...Mine hope hath he removed like a tree. He hath also kindled his wrath against me...Oh that my words were written! oh that they were printed in a book! That they were graven with an iron pen and lead in the rock forever! For I know that my redeemer liveth..." (Job 19:1-27)

Again, I consider Job to be the "poster child" for extreme suffering by an undeserving fellow. Here he certainly admits to sinking pretty low, losing almost all hope, and of doubting God's wisdom and care.

I love it when he cries out that he wishes his story was written down and preserved forever! (And then it actually was, under the inspirational guidance of the Holy Spirit! – II Tim. 3:16-17; II Peter 1:20-21) So why did God record this man's story? It certainly is not an easy one to read. What did God want Job to learn and then, through his testimony, want us likewise to be informed? Lots of things, I believe, but here is just a few.

1. Divine silence does not mean divine absence. God remained silent for quite some time, providing no reasons, answers, or even comfort. But He was not absent. He was very present and very involved in this entire season of incredible suffering, even having initiated it! (1:1-12)

2. Human suffering does not mean rejection. God had not rejected Job, in fact, Job was right in the middle of God's real-time plan for him. God had not run off; He was actively working on Job and others the whole time. God was not

finished with him; He was employing some sharper tools as He sculpted Job's complete testimony. (Rom. 8:18-39; I Peter 4:12-14)

3. Becoming self-focused and dwelling on our own pain can cause us to lose sight of God's bigger picture and plan.

4. Getting so low can force us to look upward and trust our wonderful God. God gets our attention and draws us much closer to Him.

I love why Job wanted his experiences recorded for perpetuity. It was so that readers of all generations will come to know his God the way He had come to know and grew to trust Him more. Notice his words in 19:23-27.

"...with an iron pen and lead forever! For I know that my redeemer liveth, and that he shall stand at the latter day upon the earth: and though after my skin worms destroy this body, yet in my flesh shall I see God...though my reins be consumed within me." Here and in several other places he makes it clear that his faith in God was strong and that he would continue to cling to Him. We can do the same.

For Prayer Today
- Pray for yourself and others whenever you are feeling low and alone. Cling to Job's God who accomplished His plan for Job and rewarded him in the end.

Personal Notes and Responses

Our Witness Protection Program

"But ye shall receive power, after that the Holy Ghost is come upon you: and ye shall be witnesses unto me both in Jerusalem, and in all Judea, and in Samaria, and unto the uttermost part of the earth." (Acts 1:8) "Therefore, if any man be in Christ, he is a new creature: old things are passed away; behold, all things are become new...Now then we are ambassadors for Christ, as though God did beseech you by us: we pray you in Christ's stead, be ye reconciled to God. For he hath made him to be sin for us, who knew no sin; that we might be made the righteousness of God in him." (II Cor. 5:17-21)

The witness protection programs that are allegedly offered are done so for those who provide vital evidence against some criminal behavior that produces convictions and appropriate penalties. It may free them from the penalties of their own criminal behavior and seeks to protect them by changing their identity and can involve dramatic changes in location or vocation, etc. They can then live a new life, free of their old one, and hopefully and safely lead productive lives.

When we repented of our sin and put our trust completely in Christ to save us, we were then forgiven and freed from our sinful past, as well. We also entered a "witness program"! Christ changed our identity from that of a sinful unbeliever who was facing the death penalty, into a new creation with a new life to be lived for Him. We became witnesses about Jesus Christ and are to be testifying often of His saving grace and love to the many around us who are still bound to their spiritually criminal lives.

In this case, it is not our physical lives that may need to be protected. It is our testimonies, our words of witness about our Savior. How can we protect our deliveries of such an eternally important message to those in desperate need of it? Our lifestyle plays an important role in this and Paul in Ephesians provides some concise bullet-point guidelines on it. How are we then to live out our new identities and carry out our new mission?

1. We are to walk worthy of our calling, our spiritual vocation, with humility, gentleness, longsuffering, patient love, and peaceful unity with other believers. (Eph. 4:1-3)

2. We are to walk in love, imitating Christ's sacrificial love for us. (Eph. 5:1-2)

3. We are to walk in the light, no longer returning to walk in the darkness of sinful attitudes, practices, and desires. (5:3-14)

4. We are to walk in wisdom, not foolishly, but with God's wisdom regarding His will for each day of our lives. (5:15-17)

5. We are to walk under the control and influence of the Holy Spirit through God's Word, allowing His fruit to be produced in us. (5:18-21; Col.3:16-17)

When we choose to walk in other ways, our testimony about Christ becomes suspect, our trust with people can be broken, and our ambassadorship can be seriously damaged. Please allow your new lifestyle to provide corroborating evidence to your verbal witness of what Christ can do for those who trust Him.

For Prayer Today
-   Thank God for making you a witness for Him and ask Him for a fresh "assignment".

Personal Notes and Responses
_____

ETERNAL ENCOURAGEMENTS #122

'Tis the Season!

"While the earth remaineth, seedtime and harvest, and cold and heat, and summer and winter, and day and night shall not cease." (Genesis 8:22) " Although the fig tree shall not blossom, neither shall fruit be in the vines; the labour of the olive shall fail, and the fields shall yield no meat; the flock shall be cut off from the fold, and there shall be no herd in the stalls: yet I will rejoice in the LORD, I will joy in the God of my salvation." (Habakkuk 3:17-18) "But we all, with open face, beholding as in a glass the glory of the Lord, are changed into the same image from glory to glory, even as by the Spirit of the Lord." (II Cor. 3:18)

I almost titled this piece, "'Tis My Season!" since we are reaching the middle of my all-time favorite season, autumn. I just love the changes this season brings, the crisp coolness, the creative color scheme, and even the "shorter" days. Here in Amish country, the broad textures and shades of the landscapes dramatically change as harvest time develops and the festivities and traditions of this season are enjoyed.

I am thankful to live in an area where dramatic seasonal changes can be expected and enjoyed every year, as God promised after the flood. We can anticipate them and prepare for them.

But not all changes are seasonal; some are quite sporadic and what I call situational. Blessings and tragedies often visit us unexpectantly. Little ones are birthed and many family members and friends die and leave us grieving. Dramatic weather patterns appear on the horizon, business failures take place, illnesses invade a household. Marriages crumble; children or grandchildren break our hearts. Just our aging process alone becomes quite challenging.

Many of us have great difficulty handling or surviving the difficulties that these situations produce. We can feel overwhelmed, discouraged, fearful, or depressed. Then we must remember that

God is always at work in us, making gradual changes in our character and maturity, through the seasonal and situational drama that take place around us. (Rom. 8:18-39)

At salvation, God changes us into new creations, with new and eternal life. Then He employs lots of challenges and changes in our lives to grow us toward maturity in our relationship with Him. We learn from His Word, depend on Him for everything, and become more and more like Jesus Christ. And these spiritual transformations that He develops in us, enable us to handle all the seasonal and situational challenges of life.

Yes, different seasons will come and go. Difficult situations may challenge or threaten us. But as we continue to grow in the Lord, we will be able to rejoice in our God and to trust in His sovereign will and care for us. Read again Habakkuk's testimony about this in our text today.

For Prayer Today

- Ask God to continue to mature you into Christ-likeness and enable you to handle the challenges of life with His strength and joy.

Personal Notes and Responses

ETERNAL ENCOURAGEMENTS #123

Memorable Music by Moses

"Now therefore write ye this song for you, and teach it to the children of Israel: put it in their mouths, that this song may be a witness for me against the children of Israel...And it shall come to pass, when many evils and troubles are befallen them, that this song shall testify against them as a witness; for it shall not be forgotten out of the mouths of their seed...Moses therefore, wrote this song the same day, and taught it to the children of Israel." (Deut.31:19-32:43)

I find it intriguing that some of what God wanted Israel to know and to remember, even throughout future generations, was put to music. God ordered Moses to "record" the God-inspired lyrics of a piece of music that would then become known by the clever and creative title of "The Song of Moses". And we still have it in Deuteronomy 32; all the ballad-like lyrics are there. Top of the wilderness (country) charts in his day, I imagine.

It was a song to be remembered as it would remind future Jewish generations of the past mercy and goodness of God to them as well as clearly warn them of the tragedies that would come their way through any future disobedience and idolatry.

Another vocalist and instrumentalist, David, the sweet psalmist of Israel, was used by God to record a large collection of musical admonitions and worshipful adulations of God. Most of these inspired pieces were sung often by the Israelites and corporately used in times and places of worship.

Perhaps we have all discovered that we more easily remember things that have been set to music, sometimes for many decades. Remember the musical jingles that were used to advertise many of our consumer products of long ago? Educators are finding new and expanded uses for music in the classroom and churches continue to employ it perhaps more extensively than ever before.

The passage above caught my attention a few weeks ago because our son and daughter-in-love have been singing several hymns and newer choruses to their children on most nights before bed. And our grandchildren are learning them, P

Recently, while helping out in their kitchen, we heard our 3 year old singing at the top of his lungs from the living room, "Hallelujah, All I Have is Christ" repetitively, while at the same time, almost competitively, from his high chair in the dining room our 2 year old was bellowing "Holy, Holy, Holy...!" Once during toy cleanup time, they started singing "On a hill far away, stood an old rugged cross..." which, though when sung loudly from a bathroom at 6:00 AM before anyone else has "arisen", sounds a bit more rugged.

Even God, who wants His people not to forget certain truths about Him and His care for them, made use of music that was to be taught to each succeeding generation! Are we doing that?

"Let the word of Christ dwell in you richly in all wisdom; teaching and admonishing one another in psalms and hymns and spiritual songs, singing with grace in your hearts to the Lord." (Col. 3:16)

For Prayer Today
- Thank God for the gift of music and its usefulness in advancing His kingdom.

Personal Notes and Responses

ETERNAL ENCOURAGEMENTS #124

To Err is Human; to Forgive, Canine.

"Let all bitterness, and wrath, and anger, and clamor, and evil speaking, be put away from you, with all malice: And be ye kind one to another, tenderhearted, forgiving one another, even as God for Christ's sake hath forgiven you." (Eph. 4:31-32) "Then came Peter to him, and said, Lord, how of shall my brother sin against me, and I forgive him? till seven times? Jesus saith unto him, I say not unto thee, Until seven times: but, Until seventy times seven..."' *(Matt. 18:21-35)*

It has been reported that dogs instinctively "forgive" their owners, no matter what the earlier offence might have been (exceptions being serious abuse). Upon just the sight of their masters they will race enthusiastically and happily toward them and lavish all kinds of affection upon them. They seem not even to remember any offence and are eager to continue any relationship without anger or bitterness. They refuse to harbor grudges, practice avoidance, or build walls.

Sadly, humans, even Christians are often very slow to forgive. Forgiveness seems not instinctive to them. It is not their default setting. They often immerse themselves in anger and resentment and live in poisonous bitterness even for years.

We might note several admonitions from the passages above on this important subject. We can and must forgive others who have sinned against us. It involves at least three steps.
1. **Removal** of the offense, to send it away, to cancel the debt.
2. **Refusal** to bring it up again. Do not hold it against the person again.
3. **Renewal** of the relationship if it is at all possible. Note the kindness needed here.

Said another way…

1. **Do not nurse** the wounds. Schedule no pity parties. Do not keep defending yourself or justifying any bitterness or anger on your part.

2. **Do not rehearse** the offence to others. Go silent about the situation. Do not keep talking about it to others, seeking sympathy or support for your hurts.

3. **Do not curse** it or them. Do not desire judgment on the offender. Do not seek any form of revenge. Let God deal with that, if necessary. (Rom. 12:14-21) Pour on the tender-hearted love and forgiveness, just as God has already done for you!

I so wish we could witness many such teary-eyed, humble and happy reunions among God's people who have been estranged from one another but have been brought together again in joyful expressions of forgiveness. Think of all the broken marriages that could be restored! Wouldn't that be tremendous!?

We ought to get quite excited over this, though we probably wouldn't need to jump up and down and slobber all over each other.

For Prayer Today
-   Pray that God will humble people and move them to restore their broken relationships with His grace and love.

Personal Notes and Responses

Grace AND Truth

"In the beginning was the Word, and the Word was with God, and the Word was God...And the Word was made flesh, and dwelt among us, (and we beheld his glory, the glory as of the only begotten of the Father), **full of grace and truth***...And of his fullness have all we received, and grace for grace. For the law was given by Moses, but* **grace and truth** *came by Jesus Christ." (John 1:1, 14-17)*

As the apostle John began his record of the life of Jesus Christ on earth, he clarified the fact that this One who was born of a virgin and walked among them was indeed the Eternal, Creator-God. But notice how John describes Jesus in these verses.

Under their studied gaze of Christ over 3 years of time, John and others identified the glorious perfections of God Himself. They also came to know that Jesus was the complete expression of two components – grace and truth.

Fullness of Grace – Jesus completely and precisely personified grace – that quality of providing for others who do not deserve it the manifold goodness of God. The giving-ness of God was seen as He freely provided compassion, love, forgiveness, and salvation to the undeserving. He gently touched the untouchables; freed those enslaved to sin, forgave the sinners, fed the hungry, and willingly paid the ultimate price for those with hardened, rebellious hearts who were rejecting Him. (Rom. 5:6-10)

Fullness of Truth – Jesus demonstrated to all that He was truth incarnate. He was the source and the eternal expression of truth. What He spoke was always truth. There was no falsehood or deceptive lies in Him. Truth is not relative or subject to opinion or shading. Jesus didn't hide it or dilute it. True truth is absolute. What God says is true and must be believed and obeyed with no exceptions. (Rom. 3:23-26; 6:23; Eph. 2:1-9)

If we are followers of Christ, we must strive to be expressive of both grace and truth, as well. To adequately represent Him to people, both elements should be obviously present.

Unfortunately, many believers and some churches are driven more by one or the other. Some choose to declare cold truth in the faces of the least expecting and often at inappropriate times and ways. A quickness to judge or condemn and a slowness to love and forgive can easily drive people away from our Savior. Others are so full of grace and love that they never seem to get around to sharing the truths of the gospel to people who may need it most. To think we are loving people without somehow warning them of their need of a Savior may not be love at all.

What people around us need to see are believers who with an attitude of love and grace, care enough for them to tell them the truth about themselves and of God's saving grace available to them.

We may not become completely "full" of both of these, but can we do better than we may be doing? If we are strong on grace, can we grow to recognize and to faithfully share the truths of the gospel with others? If we are strong on truth, can we learn to communicate it appropriately with compassion and love from God?

For Prayer Today
- Ask God to make you an effective communicator of both grace and truth from Him.

Personal Notes and Responses

Feeling Weary and Alone?

"I cried unto the LORD with my voice…I poured out my complaint before him; I shewed before him my trouble. When my spirit was overwhelmed within me…I looked on my right hand, and beheld, but there was no man that would know me: refuge failed me; no man careth for my soul…Attend unto my cry; for I am brought very low…" (Psalm 142)

David had been anointed to be Israel's next king and was extremely popular among the citizenry for his military courage and many victories. But once again, he was on the run from the present monarch, King Saul, who jealously hated him and determined to kill him. As David prayed the above words he was hiding in a cave while nearby, Saul and his soldiers combed the hills for him.

David was not alone; he had about 400 followers but they were not that helpful to him. They are described in I Samuel, "…every one that was in distress, and every one that0 was in debt, and every one that was discontented, gathered themselves unto him;" (22:1-2) Likewise, we may feel alone even though surrounded by people, especially if those people are those whom we are expected to serve or lead. Such relationships can discourage and drain us further, rather than encourage or strengthen us.

Are you feeling that way today? That deep within your heart you are all alone and that no one really cares for your soul?

Though you may indeed feel that way, that is not true. As David knew, there is One who really does care and can help us in such times of despair. So, once again he turned his exhausted and broken heart to God for the reassurance and encouragement that he needed. He continued His cry to God but with these words.

"I cried unto thee, O LORD: I said, Thou art my refuge and my portion in the land of the living. Attend unto my cry…deliver me from my persecutors; for they are stronger than I. Bring my soul out of prison, that I may praise thy name: the righteous shall compass me about; for thou shalt deal bountifully with me." (Psalm 142:5-7)

We can do the same in our dark and lonely times. We can talk to God and express honestly our feelings and fears to Him. We can state our confidence in God and in His truthfulness in the Scriptures. We can trust His promises and provision and claim them personally. We can resume praising Him and rejoicing in His faithfulness and look forward confidently to more of His bountiful care.

And, as we do so, He will provide the comfort and encouragement, the rest and refreshment for our soul. He will strengthen us for the task in the situation we find ourselves. He will renew our desires to serve Him and to help those around us with His grace and love, no matter how hard and daunting the challenges may be. And, our relationship with God will grow more precious and important daily for whatever the future may bring.

For Prayer Today
-     If needed, pray like David prayed, casting all your cares on the One who cares for you.

Personal Notes and Responses

Devilish Devices

"Be sober, be vigilant; because your adversary the devil, as a roaring lion, walketh about, seeking whom he may devour: whom resist steadfast in the faith..." (I Peter 5:8) "...Put on the whole armor of God, that ye may be able to stand against the wiles of the devil..." (Eph. 6:10-18) "Ye are of your father the devil, and the lusts of your father ye will do...when he speaketh a lie, he speaketh of his own, for he is a liar, and the father of it." (John 8:44) "To whom ye forgive any thing, I forgive also...for your sakes forgave I it in the person of Christ; lest Satan should get an advantage of us: for we are not ignorant of his devices." (II Cor. 2:10-11)

Regardless of whatever you may think or imagine about this one called Satan or the devil, the Bible makes it very clear that he is real, he is a fallen angel who leads hosts of other such beings, and is devoted to the destruction of God's plan for this world and its people. He shows up early in Genesis and is a major player in the end time events of Revelation and is mentioned many times in between. He is an enemy of all who have trusted Christ and he has his "wiles", carefully devised strategies, for impacting God's people. Though we need not fear him, it may be wise to review his strategic methods that are designed against us.

1. **He uses doubt**. He caused Eve to reconsider God's Word to her and to doubt and misinterpret its accuracy. (Gen. 3:1-6)
2. **He uses deceit**. He cleverly lies and deceives many with falsehoods, half-truths, and wrong views of reality. He is a great deceiver and never speaks the truth. (Gen. 3:1-4; John 8:44)
3. **He uses our natural desires** that God gave us for good things and turns them toward evil. Satan appeals to the lusts of the flesh, the lust of the eyes, and our inward pride to lure us into sinful practices. (Gen. 3:1-6; Matt. 4:1-11)
4. **He uses his domain, his dominion**. This sin-cursed world is in his grasp; he is the god of this world, which provides

us many sinful and devilish opportunities to engage in evil and to be led away from God's plan and purposes. (Eph. 2:1-3; I John 2:15-17; Eph. 6:10-18)

5. **He even can use our decisions** and dealings regarding a fallen family member. Paul urges a church to forgive a repentant brother, lest Satan take advantage of bitter or angry Christians who may be unwilling to forgive. (II Cor.2:3-11; Eph. 4:26-32)

Thankfully, Satan is a doomed character. His eternal defeat took place at the cross as Christ defeated and destroyed his plan and guaranteed that his eternity would be in a place of suffering. (Gen. 3:15; Heb. 2:14-15; Rev. 12:7-12; 20:7-10)

Please be aware that a very real spiritual conflict exists around us each day. Let us obey God's Word and trust Him to grant us the victory in each tempting skirmish that we may face.

For Prayer Today
- Thank God that victory over sin is ours through Jesus Christ. Ask Him to make you a good soldier of His. (II Tim. 2:1-4)

Personal Notes and Responses

An Employment Crisis

"Servants, be obedient to them that are your masters according to the flesh, with fear and trembling, in singleness of your heart, as unto Christ; not with eyeservice, as menpleasers; but as the servants of Christ, doing the will of God from the heart; with good will doing service as to the Lord, and not to men: knowing that whatsoever good thing any man doeth, the same shall he receive of the Lord, whether he be bond or free." "And whatsoever ye do, do it heartily, as to the Lord, and not unto men; knowing that of the Lord ye shall receive the reward of the inheritance: for ye serve the Lord Christ..." (Eph. 6:5-9; Col.3:22-4:1)

Throughout our country today, employers are dealing with an apparent labor shortage; they cannot find workers to hire. Perhaps this is a consequence of both the pandemic and of our government's largesse that has discouraged people from seeking jobs or maybe there are other major contributing factors. Smaller businesses especially see their future recovery as very questionable, in light of this reality. Everyone seems to be ramping up their efforts to regain a much-needed workforce.

Employment issues have become so complicated today and we know that there is no perfect job, employer, or employee. Even the twenty-year employment history of Jacob for his boss, Laban, reveals a contentious relationship and questionable business practices among both parties. (Gen. 30:25-31:55)

However, as Jacob prepares to leave that workforce, he presents his own record of his work history to his boss which might provide something of a template for the type of employee that is needed in most places today.

Jacob testifies that he recognized that his job was a stewardship, a caring for the assets of his employer and that those assets, Laban's flocks, had multiplied and prospered during Jacob's tenure (Gen.

30:29-30). When losses occurred, Jacob bore those losses himself and did not charge Laban with them (31:38-39). He shepherded Laban's flocks in all kinds of weather, drought and cold, with many sleepless nights (31:40). He refused to eat of Laban's herds though he may have had the freedom to do so (31:28). For twenty years he remained committed to the promises he made, though his circumstances and pay was deceptively changed ten times (31:6-7, 42).

Laban acknowledged that he had prospered much because God was obviously with Jacob and blessed his work exceedingly. He considered it an employment crisis that Jacob wanted to leave him to return home and made great effort to keep him but it was clear to Jacob that God wanted him to head home (30:25-30; 31:1-3). Unfortunately, the suspicion and animosity remained between them as Jacob and his family finally did depart (31:43-55).

Yes, employment relationships can be difficult and stressful. What is needed, though, are workers who are dedicated to make their boss and their company successful. They need to be unselfish, hard-working laborers in all kinds of circumstances. They must not steal or take advantage of their employer in any way for personal benefit. They should develop a long-term loyalty to the team and a daily dependance on God, pleasing Him in all their labor.

And, as they do so, He will bless their efforts exceedingly, and the employer will see God at work and be blessed as well. See also Col. 3:22-4:1 on this.

For Prayer Today
- Pray for adequate workers to be found for the companies in your area and ask God to make you an employee that displays God's grace in your workplace.

Personal Notes and Responses

Patterns of Prayer

"Give ear to my words, O LORD, consider my meditation. Hearken unto the voice of my cry, my King, and my God: for unto thee will I pray. My voice shalt thou hear in the morning, O LORD; in the morning will I direct my prayer unto thee, and will look up... Lead me, O LORD, in thy righteousness because of mine enemies; make thy way straight before my face...But let all those that put their trust in thee rejoice: let them ever shout for joy... be joyful in thee." (Psalm 5:1-12)

Most of the Psalms were not only written as pieces of music but they are also prayers. As we study many of these passages, we do notice some patterns or specific plans that seem to be employed by the Psalmist when he talked to God. As another simple primer on prayer, let's notice a few of these elements.

1. Prayer was often **verbally expressed**. I'm not ruling out silent praying but I've found it intriguing that so many times in Scripture, people prayed and cried aloud to God. "Give ear to my words..." I have also seen very dramatic and sudden answers to prayer when I have been seriously agonizing and fervently praying out loud to God.

2. Sometimes it was **very emotional**. The word "meditation" above can mean inward groaning. In David's prayers we see him express many different emotions. He wasn't just "saying prayers" or reciting some memorized ditty to God. He was expressing to God his love, his worship, his anger, his depression, his fear, his loneliness, his joy, etc.

3. Prayer was often uttered **very early** in the morning. It was a daily priority before all the other activities crowded out personal time with God. Many of us have found a morning time in the Word and in prayer very effective in calibrating ourselves spiritually for whatever the day may hold.

4. Prayer was **expectant**. The one talking to God fully expected a response from God. They "looked up" or "out"

for the answer. Paul instructed us to "Watch and pray." This is praying by faith. Do we really expect God to act in light of our requests? I hope so. God desires to do so.

5. Prayer was **very exacting**, very precise. Specific aspects of God were referenced in prayers of praise and worship. A variety of specific names of God were used to address Him for specific situations. Specific requests were uttered. General and generic prayers as "God bless the missionaries..." are not as effective in accomplishing much, in my opinion. I have been so excited often to discover that the more specific I am in prayer, the extraordinarily specific are His answers.

6. Prayer is made **exclusively** to our Heavenly Father, the Creator God of the universe and should include expressions of worship, praise, and thanksgiving to Him.

For Prayer Today
- With consideration of the above elements of David's prayer, pray openly and honestly with God today.

Personal Notes and Responses

The Journaling Journey

"For whatsoever things were written aforetime were written for our learning..." (Rom. 15:4) "Write this for a memorial in a book..." (Ex. 17:14) "And because of all this we make a sure covenant, and write it..." (Neh.9:38) "Take thee a roll of a book, and write therein all the words that I have spoken unto thee..." (Jer.36:2)

It is obvious that when God spoke His eternal mind to mankind, He wanted it to be remembered, thus He commanded and arranged that it be written down. God's Spirit oversaw its inspiration and its amazing preservation over many centuries of time and so today we still have the written Word of God. (II Tim. 3:16-17; II Peter 1:19-21)

No one is writing Scripture anymore, nor should anyone try to do so. However, there is great value in the habit of recording other matters of importance in our lives. As I continue to age, my memory capacity seems to be weakening and I need to write lots of things down if I am to remember them (if I recall where I put the paper). Young children often keep their own secret diaries about things that are important to them. As adults, perhaps we should do the same.

That practice today is called "journaling" and doing so can become quite the journey, especially if we are recording something of our personal relationship with God. Let me suggest three things about which we might record.

1. We can journal our own spiritual growth and development, things God taught us from the Word that day from our own reading, from hearing a sermon, from something a friend sent us, etc. Special verses you have memorized, ways you obeyed or applied a certain passage, etc. can also be recorded.

2. We can develop a prayer journal, especially listing very special prayer requests and how God specifically answered them. Include special passages on prayer, special promises, how God answered prayer in the past, etc.
3. We can keep track of unique "God-sightings" in our lives. These are those special occasions when God dramatically moved in our circumstances, surprised us with generous provisions, set up miraculous "divine appointments" and arrangements for us, etc.

Each entry should be dated and kept rather brief and may be more sporadic than daily. This becomes a personal record that you have been seriously paying attention to the Word and work of God throughout your life. You will find it of great value as a joyful reminder of things that matter for eternity.

It is truly appalling to me how much of what God said or has done in our lives that we forget. That is sad and detrimental to our spiritual health. Though I haven't mastered this discipline, I do highly recommend it. It can accelerate your awareness of God and your growth in His grace as His child.

This habit of journaling may feel a bit tedious. But over time you will have produced a concise record of quite a journey – your personal journey with our wonderful God! What a treasure to pass on!

For Prayer Today
-   With pen and paper in hand, pray for all that is on your heart and leave room for God's responses.

Personal Notes and Responses

ETERNAL ENCOURAGEMENTS #131

Lots of Loving Going On, But...

*"This know also, that in the last days perilous times shall come. For men shall be **lovers** of their own selves, covetous, boasters, proud, blasphemers, disobedient to parents, unthankful, unholy, without natural affection, trucebreakers, false accusers, incontinent, fierce, despisers of those that are good, traitors, heady, high-minded, **lovers** of pleasures more than lovers of God..." (II Tim. 3:1-4) "...Jesus said to him, 'Thou shalt **love** the Lord thy God with all thy heart, and with all thy soul, and with all thy mind. This is the first and great commandment. And the second is like unto it, Thou shalt **love** thy neighbor as thyself...'" (Matt. 22:37-40)*

It intrigues me to see with what Paul starts his list of characteristics of perilous times. Self-love. And yet our world touts loving oneself as vitally important, even foundational to one's self-esteem and success in this world. Let me just say that loving oneself is very natural to all of us; it doesn't have to be taught, it is inbred in all of us. We already love ourselves, probably excessively, and often that very self-focus (selfishness) is the seed bed of most of our problems in life today.

Please note that a focus on loving oneself can easily produce all those other traits that are mentioned above. Please think about it. With oneself as our primary motivation we can easily become a lover of money, proud boasters, resistant to authorities, unthankful, unloving to others, lacking self-control, brutal, headstrong, lovers of pleasures, etc. Much of this is clearly seen in young children but, left uncorrected, its appearance in adulthood can indeed become perilous.

Jesus summarized all the ten commandments into two, both involving love. The top two commandments are to love God with everything we are and then to love people, whether near or far, known or strangers. (See Good Samaritan story that follows this teaching in Luke 10:25-37.) Notice too that Jesus acknowledged that we already love ourselves when he said that we are to love others to the same extent that we love ourselves. Nowhere in Scripture are we commanded to love ourselves but we are to love others, to do unto them as we would have them do to us.

Please understand that we are not endorsing any self-hatred but simply a transference of our love to God and to others. If we would awaken each morning with a renewed realization that life is not about me or what I want or think I deserve, but that it is about knowing and loving God and then reaching out to love those around me, our lives would be transformed. For as we obey those two commands, life will take on great value and purpose and we will become excited about what God has done for us and can accomplish through His love to others. Very humbly and thankfully, we'll feel great about God and our place in life as we live in sync with His purposes and plan for us.

This works well with our children also. In fact, that is where this approach to life should be first introduced, taught, and modeled.

For Prayer Today
- Pray that our pride and self-focused lifestyles can be conquered and replaced with a genuine love for God and others.

Personal Notes and Responses

How "Wowed" Are You?

"Blessed is the man whom thou chooseth, and causest to approach unto thee ...By terrible things in righteousness wilt thou answer us..." (Psalm 65:4-5) "Make a joyful noise unto God, all ye lands...Say unto God, How terrible art thou in thy works...Come and see the works of God: he is terrible in his doing toward the children of men." (Psa. 66:1-5) "O the depth of the riches both of the wisdom and knowledge of God! how unsearchable are his judgments and his ways past finding out!" (Rom. 11:33)

Our language and its use continue to change year by year. Our attempts to express very positive and deeply felt emotions have taken on a number of iterations. "That's cool!" was an old attempt at it. "Then, "This will "knock your socks off" or this will "blow your mind" ramp up the anticipated emotional effect. Declaring "Awesome!" may do the job but its overuse by cool dudes today may have weakened its effectiveness. Besides, if you try to tell someone you were really "awed" by something it comes out sounding like a British "odd" which is not the impression you want to make.

My current favorite such expression is simply "Wow!" I find myself uttering it often in response to my great God and all He continues to do for us and others. Moments later, many times with tears in my eyes, I just praise Him, thank Him, and search for words of worship to express to Him, though they fall short often.

I must add a word of admonition here. Some church growth, leadership, or worship books today recommend that a church service should attain and maintain a "Wow Factor" or people will be less inclined to return. That is a very serious error. It should not be the music, the service, the preacher, or the kids' department that creates the desired "Wow" response. We should not have to conjure up a "wow" experience, build for it, provide special lighting for it, or program for it. It is God alone who is worthy of our "wow" or of our worship. The more we get to know Him and to see His hand in our lives, wherever we may be, the more often our hearts will burst out with praise to our awesome God.

If the Bible studies or sermons just seem dull and not important, you are missing out on what God wants to say today. If you are not praying fervently and specifically for your needs, you will not see God's amazing care. If you are not trusting Him to guide your day into some "divine appointments", you will doubt His presence with you and His plan to use you for His glory. You will not be "wowed" by God and will not respond in humble worship of Him.

The refrain of a new song from Majesty Music says, that God's incredible grace and power should overwhelm, overshadow, and overcome us so much that our mind and mouth should be overflowing with our worship and praise to Him.

May we be "wowed" by God alone frequently and may we respond with love and gratitude to Him. (And, you might want to hang on to your socks!)

For Prayer Today
-    Take time today just to worship and praise our great God!

Personal Notes and Responses

ETERNAL ENCOURAGEMENTS #133

Way Over the Top!

"...Now unto him that is able to do exceedingly abundantly above all that we ask or think, according to the power that worketh in us, unto him be glory in the church by Christ Jesus throughout all ages, world without end. Amen." (Eph. 3:14-21)

The extended passage above indicates that as God's children we can grow to know the many grand dimensions of God's love for us and of His unlimited power that is able to do far more for, in, or through us than we could ever imagine. I continue to be thrilled with these truths.

In this more-lighthearted piece today I want to share with you a fun story of how we tried to give my wife's parents a taste of this one Christmas.

My in-laws, usually living life on its more serious side, appeared to be more dour and troubled than usual, as we hosted a Thanksgiving dinner with them in West Virginia about 15 years ago. Near meal's end, they opened up to share a growing, serious problem that they were facing with concern and consternation. They were on their last tube of their life-long favored toothpaste and they could not find more anywhere. They had been rationing that last tube carefully, but their deep anxiety was very evident. Making a change of toothpaste, then in their eighties, was inconceivable.

We were very compassionate in our response while smiling broadly on the inside where a special plan was being born. This was going to be a lot of fun!

On Christmas morning we insisted that they open their gifts first. I prepared dad for what appeared to be a long walking stick, suggesting that the day would come soon when he'd need more support as he moved about, etc. He responded with frowns and grimaces as I handed him his gift.

As he peeled off the wrapping, he began to giggle and was soon accompanied by mother shrieking with joyful laughter. Explosions of teary outbursts continued as they uncovered about five large boxes of their long-loved item. The next gift was of the shape and feel of a picture frame, but it turned out to be another four cartons taped together that way. More excited laughter, slapping each other, kicking up their heels, cheering, etc. Then came a heavier package of another nine tubes. More jubilation from all of us followed as we laughed ourselves silly over such a celebration.

Yes, we got it all on tape. Debra and I watched it again recently and laughed again over it. But it reminded me how often I agonize over some pretty small issues or needs and how I seem to forget that I have a heavenly Father who can do far above all I could ever imagine with my problems.

Sometimes I just need another good "brush" with Eph. 3 for a special "Gleem" of light from heaven.

"Blessed be the Lord, who daily loadeth us with benefits, even the God of our salvation." (Psalm 68:19)

For Prayer Today
- Give special thanks to God for those occasions when He has overwhelmed you with His love and power.

Personal Notes and Responses

The Downsides of Doubting God

"If any of you lack wisdom, let him ask of God, that giveth to all men liberally, and upbraideth not; and it shall be given him. But let him ask in faith, nothing wavering. For he that wavereth is like a wave of the sea driven with the wind and tossed. For let not that man think that he shall receive any thing of the Lord. A double-minded man is unstable in all his ways." (James 1:5-8) "… Trust in the LORD, and do good; so shalt thou dwell in the land, and verily thou shalt be fed." (Psalm 37:1-7) "Trust in the LORD with all thine heart; and lean not unto thine own understanding. In all thy ways acknowledge him, and he shall direct thy paths..." (Prov. 3:5-7)

Probably none of us who follow Christ would claim not to believe in God. We would categorically state that we do trust in God; we've trusted in Him through Christ for our eternity and we are trusting Him for our everyday needs. However, if we were totally honest, perhaps, we'd admit that sometimes some doubt creeps in. James certainly addresses that possibility.

Why do we sometimes doubt God's Word or question His promises? Maybe we think that our situation is too small for Him to care about it or that it is too large and complicated that it seems impossible, even for Him to handle it. Maybe we suppose that God is too busy and too focused on the greater needs of the world and that He certainly shouldn't be bothered by little me. Maybe our past haunts us yet and we doubt His assured forgiveness and so we feel that we do not "deserve" any of His attention.

What are the practical results of all these doubts in relation to our God? Read Psalm 37:1-11 and see some of the downsides of doubting God.

1. We focus more on the wicked and their ways, even sometimes envying them instead of staying focused on God. (37:1-2, 8; Prov. 24:1, 19)
2. We fret and worry about the evil threats around us and lose the rest and peace that God can provide. (37:1-2, 7)
3. We fear the wicked, often forgetting that the day of their demise will come. (37:7-15; Ex. 14:13, 14; Josh. 1:9)
4. We feed on our own wisdom, schemes, cleverness, and resources, leaning on our own understanding, instead of on the faithfulness of God. (Prov. 3:5-8; Psa. 37:3)
5. We fight, often taking matters into our own hands and erupt with harmful anger and wrath. (37:7-9)
6. Sometimes we flee from the things that God has asked us to do, sensing our own weaknesses, since we are doubting God. (Psalm 11, 37:12-40)
7. We even fail in prayer when we pray while not really trusting God. (James 1:5-8; 4:1-3)

We say, "We are only human!" as an excuse for doubting God's Word. It is true that as newer believers, our faith may be small but as we feed on the Scriptures and walk with God, we will sense growth and maturing of our ability to trust God. Notice the reassurance in Psalm 37:39-40.

For Prayer Today

"Increase my faith", even as the disciples asked the Lord to do. (Luke 17:1-6)

Personal Notes and Responses

Reasons to Sing

"Rejoice in the LORD, O ye righteous: for praise is comely for the upright. Praise the LORD with harp: sing unto him with the psaltery and an instrument of ten strings. Sing unto him a new song; play skillfully with a loud noise. For the word of the LORD is right; and all his works are done in truth. He loveth righteousness and judgment: the earth is full of the goodness of the LORD. By the word of the LORD were the heavens made; and all the host of them by the breath of his mouth...The LORD bringeth the counsel of the heathen to nought: he maketh the devices of the people of none effect..." (Psalm 33:1-22)

We have established earlier that God, as Creator, is the originator of music. The human capacity to communicate musically stems directly from God's design of such organs as vocal cords, diaphragm, lungs, brain, tongue, etc. The components of music, the scales, notes, chords, tones, etc. were His idea. Our ability to hear, understand, and appreciate musical compositions is by His creation. And, in many of the Psalms, there are clear expressions of God's worthiness of receiving musical expressions of worship and of His joy in hearing it.

The psalmist and instrumentalist, David, urges that the righteous be involved in expressing praise to God musically. He here gives us some reasons we should do so.

1. We should sing praise to God because of His character. (Psa. 33:1-5) Our God is righteous, truthful, just, and good. He loves righteousness and to hear His righteous people singing to Him. What a great God He is!
2. We should sing praise to God because He is the Creator. (33:6-9) He spoke; He commanded and all of creation came into existence. Think about that and "let all the inhabitants of the world stand in awe of him." Then let them sing!

3. We should sing praise to God because He is in control. (33:10-17) He is sovereign over individuals and over the nations. He rules and reigns and His counsel will be accomplished. No king or no army can thwart or overcome the power of our God. That's security!

4. We should sing praise to God because He cares for His own. (33:18-22) His eyes are on us; He keeps us alive; He is our help and our shield! The God of the universe is deeply involved in our care! Incredible!

At least fifty times in the Bible, God's people are commanded to sing. God has created us to do so. We have lots of spiritual reasons to sing to Him and about Him. We have many occasions to sing, in our churches, in the car, at home, and, yes, in the shower. We can teach our children to sing praises to God and sing with them. And when we are singing to our great God, it is worship that pleases Him.

Please do not ignore this repeated command. Sing to the Lord! Frequently. Wherever you may be. When with other believers in church, join heartily in singing praise to our wonderful God. Do not withhold such worship from God.

For Prayer Today
- Sing a song of praise to God today!

Personal Notes and Responses

Fighting Fear

"...For God hath not given us the spirit of fear; but of power, and of love, and of a sound mind. Be not thou therefore ashamed of the testimony of our Lord, nor of me His prisoner: but be thou partaker of the afflictions of the gospel according to the power of God..." (II Timothy 1:6-12) "Herein is our love made perfect, that we may have boldness in the day of judgment: because as he is, so are we in this world. There is no fear in love; but perfect love casteth out fear: because fear hath torment. He that feareth is not made perfect in love." (I John 4:17-18)

For most people, some degree of initial fear can be a helpful default setting in life. It is almost an automatic warning that some threat or danger is near. It urges us to pay attention, to enact caution, to get prepared for whatever is about to happen.

However, many people today seem to live day and night in fear. It robs them of peace. It keeps them awake at night. It creates uncertainty and timidity even in the basic routines and responsibilities of life. It provides a level of personal torture as it eats away at us. It intimidates us and drives us away from meaningful relationships and from important jobs and ministries. It becomes a powerfully captivating force under which people live in bondage every day.

What does the Bible say about all of this? It is clear that we are not to live in fear, no matter what circumstances we may be facing. It is clear that we are to live by faith, trusting our God to care for us and to accomplish His will in our lives.

Here is some Scriptural "ammo" (as in "bullet points") for our battle with fear.

- God's perfect love can drive out our fears. (I John 4:18-19) When we realize how completely and eternally God loves us and controls all the details of our lives while never ceasing His love, our fears can be conquered. (Rom. 8:28-39)

- God's goodness and mercy pursues us every day and at life's end we go to live in the Father's house. (Psalm 23:1-6; John 14:1-3) As we recognize God's goodness in our lives every day and constantly praise Him for it, our fears can be defeated.
- Whenever fear takes root, we can immediately call on the Lord and trust Him with the matter. (Psalm 56:3-4, 10-11)
- At the cross Christ defeated Satan and removed the fear and the sting of death from us. (Heb. 2:14-18) We can face death with joyful confidence and expectation.
- As believers in Christ, we are never alone. He is always with us in His Spirit. There's no need to fear. (Heb. 13:5-6; Matt. 28:18-20; Isa. 41:10; 51:12-16)
- God knows even what may be unknown to us. We often fear the unknown. But God knows it all and is involved with it all. We can rest in Him. (Matt.6:25-34; Psalm 139)

For Prayer Today
- Read the above referenced Scriptures often and ask God to grow your trust in Him.

Personal Notes and Responses

ETERNAL ENCOURAGEMENTS #137

"Talking to Yourself??"

"...But Naaman was wroth, and went away, and said, Behold, I thought, He will surely come out to me, and stand, and call on the name of the LORD his God, and strike his hand over the place, and recover the leper. Are not Abana and Pharpar, rivers of Damascas, better than all the waters of Israel? may I not wash in them, and be clean? So he turned and went away in a rage..." (II Kings 5:1-19)

"And he would fain have filled his belly with the husks that the swine did eat: and no man gave unto him. And when he came to himself, he said, How many hired servants of my father's have bread enough and to spare, and I perish with hunger! I will arise and go to my father..." (Luke 15:11-32)

So, do you find yourself actually talking to yourself? (Do others hear you doing so?) I suppose it is not so bad, especially in light of the well-known fact that most of us talk to our plants and to our pets (even robotic ones), and to any number of inanimate objects. Some of this can become quite entertaining but sometimes it is evidence of very deep pains and emotions. I suppose the content and attitude of such self-talk should be the measure of its value.

The first man quoted above spoke in pride-driven anger. He had inquired if a certain prophet could call on God and heal him of his leprosy. When the prophet sent his servant to him instead of going himself, this Syrian army commander was insulted. Then he was shocked at the simple advice the man gave him to enable his healing. In his conversation with himself, he rejected the prophet's advice, believing his own ideas were far superior, and remained afflicted.

That is the way of many people who are filled with their own thoughts, opinions, and desires and who continue to reject any divine intervention or counsel. So very sad and can be terminally dangerous.

In the New Testament we find the account of the prodigal son who finally came to himself and spoke words of humble honesty about his situation and came to right conclusions about what he must do. Then he humbly followed through on them.

Fortunately, both men came to their senses and turned to the true God in faith and obedience and both men came to know physical and spiritual healing and restoration of their lives and relationships. (Please read both stories completely.)

So, whenever you catch yourself talking to yourself, do you ever pause and evaluate the conversation? Is your talk drawing you to a deeper trust in God and an appreciation of all His gracious blessings He has given you? Or does it stir up more frustration and anger and a refusal to call on God for His help?

By the way, talking to God is always far better than talking to oneself.

For Prayer Today
- Pray for those you may know who continue to tell themselves things that are not true or helpful, that God will redirect their thinking and their trust toward Him.

Personal Notes and Responses

"Somew h e r e...Under the Rainbow..."

"...and I will remember my covenant, which is between me and you and every living creature of all flesh; and the waters shall no more become a flood to destroy all flesh. And the bow shall be in the cloud; and I will look upon it, that I may remember the everlasting covenant between God and every living creature of all flesh that is upon the earth." (Gen. 9:8-17)

It was over thirty years ago when my home church in eastern Pennsylvania called their third senior pastor. He and his wife and their five children were a delight to all of us and God's blessings were enjoyed by all as they began their ministry among us. But we also bonded with them very deeply after a very sad incident took place.

Not many months after joining us, the family was biking together somewhere in Maryland when a large bus, while making a tight turn with its rear wheel jumping a curb, struck and crushed their youngest son, at the age of seven.

I remember so agonizingly well how this tragedy forged our hearts together with this dear family as we grieved and wept together. I was asked to conduct the memorial service and the Lord led me to use a text from II Kings 4 in which friends of the prophet, Elisha, are grieving the sudden death of their only son. As the mother rushes off to find Elisha, his servant approaches her and asks, "Is it well with thee? Is it well with thy husband? Is it well with the child?" She answers, "It is well." (Read the entire story in II Kings 4.) In spite of the deep grief and heartache that we all felt, because this family was trusting the Lord, it was "well" with them. And, because their precious son had earlier repented of his sin and trusted Jesus to save him, we could say with certainty, "Yes, it is well with him, as well." He was with the Lord. That was a very difficult season but our church family of around 700 circled the wagons around their new pastor and family and moved through that valley together.

It was many months later when they discovered their camera that they had stashed away during their move and realized that there was still film in it. Upon getting it developed and not remembering what it contained, they made an awesome discovery. There was a somewhat distant shot of their young son and above him was a beautiful rainbow!

The sight of that bow in the clouds and the reminder that God had promised to restrain such a watery judgment from the earth was a gracious sign from Him that their son was indeed under the care of his promise-keeping, Heavenly Father.

We often do not understand why things happen, even why God seems to allow severe trials to come our way. But He is a good and gracious God who has demonstrated His love for us by giving up His own Son to suffer, bleed, and die in our place so that, through faith in Him, it can be well with us as well, both in this life and throughout eternity.

For Prayer Today
-    Pray for family, friends, or co-workers who have suffered severe losses, that they will find God to be the source of saving grace and comfort.

Personal Notes and Responses

That Mental Tape Player

"Finally, brethren, whatsoever things are true, whatsoever things are honest, whatsoever things are just, whatsoever things are pure, whatsoever things are lovely, whatsoever things are of good report; if there be any virtue. and if there be any praise, think on these things." (Phil. 4:8) "I will meditate in thy precepts, and have respect unto thy ways. I will delight myself in thy statutes: I will not forget thy word." (Psalm 119:15-16)

You may think far less of me for this but, I will admit to totally enjoying most "musicals", especially the old ones and now all the ones being performed near us here in Ohio. I value them so much that I always purchase the soundtracks and find myself playing them rather often. One benefit of that is that I get to relive the performances repeatedly in my mind's eye. I can actually see again the actors, their environments, and all the fun interactions and drama between them. They are not just fun songs; they become powerful reprises of dramatic storylines. Otherwise, they would fade from my memory and thus from my enjoyment.

I have learned that many people have made a habit of playing repeatedly certain soundtracks in their minds, especially of the difficult and tragic episodes in their lives. And as they play them over and over again, they get to "relive" those experiences and to "re-feel" all the emotions and to re-suffer all the injuries and indignities, sometimes daily. And doing so compounds their sad effects and complicates their lives with ongoing discouragement, despair, and angry bitterness.

(I am not referring to those with memory losses or damages due to injuries or dementia/Alzheimer's.) I am referring to those who choose to dwell on past hurts, reviewing them mentally often, and bringing them up in every conversation they enter. Perhaps it results from irritating or raw scars from past betrayals or abuses.

It may be the aftermath of being taken advantage of or of someone else receiving promotions that the person deserved. Possibly many years of medical trials and disappointments have left their mark on the soul. But mentally replaying those episodes repeatedly will not help the healing and restoration of a life.

Phil. 4:8 prescribes that we think or meditate on certain things. This involves a specific act of choosing and it involves a certain type of content.

Let's not just think about whatever is "in the air" at the time or let our minds drift in just any direction. Let's make hard choices to focus on specific matters. And let those matters be representative of the kinds of realities in 4:8. Let's also meditate on the Scriptures and let them replay again and again throughout every day.

Many of the truths and promises of God's Word are so wonderfully expressed in the hymns of our faith. Singing them silently or aloud may even provide you with a "musical" version of life lived with the blessings of God.

And playing those "tapes" over and over again will have a very positive effect on your spiritual health, your outlook on the future, and your daily walk with God!!

For Prayer Today
-      Ask God to control your thought life through the day in ways that please Him. (Psalm 19:14)

Personal Notes and Responses

Games People Play

"Whither shall I go from thy spirit? or whither shall I flee from thy presence? If I ascend up into heaven, thou art there: If I make my bed in hell, behold thou art there...If I say, Surely the darkness shall cover me...yea, the darkness hideth not from thee..." (Psalm 139:7-12) "Beware ye of the leaven of the Pharisees, which is hypocrisy. For there is nothing covered, that shall not be revealed; neither hid, that shall not be known." (Luke 12:1-2) "Be not deceived; God is not mocked: for whatsoever a man soweth, that shall he also reap." (Gal. 6:7)

I enjoy playing games, especially word games and ping pong, though I can't seem to find anyone to beat anymore. That may be the reason I am playing fewer games these days, plus our grandchildren are too young for me to take any pleasure in defeating them for entertainment purposes. (I do have some propriety left!)

Game playing can provide a welcome break from the stresses of life but then it is time to get back to work. The meaning of life does not entail racking up victories and breaking gaming records. Sadly, some folks never stop playing games. Here are a few favorites.

1. The **"Hypocritic Oaf Game"** – (You've heard of the "Hippocratic Oath." This is not it.) This is played out among people wearing masks, pretending to be what they are not and seeking to move through life without anyone discovering their true identity or character. They are proud, sometimes pompous people who believe that they are the center of the universe, that their opinions are best, and that they need no one. They love to be noticed and praised. They'd love to be the bride at every wedding and the corpse at every funeral.

   Jesus had no time at all for this game or its phony players and expressed harsh condemnation of all forms of it. (Matt. 6: 1-18; Matt. 23)

2. **"Hide but Don't Seek"** This one is a favorite at church services and other gatherings. During a service, someone notices someone or even an entire family is absent. Their name is mentioned and feeble inquiries are made but no plans are set to send out a search party or to seek to make contact with the missing. Interestingly, many of those people are hoping not to be found. They find every excuse to be among the missing and hard to locate. Showing up is not that important anyway. Many confess to be able to worship God on the golf course. Actually, they are just playing games on God's course. And since they are intent on not being found and little effort is made to locate them and bring them back, they remain among the missing for many years and,–no one wins. (Heb. 10:23-25 provides instructions regarding this game.)

3. **"Harvesting Happiness"** is a mind game that can be played by a single person who has convinced himself that he can ignore God and sow all kinds of sinful seed throughout life and in the end he can eat, drink, and be happy, with no accountability for the sins of the past. Read Gal. 6:7-9 and Luke 12:15-21 for the warning labels on this dangerous game.

Continuing to play at these types of games can make losers of everyone!

For Prayer Today

- Ask God to keep you serious about life's most important matters.

Personal Notes and Responses

ETERNAL ENCOURAGEMENTS #141

Making Disciples

"...All power is given unto me in heaven and in earth. Go ye therefore, and teach all nations, baptizing them in the name of the Father, and of the Son, and of the Holy Ghost: teaching them to observe all things whatsoever I have commanded you: and, lo, I am with you alway, even to the end of the world. Amen." (Matt. 28:18-20) "And the things that thou hast heard of me among many witnesses, the same commit thou to faithful men, who shall be able to teach others also." (II Tim. 2:2) "Be ye followers of me, even as I also am of Christ." (I Cor. 11:1)

Life can be very hectic and challenging and it amazes me how busily occupied I can become with many things and then forget the most important thing. The words above were our Lord's final words, just before returning to heaven, and they were spoken with authority to His followers, His "disciples". They were commanded that, wherever they would go, they should be involved in "making disciples". Paul then repeated that command to Timothy and to others and certainly illustrated and modeled it by his own life.

The Priority of Making Disciples Its importance is seen in that it is a command that originated from the heart of our Savior, Jesus Christ. The priority is also obvious in that, without His followers leading others to know and trust Him, there is no hope that others will be saved and will join us in heaven someday. Thus, there is a serious urgency about this mission. (II Cor. 5:14-21; Rom. 9:13-15)

The Process of Making Disciples It begins when one believer speaks to someone about their need of a Savior from their sin and explains how to repent and trust Jesus Christ. But it also continues when a person makes that decision to become a Christian. We who lead them to know the Savior are to see that they are then baptized and then taught all that Christ taught His disciples. This should include helping them to become a part of a church family that will aid greatly in their maturing process and in their effectively "making disciples" as well.

This process involves mentoring, parenting, modeling, and much teaching. It is pouring one's love for Christ into the heart and life of another and helping them to see and to live all of life from God's perspective.

The Principle of Making Disciples Disciple-making is an ongoing process that should involve every follower of Christ. We should either be a disciple who is being taught by someone else or we should be a more mature disciple who is developing others.

So, where are you in this process of obeying Christ's "Great Commission?" Are you being helped along in your walk with the Lord or are you helping others with their journey?

For Prayer Today
- Ask the Lord to give you someone who can help you walk with God or to provide you someone whom you can help along in following Christ.

Personal Notes and Responses

Changing Your Family Tree

"...Ye children of Israel, turn again unto the LORD God of... Israel...and be not ye like your fathers, and like your brethren, which trespassed against the LORD God of their fathers, who therefore gave them up to desolation, as ye see. Now be ye not stiff-necked, as your fathers were, but yield yourselves unto the LORD, and enter into his sanctuary, which he hath sanctified for ever: and serve the LORD your God, that the fierceness of his wrath may turn away from you." (II Chron. 30:6-9) "...And such were some of you: but ye are washed, but you are sanctified, but ye are justified in the name of the Lord Jesus, and by the Spirit of our God. (I Cor. 6:9-11) "Therefore if any man be in Christ, he is a new creature: old things are passed away; behold, all things are become new." (II Cor. 5:17)

We have been told by some that people cannot change; they cannot be totally delivered from their past that continues to haunt them and control them. If a couple generations of parents have been heavy alcoholics, then the next few generations may very well follow suit. Many in recovery programs even after years of success are trained to introduce themselves with their old, former identity, as if that identification will help them to find continued deliverance.

The Old Testament Israelites certainly could have adopted that position. Even in their royal families, evil kings and queens seemed to produce several generations of evildoers who even seemed to try to outdo the previous generation's depravity. But every so often something happened to change things for a generation or two. What made the difference? It began when people turned from their sin in repentance, humbled themselves, and turned back to a relationship with God. Freedom from sin's bondage is made possible; old habits can be broken and new-creation lifestyles can begin. Darkness can be overcome with the light – all by the powerful grace of God.

I was unexpectedly reminded of this truth as I drove home one night last week. I was listening to a Christian station when suddenly I heard a sound from my distant past, the restrained but swelling sound of an organ played dramatically. I recognized it immediately as the theme music of the radio drama program produced by Pacific Garden Mission in Chicago called, "Unshackled". As young kids, we eagerly listened to it each Sunday night after church as the true stories of men and women, bound in sin's awful grip for years, had found themselves "Unshackled" to live for God.

God makes the difference, even today, in so many lives who turn to Him by faith and become new creations in Christ. We do not have to repeat the sins of our parents. We do not have to remain enslaved to sinful habits and lusts. We need not let sin destroy our bodies, our families, or our testimonies. We can turn to God and find lasting deliverance by His loving grace. "But where sin abounded, grace did much more abound:" (Rom. 5:20) Praise God for that!

For Prayer Today
-    Pray for someone who you know is struggling with lifetime sinful habits, that God will bring them to repentance and deliverance.

Personal Notes and Responses

The Prayer of a Cave Man

"I cried unto the LORD with my voice...I poured out my complaint before him; I shewed before him my trouble...They privily laid set a snare for me...refuge failed me; no man cared for my soul. I cried unto thee, O LORD: I said, Thou art my refuge and my portion in the land of the living. Attend unto my cry; for I am brought very low: deliver me from my persecutors; for they are stronger than I. Bring my soul out of prison..." (Psalm 142:1-7)

I've called Moses a "mountain man" for the many times God called him up Mt. Sinai to meet with Him. David, I'm calling a cave man for the many times he had to flee for his life and hide from King Saul and later from his son Absalom among the rocks and in the caves of the wilderness. God also had Joseph and Jeremiah spend some time in a pit or in a well. Joseph and Paul joined others for long stints in various prisons. Hmm.

Psalm 142 is titled "A Contemplation of David. A Prayer when he was in the cave." It may refer to the dramatic times recorded in I Samuel 22-24 when Saul was determined to hunt down David and kill him. David began to despair as he was running out of hiding places as Saul's forces surrounded him. He was lonely and feeling abandoned. Traps were everywhere; where could he turn?

To the LORD. David had quite a relationship with the Almighty God and in his times of hopelessness and helplessness, He called again on God. He realized that his real refuge of safety was not in some mountain cavern but in a Person, the Person of God. He cried out honestly to Him and was assured that God would bring him through His present distress to fulfil God's purposes for his life.

Perhaps we all have had some "mountain-top experiences" with the Lord in His Word and also found ourselves in the "pits" more times than we might admit. So have all who have sought to walk with the Lord and He has proven Himself faithful to all who have called upon Him.

Let me remind you also that it was the Father's will and plan that our Lord Jesus Christ left the glories of heaven to dwell on this sin-cursed earth, then to hang on a cross, suffering the effects of the sins of the world, being hated, despised, forsaken, and slain. He was then laid in a cavern type tomb for three days. Then from that dark place our Savior came forth, victoriously over sin and death, and later ascended back to His former glories in heaven where He awaits our victorious arrival there someday.

Even for the Son of God, our Savior, there were dark days as He dealt with sin and evil in this world. But the victory and the blessings that followed are eternal and will be shared forever by all who know, trust, and love Him.

Don't despair, my friend. Don't lose hope. Trust God and His promises; lean hard on Him in your hard times and let Him work on your behalf and for His glory.

For Prayer Today
-     From your dark and difficult place, cry out to the Lord.

Personal Notes and Responses

Healthy Refreshment

"For we have great joy and consolation in thy love, because the bowels of the saints are refreshed by thee, brother...Yea, brother, let me have joy of thee in the Lord: refresh my bowels in the Lord." (Philemon 1:7-20) "The Lord give mercy unto the house of Onesiphorus; for he oft refreshed me, and was not ashamed of my chain: but, when he was in Rome, he sought me out very diligently and found me...and in how many things he ministered unto me at Ephesus, thou knowest very well." (II Tim. 1:16-18) "Now I beseech you, brethren...that ye strive together with me in your prayers to God for me; that...I may come unto you with joy by the will of God, and may with you be refreshed." (Rom. 15:30-32)

In our busy and hectic world and in our chosen lifestyles we often find ourselves exhausted and our batteries drained. So many things can discourage, frustrate, and even debilitate us. We often need physical, emotional, mental, and spiritual refreshment and it is not effectively found in sports beverages and energy bars.

The people whose stories are recorded in Scripture were often in need of this commodity. The weekly Sabbath day of prescribed rest was for this purpose, even for the animals, the servants, and the strangers and God meant those directives very seriously. (Ex. 23:11-12; 31:12-17). Quiet, string music played by David brought refreshment to the heart and mind of Saul, even driving away distressing spirits that haunted him. (I Sam. 16:23) Sound sleep and good physical nourishment are often needed and very helpful as is spending time in the Word and heeding what God instructs us to be doing. (I Kings 19:1-21)

The New Testament highlights what can be another source of refreshment–the arrival and special fellowship of personal friends or ministry co-workers. Read again the above verses along with I Cor. 16:17-18 and II Cor. 7:13. Paul enjoyed, benefitted from, and looked forward to enjoying such fellowship with those from afar or from previous ministry relationships.

This past week, we experienced such special refreshment as several friends paid us visits and encouraged us greatly with their fellowship. They represented three different church ministries we had served over 40 years and we had a great time reminiscing and reviewing what God has been doing in and through all our lives since then. Lots of laughter added to the happy pleasure of being together again. It was refreshing to know that they haven't forgotten us and that our ministry to them in the past mattered. We trust that we also were of some refreshment to them.

Do you know of someone who needs some refreshing? Someone who seems exhausted or lonely? What can you do to provide such a blessing to them? Please do so. (Even a surprise phone call can provide such a delight.)

For Prayer Today
-     Ask the Lord to make you a very special blessing to someone today (or soon).

Personal Notes and Responses

Continuous Praise

"Seven times a day do I praise thee because of thy righteous judgments." (Psalm 119:164) "I will extol thee, my God, O King; and I will bless thy name for ever and ever. Every day will I bless thee; and I will praise thy name for ever and ever. Great is the LORD, and greatly to be praised; and his greatness is unsearchable. One generation shall praise thy works to another, and shall declare thy mighty acts. I will speak of the glorious honour of thy majesty, and of thy wonderous works...My mouth shall speak the praise of the LORD: and let all flesh bless his holy name for ever and ever." (Psalm 145)

I really do not believe that seven times a day would be sufficient to give God the glory for all He is, has done, and is doing in our lives. How about seventy times seven each day? Well, that's probably more like it but even then, that goal might fall short of what would be necessary.

I also do not think that we need to keep an account of all the occasions when we offer words or thoughts of praise to God, recording each one and trying to break our praise records often or to be more worshipful than someone else. That is certainly not the point here. Then, what is the point?

In every passage that highlights praise and worship of God we come away with these reminders.

1. **Our God is incredible**. All we know of Him overwhelms us. His glory, power, holiness, compassion, justice, knowledge, truth, sovereignty, love etc. Then we add all His incredible works throughout the past and daily in our lives and for those around us.

2. **Our worship and praise of God should be incessant**. Continuous worship and adoration of Him should fill our hearts and overflow through our mouths and in everything we do.

3. **Our praise of God should also be intentional.** Setting aside specific times for uninterrupted worship of Him should be built into our daily and weekly lives. It should be a priority in our daily schedules.

4. **Our praise of God should be inter-generational.** Our worship can be audible and conveyed to those around us and specifically in the hearing of our children and grand-children. It should not always be private but public at times. It is not just something intensely personal but can be expressed in ways that those around us are frequently reminded of the incredible greatness of our God and of their need to know and trust Him.

5. **Our praise of God is very important, personally**, as well. You never read of the Psalmists calling attention to themselves, listing their accomplishments, trying to impress their constituency. Continual acknowledgement of the glories of God reduces our pride and self-focus and keeps us humble before the God who is indeed worthy of all our worship. Our humility before Him also brings Him glory that is rightfully due to Him.

How involved are you in personal worship and praise of God each day?

For Prayer Today
- Fill your prayers today with expressions of worship and adoration of our great God.

Personal Notes and Responses

The "One Anothers"

"...For by one Spirit are we all baptized into one body, whether we be Jews or Gentiles, whether we be bond or free; and have been all made to drink into one Spirit...But now hath God set the members every one of them in the body, as it hath pleased him... that there should be no schism in the body; but that the members should have the same care one for another..." (I Cor.12:12-27) "A new commandment I give unto you, that ye love one another; as I have loved you, that ye also love one another..." (John 13:34-35)

To listen in on some of the loudest voices of today, one might come to the conclusion that life is all about "me". People are very concerned today about "my" rights, freedoms, choices, identity, preferences, body, positions, beliefs, habits, lifestyle, etc. And serious reactions can follow if anyone thwarts me or looks down upon me for any reason. No judging of others is permitted; respectful toleration or even vocal agreement is expected because "no one should be telling me what to be or do." It is "my life"!

The contrast between these attitudes and priorities and those we should have as Christians is so radically different. We are not to focus on loving ourselves, promoting ourselves, demanding our agendas, etc. Our focus must be on loving and serving God and then on loving and serving others, the two greatest commandments. (Matt. 22:35-40)

Choosing to emphasize our relationship to others in this devotional, I want to provide a simple list of commands that we are to obey toward them, as we fulfill that second greatest command. (Gal. 6:10; Luke 10:27-37) We call them the "One Anothers".

Love one another. (I Peter 1:22-23)

Gather together with one another. (Heb. 10:24-25)

Exhort one another. (Heb. 10:25) Come alongside to encourage, strengthen others.

Admonish one another. (Rom. 15:14; I Thess. 5:14) Warn, correct, counsel.

Receive one another. (Rom. 14:1; 15:7) Welcome, accept one another.

Edify one another. (Rom. 14:19; Eph. 4:29) Encourage and build others up.

Bear the burdens of one another. (Gal. 6:1-2) Help and restore others.

Comfort one another. (I Thess. 4:18; 5:11) Esp. those suffering losses.

Be like-minded toward one another. (Rom. 15:5-6) Work toward unity not divisiveness.

Forgive one another. (Col. 3:13; Eph. 4:32) No bitterness, anger, grudges.

Pray for one another. (James 5:16)

Serve one another. (Gal. 5:13)

That's quite a list, and there are more. Let me encourage you to think of a couple people who need some of what we find in this list, read the noted verses in their contexts, and then go about to provide it for them soon.

The more time and effort we spend on caring for others, the less time we will find ourselves selfishly demanding that our desires be satisfied and our agendas be accomplished each day. And, as we obey such commands, we will sense the blessing of God and His joy in our hearts as others are cared for in His name.

For Prayer Today

-   Ask the Lord to enable you to serve someone else today with His grace and love.

Personal Notes and Responses

Fresh, Flourishing, and Fruitful

"The righteous shall flourish like a palm tree: he shall grow like a cedar in Lebanon. Those that be planted in the house of the LORD shall flourish in the courts of our God. They shall still bring forth fruit in old age; they shall be fat and flourishing; to shew that the LORD is upright: he is my rock, and there Is no unrighteousness in him." (Psalm 92:12-15)

It is reported that Julie Andrews once sung something like the following words to an AARP gathering. "Maalox and nose drops and needles for knitting, walkers and handrails and new dental fittings...these are a few of my favorite things..."

Ah, yes, the gradual process of aging is difficult and fraught with serious pains and challenges. I don't think the young could handle it!

Did you notice in today's passage the mention of "old age"? And our title today is not often a description of the senior adult in our society or in our churches. And yet, God's Word informs us that these characteristics are indeed possible in our later years, especially among those who know the Lord.

The Potential of this is seen in the righteous relationship that such an individual has maintained with God. It was begun by faith in what God had provided for salvation and then grows and develops over time by trusting and obeying God daily. (92:1-4)

The Power for this is the power of God Himself. His enemies fall before Him and He can assure us of the same in our battles. Our own enemies are then defeated by that same power and we can delight in daily personal victories through Him. (92:4-11)

The Purpose for this is that the world may know that God is full of lovingkindness and faithfulness daily and that He is my Rock in whom is no unrighteousness at all. (92:1-2, 15) Older saints have the responsibility to be declaring and demonstrating God's character to a world that desperately needs Him.

Is that true with you? Are you flourishing fruitfully as you speak of God to this new generation? That is one great reason for your latter years on this earth.

One elderly woman once said to her friend, "Why, I'm getting so old that all my friends in heaven will think I didn't make it!"

And, if that is your imagined situation, I suggest that when God does call you Home, that you joyfully inform your friends then of what you've been doing all these later earthly years and of the fresh fruit that God has produced through you for eternity.

For Prayer Today
-    Ask God to help you make your later years of life really count
     for eternity in the lives of others

Personal Notes and Responses

ETERNAL ENCOURAGEMENTS #148

A U.F.O. Sighting?

"...And I looked, and, behold, a whirlwind came out of the north, a great cloud, and a fire infolding itself, and a brightness was about it...Also out of the midst thereof came the likeness of four living creatures...every one had four faces, and every one had four wings...Now as I beheld the living creatures, behold one wheel upon the earth by the living creatures, with his four faces... and their appearance and their work was as it were a wheel in the middle of a wheel...as for their rings, they were so high that they were dreadful; and their rings were full of eyes round about them four...whithersoever the spirit was to go, they went..." (Ezekiel 1:1-28)

Again, from my teenage days, I remember discussing in a youth group whether Ezekiel 1 described a UFO or not. We had some fun with this but unfortunately some Bible believers today spend far too much time deciphering the symbols of Scripture while often missing the clear message of a passage.

I'll admit that this passage does make one think of some sci-fi invention that could threaten all of life on planet earth. But that is not the focus of what God intended to communicate here. Several concise points might be made.

1. During the times before the Scriptures were completed, God did use a variety of methods and attention-getting devices to reveal Himself and His will for His people. (Heb. 1:1-2; 2:1-4) Consider the burning bush, the ten plagues, and the sound and light display accompanied by earth-shaking sensations at Mt. Sinai as God's holiness and His law were being revealed. (Ex. 19:9-25)

2. But the accompanying extravaganzas were not what was important. The message was vital and needed to be declared with authority and clarity. God endowed His prophets and preachers with the responsibility to proclaim His truth with an authoritative, "Thus saith the LORD!"

Those within the sound of those voices needed to take God's Word very seriously.

3. Today we are in possession of the complete and authoritative Word of God. It contains the total revelation of Himself and of His will for mankind. No longer needed or employed by God are the "special effects" accompanying the declaration of God's truth. Its life-changing "spiritual effects" on us are sufficient to morph and mature us into new creations that honor Him and lead others to know Him. "...Is not my word as a fire...and like a hammer that breaketh the rock in pieces?" (Jer. 23:28-29) "...the word of God is quick, and powerful, and sharper..." (Heb. 4:12-13)

4. Beware of those today, who seek for spectacular demonstrations or fresh visions from God. Even in the prophet Jeremiah's day we read, "I have heard what the prophets have said who prophesy lies in My name saying, 'I have dreamed, I have dreamed...they are prophets of the deceit of their own heart who try to make people forget My name by their dreams...Therefore, behold, I am against them..." (Jer. 23:25-40)

Let us get all our messages from God from His written Word and be obedient to them. Let's allow His Word to powerfully change us. (II Tim. 3:15-17)

(By the way, note the "Beam me up, Scotty" event in Ezek. 3:10-15). Hmm.

For Prayer Today
-   Thank God for His completed Word to us!

Personal Notes and Responses

ETERNAL ENCOURAGEMENTS #149

God's Not-So-Hidden Agenda

"And the very God of peace sanctify you wholly; and I pray God your whole spirit and soul and body be preserved blameless unto the coming of our Lord Jesus Christ. Faithful is he that calleth you, who also will do it." (I Thess. 5:23-24) "Now the God of peace, that brought again from the dead our Lord Jesus, that great shepherd of the sheep.. make you perfect in every good work to do his will, working in you that which is wellpleasing in his sight through Jesus Christ; to whom be glory for ever and ever. Amen." (Heb. 13:20-21)

Do you ever wonder why God doesn't whisk you right into heaven the very moment you place your trust in Christ? The short answer is that He has just begun to work in you, on you, and through you to accomplish His ultimate purposes for you. We see something of His agenda in I Thess. 5.

1. **The Direction of God's Agenda** – He plans to "sanctify" us, to set us apart, to grow us in holiness, so that we become more and more like Christ. He is moving us away from our sinful past and toward victory and service for Him. (Rom. 6)

2. **The Dimensions of God's Agenda** – He desires to work on us "completely" so that our total self is then transformed and preserved for Christ's return. It is a total life "makeover" God's way. "…old things have passed away; all things become new." (II Cor. 5:17)

3. **The Details of God's Agenda** – The threefold parts of man are included.

   a. The Spirit – We were spiritually dead before coming to Christ but then were made alive spiritually and can now know God, understand His Word, and worship and serve Him appropriately. (Eph. 2:1-3; I Cor. 2:9-16; John 4:23-24)

   b. The Soul – the real inner part of man, his mind, emotions, and will are being renewed by the Holy Spirit

> through the Word of God so that our thinking, feeling, and decision-making line up more and more with God's will. (Rom. 12:1-2; I Thess. 4:1-7)
>
> c. The Body – We are to present even our bodies to God as a living sacrifice in which we can then serve Him and be the evidence that His will is good, acceptable and perfect. (Rom. 12:1-2; I Cor. 6:19-20; I Thess. 4:1-7)

4. **The Destination of God's Agenda** – As He transforms our total being, what is His purpose? Where is He going with all this? His predetermined plan is that our lives be lived in service for Him, that we be thoroughly equipped for every good work, that we become servants of righteousness, and effective disciple-makers of others from every nation on earth. (II Timothy 3:16-17; Eph. 2:10; Romans 6:17-22; Matt. 28:18-20)

What an incredible agenda that is! You and I may not feel up to it; we may doubt that He can get it all done. But...

"...being confident of this very thing, that he which hath begun a good work in you will perform it until the day of Jesus Christ:" (Phil. 1:6) "...Faithful is he that calleth you, who also will do it." (I Thess. 5:23-24)

For Prayer Today
- Ask God to make more progress in growing and maturing you this day.

Personal Notes and Responses

Eternal Encouragements #150

TRECESP

"Be kindly affectioned one to another with brotherly love; in honour preferring one another;" (Rom. 12:10) "Render therefore to all their dues: tribute to whom tribute is due, custom to whom custom; fear to whom fear; honour to whom honour." (Rom. 13:7) "Honour thy father and thy mother..." (Eph. 6:2) "Honour all men. Love the brotherhood. Fear God. Honour the king." (I Peter 2:17) "Thou shalt rise up before the hoary head, and honour the face of the old man, and fear thy God..." (Lev. 19:32)

Ever since I shifted into a semi-retired state and moved into a retirement community, we have been inundated with opportunities to do puzzles. The toughest for me are those where the letters of words are scrambled, challenging you to identify and spell the word correctly. Thus, the title above.

I'm sure you have figured that one out by now. It is the word "Respect". But just identifying a word does not guarantee a knowledge of its definition or proper use of it in real life. I believe the definition of "respect" today has been forgotten through much disuse and abuse.

Respect can be defined as to show honor or reverence to someone or something. It is to recognize someone's or something's high value and importance and to demonstrate such in a variety of ways. Let's use an acrostic (with "answers" provided) to further unpack this concept.

Respect can be and should be shown by our...

Responses – When approached or spoken to, respectful listening and responding is in order. Silence is disrespectful. (Prov. 4:1, 20; 18:13)

Eyes – by looking directly at the person speaking with an attentive gaze, not being distracted by others, not glaring at people or showing scorn. (Prov. 30:17; 26:18-19)

308

Speech – Words and tone of voice should be void of nastiness, anger, disrespect; courteous terms "Sir, Mr., Mrs., Pastor," etc. can convey respect. (Prov. 4:24; 10:32; 12:18; Dan. 6:21)

Posture – Respect is seen by sitting up, standing when people enter a room, shaking hands, etc. Slouching, not standing, not focusing on the other person, etc. shows disrespect. (Lev. 19:32)

Expressions and gestures – Our countenance and emotional movements communicate. (Acts 23:1-5; I Cor. 16:20)

Courtesies – Formerly common manners and kindnesses should be employed. No rudeness, interrupting, etc. Express gratitude sincerely, etc. (Acts 26:1-3)

Truthfulness – Always being honest and trustworthy shows great respect to all. (Eph. 4:15, 25; Prov. 12:17; 14:5, 25)

Actually, this isn't just some clever word game. In our world today, many of us have the responsibility of caring for our ailing and aging family members and friends, not usually an easy task. Let's pull out all the stops and use every form of utmost respect and love as we care for them.

Perhaps you can also use some of this material to teach the next generation or two about this important concept, as well.

For Prayer Today
-   Pray much for the many who are enduring difficult disrespect and abuse, that God will protect them and deliver them.
-   Pray for all who are in the trenches caring for others, that genuine love and respect will motivate and guide all they do for those in their care.

Personal Notes and Responses

Our Final Destination

"And I saw a new heaven and a new earth: for the first heaven and the first earth were passed away...And I heard a great voice out of heaven saying, Behold, the tabernacle of God is with men, and he will dwell with them, and they shall be his people, and God himself shall be with them, and be their God. And God shall wipe away all tears from their eyes; and there shall be no more death, neither sorrow, nor crying, neither shall there be any more pain: for the former things are passed away. And he that sat upon the throne said, Behold, I make all things new." (Rev. 21:1-5)

Perhaps, the ultimate "eternal encouragement" for us is that the God who keeps all His promises has guaranteed for us an eternal home in His presence. It may surprise us to hear that though the present heaven is the destiny of all believers in Jesus Christ at the time of our earthly deaths or at the rapture (II Cor. 5:1-8; John 14:1-3; I Cor. 15:50-58; I Thess. 4:13-18), technically, that is not our ultimate destination.

A number of events will take place between our arrival in the present heaven and later, in our future home. On earth a seven-year period of judgment will take place, (Rev. 6-18; Matt. 24-25) followed by the return of Jesus Christ to earth with His saints (Rev. 19). God will then fulfill His promises to Israel in a one-thousand-year earthly kingdom with Jesus Christ ruling the world from Jerusalem (Rev. 20). There will then be the final resurrection and judgment of all unbelievers (Rev. 20:11-15). Then God will create a totally new heavens and earth for all His followers with a massive new Jerusalem as its centerpiece (Rev. 21-22; Isaiah 65:17-19; 66:22-24). See also II Peter 3:1-13 for a serious warning about the certainty of these final events.

But today, please focus on some of the blessings we will experience in our new and final home. Try to imagine this. This will be a time and place without any more death, sorrow, crying, or pain. This is because there will be no more sin, corruption, defilement, or wickedness. The curse of sin and all unbelieving sinners will be absent as well. (Rev. 21:8, 27; 22:15; 20:11-15).

This is not fantasy or science-fiction. These passages finalize all that God wanted us to know, even about the future, and we need to study and believe God's Word as true. For those who trust and follow Christ, all ends so very well. Actually, it doesn't end at all. The blessings of God will continue forever! Eternally!

This, I believe, is some of what Paul was referring to as he sought to encourage his readers. "For I consider that the sufferings of this present time are not worthy to be compared with the glory which shall be revealed in us..." (Rom. 8:18-39)

Like Abraham and many others, let's look forward to our future home with expectant joy as we travel through our present earthly world, trusting and serving our faithful God. (Heb. 11:8-10, 13-16).

For Prayer Today

-   Thank God for promising and preparing for our forever home. Ask God to help you rescue others from their sin through the gospel so that they can join you there.

Personal Notes and Responses

ETERNAL ENCOURAGEMENTS #152

The Supernatural Fruit of Love

"But the fruit of the Spirit is love..." (Gal. 5:22) "Hereby perceive we the love of God, because he laid down his life for us: and we ought to lay down our lives for the brethren." (I John 3:16) "He that loveth not knoweth not God; for God is love."(I John 4:8) "Beloved, if God so loved us, we ought also to love one another." (I John 4:11) "By this shall all men know that ye are my disciples, if ye have love one to another." (John 13:35)

Recently, we noticed that as our heavenly Gardener, God expects to produce fruit in our lives that would mature us and reflect the very character of Christ. Paul in Galatians 5 calls it the "fruit of the Spirit", fruit produced by God the Holy Spirit. It would not be natural or physical fruit; it would be spiritual fruit. To emphasize more of its nature, I am calling it "supernatural fruit".

What makes it supernatural? It is germinated and grown by God Himself. This is not organic, home-grown, self-picked, on-sale fruit. This is heavenly seed grown in a human soul with supernatural power and potential. It is super fruit!

In Galatians 5, this fruit is first characterized as "love". Supernatural love!

1. Supernatural love is a totally unselfish love, seeing and contributing to the value of others. It is to be directed first back to God and then to others. It has the capacity to be expressed even to "all the world" through the believer, to family, neighbors, even enemies! (John 3:16; Matt. 5:43-48) This is so far beyond the reach of normal, human love. It's supernatural!

2. It is love that is expressed in deeds, not in thought, intentions, or words only. It is a giving, sharing, caring kind of love, one that is willing to sacrifice or to be inconvenienced for others. (I John 3:16-18; 4:7-11)

3. It is love that stands out far above other forms of love and as such, reveals God's presence in our lives and can convince the world that we are followers of Christ. (I John 4:12-21; John 13:34-35) It provides hard evidence that Jesus is real and can change lives.

John tells us that we can indeed and should love God because He first loved us. (I John 4:19) Do you realize how supernatural it was for God to love you while you were still an unrepentant sinner and to provide a Savior for you? Then, upon trusting Christ, He lavishes His gracious and abundant love into our hearts and promises never to cease His love for us. (Rom. 5:5-11; 8:35-39)

We have become the recipients and the conveyors of heavenly, supernatural love! How is your crop growing in your soul's soil these days?

For Prayer Today

-   Ask God to plant a new crop of His Heavenly love in your heart today. Often it gets trampled or neglected by the fears and anxieties that crowd it.
-   Ask Him to make you discontent with loving others as others love. Ask for opportunities to express this super-love to someone around you today.

Personal Notes and Responses

ETERNAL ENCOURAGEMENTS #153

The Supernatural Fruit of Joy

"But the fruit of the Spirit is...joy..." (Gal. 5:22-23) "... I have chosen you, and ordained you, that ye should go and bring forth fruit, and that your fruit should remain..." "These things have I spoken unto you that my joy might remain in you, and that your joy might be full." (John 15:16, 11) "Hitherto have ye asked nothing in my name: ask, and ye shall receive, that your joy may be full." (John 16:24)

My wife and I were on our front porch for a while last night and took note that a second "crop" of floral plants were beginning to bloom, among them being a couple we could not identify.

Like the newest "mystery flowers" we discovered last night, there may be some confusion about this second "variety" of the fruit of the Spirit called "joy".

So, what is this supernaturally produced fruit of joy; how does it grow; can it flourish in rocky soil, how do we irrigate it sufficiently; is it an indoor or outdoor plant, etc.????

This **"joy-fruit"** involves a pervasive overall sense of well-being and a delight in knowing all is well in our relationship with God. (Zeph. 3:14-17) It is seeded by the truths of our salvation. Through trusting Christ alone we can know **joy's fullness** and be rejoicing in the Lord always as we realize that our **joy's focus** should be in Him. (Phil. 4:4; I Thess. 5:16) We can experience **joy's freedom**, even if imprisoned by trials (Phil.1:12-18; Acts 16:22-34). We can enjoy **joy's fellowship** as we interact with believers and pray for them (Phil. 1:3-5). We can bloom with the **joy of faith** as we pray and see God answer our requests (John 16:23-24). The **joy of forgiveness** blossoms brilliantly as we confess our sins to God and know the sweet fragrance of His cleansing and forgiveness (Psalm 51:12; I John 1:4, 8-10). We can spread **joy's fertilizer** (Supernatural Miracle Grow) in the garden of our hearts as we abide in Christ and let His Word abide in us. (John 15:7; Psalm 1:1-3) And we can anticipate our **future of joy** with the Lord and His family eternally (**forever joy!**) (Matt. 25:21, 23; I Thess. 2:19-20; Rev. 19:7)

Wow! What a bountiful harvest of the Spiritual fruit of joy. It can grow year-round, indoors or outdoors. It will produce a heavenly delight that will lighten our burdens and brighten all those who taste of it. Our Heavenly Gardner wants us to be full of the fruit of joy!

For Prayer Today

- Ask God to grow a fresh crop of His joy in your heart, in your family, etc.
- Ask Him to help you weed out of your heart anything that may be choking out your joy. Then ask Him to not allow you to hide this fruit in your heart but to let it out publicly so others can benefit from it. Our world needs this super-fruit desperately.

Personal Notes and Responses

The Supernatural Fruit of Peace

"But the fruit of the Spirit is love, joy, peace..." (Gal. 5:22-23)
"Peace I leave you, my peace I give unto you: not as the world giveth, give I unto you. Let not your heart be troubled, neither let it be afraid." (John 14:27) "These things I have spoken unto you, that in me ye might have peace. In the world ye shall have tribulation: but be of good cheer; I have overcome the world." (John 16:33) "...and the peace of God, which passeth all understanding, shall keep your hearts and minds through Christ Jesus." (Phil. 4:7)

This third installment on the "fruit of the Spirit" tells us that God wants to grow in our heart's soil His variety of peace, a supernatural inward tranquility of mind that drives away the fears and anxieties of our lives. It is an inward realization that all is well between us and God and that He is in control of all things and cares for us.

1. **The Root of this Super-Peace** is grounded in what God has done and continues to do for us. "Therefore, having been justified by faith, we have peace with God through our Lord Jesus Christ." (Rom. 5:1, 6-11; Eph. 2:1-5, 11-18) Since we have been officially declared righteous when we trusted Christ, the warfare between us and God has ended; we have peace with Him! Because Christ is our peace, He has also removed the walls between us and others and relational peace with others can be realized in Christ.

2. **The Fruit of this Super-Peace** Though it seems to be somewhat rare, unfortunately, even among Christians, let me try to describe its "taste". Many are concerned about what they eat these days. Some want things that are "fat-free, sugar-free, fun-free, gluten-free", etc. (I'm still trying to be "glutton-free".) This peace is not only "free" of some things, but will also drive out those same weedy qualities that are often found to be weakening our spiritual health!

Check out, not the _{fine print}, but the **bold print** below for this information.

    a.   **It is "fear-free"!** Though our world can be a fearful place, trusting that God is with us and cares for us, and is in control can drive away the fears that torture and paralyze us. (John 14:27; I John 4:17-19)

    b.   **It is "worry-free"!** As we learn to pray about everything, we will have His all-surpassing peace, and thus will need to worry about nothing! For more helpful information, consult Phil. 4:1-9 thoughtfully.

"Thou wilt keep him in perfect peace, whose mind is stayed on thee: because he trusteth in thee." (Isaiah 26:3)

So, is your heart's garden a place that is densely choked with the worldly weeds of fear and worry, or is it a tranquil and beautiful place of peace and serenity because the Gardener in whom you have complete trust is growing a healthy crop of His powerful, protective peace?

For Prayer Today

-    Make a list of everything that robs you of real peace, then ask God to help you to trust Him with those matters and to fill your heart with His super-peace.

Personal Notes and Responses

The Supernatural Fruit of...
Loonnngggsssssuuufffeerrriiinnngggg

*"But the fruit of the Spirit is love, joy, peace, longsuffering..."
(Gal. 5:22) "...And not only so, but we glory in tribulations also:
knowing that tribulation worketh patience; and patience, experience; and experience, hope: and hope maketh not ashamed;
because the love of God is shed abroad in our hearts by the Holy
Ghost which is given unto us." (Rom. 5:1-5)*

A number of years ago, I preached a series on the fruit of the Holy
Spirit and as an object lesson, I used a different piece of fruit to
illustrate or represent each aspect of the Spirit's fruit in our lives.
I think I used an apple to represent love and a banana with its
chronic scoliosis of the spine, to illustrate a smiley joy. When I
came to longsuffering I did not hesitate to choose a grapefruit. I
eat them and enjoy them if very chilled but it is not my favorite
fruit. It often has a strong sour or bitter kick that has me wincing
and squinting and others at the table often "suffer" as we end
up squirting each other as we gouge our way through the fruit.
Similarly, longsuffering is not my favorite variety of Spiritual fruit.
It actually is the ability, the stamina, the endurance, and the perseverance that will enable us to suffer llllllooooonnnnnnggggg!!!!!
Can you imagine that?!

I want to sign up for short-suffering. I'll go to the very Brief-Pain
Clinic gladly. I don't want long-term pain, complicated problems,
or nasty people to hang around. I don't want to become good at
suffering; I want to out-run it, hide from it. And, no thanks; I don't
need a second helping of grapefruit.

But God knows how much we need this quality because He knows
how much pain He plans to use to mature and equip us for His service. In addition to Romans 5, remind yourself of Romans 8:18-39
and James 1:1-8 and rejoice again that trials indicate that God is

indeed at work in our lives, growing us, maturing and equipping us for the harder times of life. He is also developing this in us for another very good reason.

It is so that we can help others in genuine ways. II Cor. 1:3-7 tells us that God takes us through trials while helping us so that we can reach out to others who are suffering and share with them the same help that God gave to us.

Please remember that many around us are suffering-long and need some help. They need some long-supporting, long-loving, long-helping, long-praying, long-encouraging. Not short-term, brief help, but long-term patience, perseverance, and love and, by God's grace, many of us have "been to school" for this.

For Prayer Today
-   Make a list of those who have been suffering-long and pray fervently for them.
-   Ask God to continue to develop this quality in you for your growth and the good of others.

Personal Notes and Responses

ETERNAL ENCOURAGEMENTS #156

The Supernatural Fruit of Gentleness

"But the fruit of the Spirit is love, joy, peace, longsuffering, gen-
tleness... (Gal. 5:22) "Come unto me, all ye that labour and are
heavy laden, and I will give you rest. Take my yoke upon you,
and learn of me; for I am meek and lowly in heart: and ye shall
find rest unto your souls..." (Matt. 11:28-30) "And the servant of
the Lord must not strive; but be gentle unto all men, apt to teach,
patient, in meekness instructing those that oppose themselves..."
(II Tim. 2:24-26)

As we have seen in past devotionals, God wants to produce powerful fruit in our lives such as His brand of love, joy, peace, longsuffering, and now, "kindness". This is not "the milk of human
kindness" but the super-fruit of God's kindness.

The definition of this term involves, "a gentleness of heart, a
sweetness of temper, a kind, loving politeness" and is descriptive
of God's heart toward people. Even before we were saved, when
we were filled with disobedience, malice, envy, hatred, etc, "...the
kindness and the love of God our Savior toward men appeared...
according to his mercy he saved us..." (Titus 3:3-5). His kindness
toward us will continue throughout the future, as well "that in the
ages to come he might show the exceeding riches of his grace in
his kindness toward us..." (Eph. 2:7). It is this same demonstra-
tion of loving kindness that we should be growing and sharing
with others.

Unfortunately, in our world today, this type of fruit seems rare
while its very opposite is flourishing. Cold unkindness, harshness,
crabbiness, and rudeness abound like thick weeds that threaten
to choke out such kindness. Suspicion and fear make us hesitant
to reach out with kindness to some people. We want to become
feisty and defend our position, fight for our "rights", out-shout
the voices of hatred and animosity. Soon we become just like

these other people and thus lose our testimony and our opportunity to demonstrate genuine loving-kindness to those who may not deserve it but who do desperately need it.

Luke 6:27-36 is a challenging admonition to us all. In addition to the "golden rule", is the challenge to love, bless, do good, and give to difficult people, even those considered our enemies, without expecting to receive good in return. And the reason given for this radically expected behavior? It is so that we will be recognized as "sons of the Most High. For He is kind to the unthankful and evil."

Let's think about this.

For Prayer Today

- Ask God to grow a fresh batch of kindness in your heart, a large crop that you can then share with many different kinds of people.
- If you have been unkind to someone, apologize to them for the awful weeds that they have received from you. Ask God to forgive you and to heal that human relationship, as is possible. (Eph. 4:31-32)

Personal Notes and Responses

ETERNAL ENCOURAGEMENTS #157

The Supernatural Fruit of Goodness

"But the fruit of the Spirit is love, joy, peace, longsuffering, gentleness, goodness..." (Gal. 5:22-23) "Woe unto them that call evil good, and good evil; that put darkness for light, and light for darkness..." (Isaiah 5:20) "Abhor that which is evil; cleave to that which is good." (Rom. 12:9)

We currently live in the middle of an Amish community where farming is a way of life. Surrounded everywhere by flourishing fruit, vegetable, and floral growth, it is clear that these farmers and gardeners know the difference between healthy crops and poisonous weeds. There is no confusion there.

But we live in a day when so many are confusing the produce that is growing in people's lives. That seems especially the case in regard to this fruit of goodness. Some deny both the responsibility to call anything good or bad and that there is any standard for indicating their differences. Rights and wrongs are blurry concepts today and no one should determine or dictate what another person's standards should be. Judges and fruit inspectors are not permitted.

God wants to produce the fruit of goodness in the hearts of His family. Its identifying qualities are those of being upright, virtuous, morally honorable, beneficent to others, and pleasing to God. God Himself is the authoritative standard for goodness. God is good and determines what goodness is! (Psa. 119:68; 100:5; 86:5; 145:9; Jer. 33:11; James 1:13, 17)

As God grows a great crop of goodness in our hearts, we will then be able to do the following:

Demonstrate that God's will is really good, acceptable and perfect (Rom. 12:1-2).

1. Discern the difference between good and evil and thus enable us to abhor evil and cling to the good (Rom. 12:9).
2. Defeat evil by doing good (Rom. 12:17-21; I Peter 3:8-17).
3. Disciple others to do good (Heb.10:23-25).
4. Declare God's goodness by being zealous to do good works to many others each day (Titus 2:11-15; Eph. 2:8-10; Matt. 5:14-16).
5. Let's thank God for His incredible goodness to us and for planting in us that same character. Let's not play around with the evil weeds of life but sow seeds of God's goodness in the hearts of those who need Him.

For Prayer Today

- Ask the Lord to allow you to show His goodness to others today so that they may "…taste and see that the LORD is good…" and how "…blessed is the man (person) that trusteth in him." (Psalm 34:8)

Personal Notes and Responses

ETERNAL ENCOURAGEMENTS #158

The Supernatural Fruit of Faithfulness

"But the fruit of the Spirit is love, joy, peace, longsuffering, gentleness, goodness, faith..." (Gal. 5:22-23), "For by grace are ye saved through faith; and that not of yourselves: it is the gift of God..."(Eph. 2:8-9) "So then faith cometh by hearing, and hearing by the word of God." (Rom. 10:17) "The just shall live by faith." (Rom. 1:17) "Now faith is the substance of things hoped for, the evidence of things not seen...But without faith it is impossible to please him..." (Heb. 12:1-6)

This next super-fruit that the Holy Spirit produces in the hearts of God's people is that of faith or faithfulness. Having faith speaks of possessing an unwavering confidence, a firm persuasion, a placing of our trust, our reliance, and our total dependence on a truth, an item, or a person. Whether it be a point of doctrine, a piece of furniture, or a personal God, we express our faith in it by totally believing and resting in it.

The brand of faith that pleases God and triggers His deep involvement in our lives is not our faith in ourselves or in a religious organization, but faith totally in Him. When we acknowledge our sin and place our faith in Jesus Christ's sacrifice for our sins to save us, we become children of God (John 1:12) and then can begin living the rest of our lives by faith, by trusting God in everything. (Prov. 3:5-7)

The Bible describes God as faithful, One who is worthy of our reliance on Him. He is trustworthy and will always be faithful to His children, His own character, and His promises. (Deut. 7:9; Lam. 3:22-23; Rev.19:11; I Thess. 5:23-24; I Cor. 10:13) We can and need to trust Him at all times and for all situations.

As we walk by faith in God and discover more of His gracious faithfulness, He will be producing in us a similar faithfulness. As we trust, rely, and depend on God, we will become increasingly trustworthy, reliable, and dependable to God and to others. We will be faithful to Him, to our promises, and to the relationships and responsibilities that God gives us. Our faithfulness will illustrate God's faithfulness to others. (I Cor. 4:2; Num.12:7; I Sam. 22:14; Titus 2:9-10; Prov. 25:13)

Twice now, in clear view of a group of people, I have hurriedly slammed myself into a plate-glass-imagined doorway, not realizing that the lighted way in front of me was not a doorway at all. I ran into the hard "evidence of things not seen"! (Heb.11:1) Ouch! *Ouch!*

When we walk daily by faith in our invisible God, He provides hard evidence of His love and grace, of His generous provisions, and of His faithfulness to us. Our growing faith in Him reveals His faithfulness to us – and to others around who may be watching our lives, who often need hard evidence that a faithful God exists at all. If we do not live by faith and just live like everyone else, that evidence remains invisible and quite unconvincing to them.

For Prayer Today
- Ask God to grow your faith, your ability to trust Him and to become more trustworthy to others.

Personal Notes and Responses

The Supernatural Fruit of Meekness

"But the fruit of the Spirit is love, joy, peace, longsuffering, gentleness, goodness, faith, meekness..." (Gal. 5:22-23) "Come unto me, all ye that labour and are heavy laden, and I will give you rest. Take my yoke upon you, and learn of me; for I am meek and lowly in heart: and ye shall find rest unto your souls..." (Matt. 11:28-30)

If you are running around heavily burdened about all the inequities of life or angered by personal slights and unfairness, you will never know real rest. If you refuse to accept any personal unfairness, are always protecting your rights and your turf with a chip on your shoulder, you will never know the peace God can provide. But, if you quietly allow God to handle these things and then address them with humble meekness, you will enjoy the inward tranquility that Jesus can provide.

We are blessed to know that this "meekness" is another description of the fruit of the Spirit that God wants to grow in our lives. This term is defined as – to be humble and gentle in the face of adversity or when facing intimidation, slander, etc. It is experiencing unfair difficulty with humble acceptance and without bitterness or anger. It is strength under control, the strength to control one's emotions during periods of perceived unfair or unjust circumstances.

It is illustrated by how Moses let God handle things when he was receiving family criticism of his wife (Numbers 12:1-13). David demonstrated it when he was frequently being cursed and the target of rocks being thrown at him by an enemy (II Sam. 16:5-14). Christ demonstrated His meekness as He responded to the taunts and tortures of His passion week of suffering (I Peter 2:18-23). Like Moses and David, He trusted His unfair situation to the Father in heaven and proceeded to do His will on earth.

Maybe you don't sense a need for this fruit. What good is it, really? This super-fruit of meekness can be helpful when trying to restore a wandering or fallen brother (Gal. 6:1) or when attempting to express real forgiveness to others (Col. 3:12-13). It can be useful when we are out and about doing good works for some undeserving others (James 3:13) or when we are inside reading and studying God's Word (James 1:21). And, of course, it is super-handy when we find ourselves suffering for doing right, as a Christian (I Peter 2:19-25; 4:12-19).

What a super-testimony we could have for Christ before others as they watch us handle life's unfair harshness with this super-fruit of meekness as we trust God with it all. (I Peter 2:11-12; Matt. 5:11-16).

For Prayer Today
- Ask the Lord to grow in you this trait of meekness as you struggle with so much of life that seems so wrong or unfair.
- Thank God for the truth that He will handle these things in His way and time and that we do not have to straighten everything out ourselves.

Personal Notes and Responses

ETERNAL ENCOURAGEMENTS #160

The Supernatural Fruit of Self-Control

"This I say then, Walk in the Spirit, and ye shall not fulfill the lust of the flesh. For the flesh lusteth against the Spirit, and the Spirit against the flesh: and these are contrary the one to the other: so that ye cannot do the things that ye would...Now the works of the flesh are manifest, which are these...but the fruit of the Spirit is love, joy, peace, longsuffering, gentleness, goodness, faith, meekness, temperance..." (Gal. 5:16-22)

As we draw toward a conclusion of our study of the super-fruit that the Holy Spirit wants to grow in us, we are reminded above that all is not well in the garden of our hearts. It is not always peaceful and serene. It is actually a war-zone as a daily battle is being waged in our hearts between the Spirit of God and our own souls. Yes, we may be saved from sin through trusting Christ as our Savior but our flesh with its appetites is still heavily influenced by strong inward desires and manifold temptations around us. Thus is emphasized the need for this final brand of super-fruit, self-control.

By way of definition, the term means "to hold oneself in, to hold fleshly desires in check, to have control of the sensual passions". This is not "will-power". (I have plenty of will-power! I *will* super-size my fries. I *will* have seconds on ice cream. I *will* sleep in. I *will* avoid exercise. I *will* tune in to that seductive show or website.) No, this is actually a spiritual super-fruit of *"won't power."*

We are to cooperate with the Holy Spirit as He develops in us this spiritual control capacity. We are to walk daily according to God's will and Word. We are to turn away from things that will diminish our testimony for God and stunt our spiritual health. We are to be spiritually disciplined to resist sin and to grow strong in God's grace. We are to be under the control of God's Spirit.

Whatever we allow to "fill us" ends up controlling us. It may be anger, lust, envy, greed, fear, alcohol, etc. We must ask the Holy Spirit daily to fill or control us so that we walk with Him and under His control. (Eph. 5:18-21; Col. 3:12-17) This "self-control" is actually putting oneself under the Spirit of God's control. As we do so, we will not find ourselves committing the despicable works of the flesh. See that list in Gal. 5:19-21.

What will this piece of fruit taste like? It will taste like maturity (II Peter 1:5-9), moral purity (I Cor. 6:15-7:9), victory (I Cor. 9:24-27; Rom. 6:1-23; 7:1-25), and effective ministry to others (Titus 1:5-9). If we lack this fruit, we will remain spiritual babies demanding that our desires be fulfilled, addicted to playing in the immoral mud puddles of this world, living in frequent discouragement and defeat, and will not be able to bless and encourage others in the Lord.

Let's ask God to "Miracle-Gro" this important fruit in our lives. We so need it!

For Prayer Today
-   If you know your garden is deficient in this area, plead with God to take control of you and to develop this "Spirit-control" in your life.

Personal Notes and Responses

ETERNAL ENCOURAGEMENTS #161

Will God Ever Give Us Something that is Not Good for Us? (An Introduction to the series, "Symptoms of Soul Sickness")

"Then believed they his words; they sang his praise. They soon forgat his works; they waited not for his counsel: but lusted exceedingly in the wilderness, and tempted God in the desert. And he gave them their request; but sent leanness into their soul." (Psalm 106:12-15)
"Then all the elders of Israel...came to Samuel...and said unto him, Behold, thou art old, and thy sons walk not in thy ways: now make us a king to judge us like all the nations...And the LORD said to Samuel, Hearken unto the voice of the people in all that they say unto thee: for they have not rejected thee, but they have rejected me, that I should not reign over them." (I Sam. 8:4-7)

According to the Scriptures, the answer to our title question is clearly a "Yes"! Consider first, three general thoughts.

1. God wants His people to be spiritually healthy. (Psalm 106:1-12; 78:12-16, 23-30; 1:1-3) He desires that our souls be free of sin and guilt so that they can grow and flourish in their worship and service for God, bearing His fruit and good works to others. (John 15:1-16; Eph. 2:8-10; Titus 3:5-8)

2. We often want to be happy, to have our own selfish desires fulfilled. (Psalm 106:13-15; 78:18-20, 29-30) Israel certainly illustrated this in these passages. Not content with God's provision, they yearned and yelled for more, better, different, etc.)

3. God can and does often grant to us our selfish requests but then allows us to suffer the consequences of our demands, producing spiritual ill-health, weakness, and sometimes death. (Psalm 106:16; 78:30-33)

We see these generalities played out in several instances in the Bible. We see in the passages above that Israel repeatedly demanded of and tested God in the wilderness. He often responded by granting their demands but also provided the accompanying consequences of their choices.

The same scenario is seen when Israel rejected God's rulership over them and demanded a human king just like the surrounding nations had. God graciously warned them of the dire consequences of such a choice but then fulfilled their demands with a terrible king. (I Samuel 8-9, etc.)

Perhaps closer to home is the process depicted in Romans 1:18-32 where three times it acknowledges that when mankind resists God's rule of life and desires some other form of lifestyle, values, or agenda, that God seems to step back and allows man to fulfill their selfish and sinful desires. (1:24-28) But the consequences follow with deeper degradation and bondage to the power of sin and all kinds of evil. (1:29-32) God "grants" mankind's requests but sends leanness, weakness, and sickness to their souls.

For God's people, this can take on the form of loving but firm disciplinary action on the part of our Heavenly Father. (I Cor. 11:27-30; Heb. 12:5-11)

In this series of devotionals, we will return to Psalm 106 to examine what some of the symptoms of ill spiritual health looks like. Lately, we've been examining ourselves for evidences of this worldwide virus in our bodies. Let's also examine our souls for symptoms of serious spiritual illness.

For Prayer Today
- Ask God to make you and keep you spiritually healthy, that He will strengthen you to avoid fulfilling sinful desires that will erode and infect your soul's health.

Personal Notes and Responses

Symptoms of Soul Sickness – Part 1

"...lusted exceedingly in the wilderness, and tempted God in the desert. And he gave them their request; but sent leanness to their soul. They envied Moses also in the camp, and Aaron the saint of the LORD..." (Psalm 106:14-18) "... and they rose up before Moses, with certain of the children of Israel, two hundred and fifty princes of the assembly...gathered themselves together against Moses and against Aaron, and said unto them, Ye take too much upon you...Wherefore then lift ye up yourselves above the congregation of the LORD...?" (Numbers 16:1-50)

The covid virus's spread has kept us alerted to a variety of symptoms that can result from its infectious arrival. A knowledge of these has been helpful to discover and track its path through the worldwide community as well as to administer treatments to fight it. A very medical world-war continues to be fought for physical health and life even as thousands of lives are being lost in this battle.

In our previous devotional we saw that in response to Israel's rejection of God's plan for them and their insistence on their own agenda and lifestyle, God sometimes "backed off" and let them have their way. But in doing so He allowed the consequences of their rebellious choices to play out in their lives and nation. Thus they experienced, instead of fat and robust spiritual health, a sickening and weakening within their souls, very serious symptoms that, without proper spiritual treatment brought tragic results to thousands of people.

Psalm 106 continues with what we might imagine as a patient's medical chart listing a number of the symptoms of such soul sickness. The first one in this list is that of a rejection of God-appointed leadership. Perhaps "generically", it is an independent spirit of pride.

God had clearly appointed Moses (politically) and Aaron (religiously) to lead His people. But when those people became disgruntled with their conditions, they went after the leadership, doubting their authority, threatening to remove them, and even planning to desecrate the system of the priesthood by their rebellion. God dramatically stepped into the picture and thousands of deaths occurred. So terribly tragic!

There are no perfect spiritual leaders today, even as both Moses and Aaron also fell far short of that standard. But God still calls individuals to oversee, to lead, to teach, and to care for His people. Plus, today we have God's completed Word from which we learn directly what God expects of us.

One of the first symptoms of spiritual illness is when we stop listening to God's Word and to His called servants. We stop tuning in to their sermons. We reject their biblical counsel and advice. We cease reading and meditating on God's Word. We do not make decisions based on God's will. Instead, we develop an independent spirit, an attitude and approach to every day that declares that we know best, that our wisdom is sufficient, that no one can tell us how to handle our lives or our families, and that we can do without God and His Word.

This sinful malady may develop gradually on the inside, but God sees the heart and this arrogant pride, even in microscopic form, can bring great destruction.

For Prayer Today
- Ask the Lord to keep you hungry and humbly dependent on Him and His Word.

Personal Notes and Responses
_____

Symptoms of Soul Sickness – Part 2

*"...And he gave them their request; but sent leanness to their soul...
They made a calf in Horeb and worshipped the molten image.
Thus they changed their glory into the similitude of an ox that
eateth grass. They forgat God their saviour, which had done great
things in Egypt..." (Psalm 106:12-23) "Thou shalt have no other
gods before me. Thou shalt not make unto thee any graven image...
thou shalt not bow down thyself to them, nor serve them..." (Ex.
20:3-6) "...these men have set up their idols in their heart, and
put the stumblingblock of their iniquity before their face...they
are all estranged from me through their idols...Repent, and turn
yourselves from your idols..." (Ezekiel 14:1-11)*

Returning to Psalm 106, we are reminded that due to Israel's stubborn selfishness, God "...gave them their request but sent leanness to their soul." This sickened and weakened spiritual condition brought on further devastating conditions, the symptoms of which we are noting in this brief series. The first one mentioned in the text was that they began to resist the leadership of those God had given to lead them and to reject God's Word from them. (Psa. 106:15-18; Num. 16)

The second symptom in the text above is that they chose to create other "gods" to whom they bowed down and worshipped. This very dramatic "golden calf" episode is told in Ex. 32 and it is shocking in many ways. While Moses is on Mt. Sinai receiving the laws of the holy God, down below the sinfulness of man goes viral in the camp. Taking advantage of Moses' absence, the people demand a god they can see and Aaron complies, even declaring that this newly crafted image is "...thy gods, O Israel, which brought thee up out of the land of Egypt." and facilitating their sensual worship of it! (Ex. 32:1-6) God's wrath is kindled on the mount, Moses pleads for God's mercy, then rushes down to confront the evil, smashing the tablets. Aaron lies about it, defending it, and dire consequences fall.

We call this sin "idolatry" and the serious essence of it is when we replace the glory of God with the glory of some other object, person, pleasure, etc. It is a sin of the heart that becomes evident on the outside by the attention we give to it and the price we pay for it. Whenever we "idolize" something, we, to some extent, find ourselves worshipping it, prioritizing it, gloating about it, loving and serving it far more than we do with God Himself. It dethrones God in our hearts and replaces Him with all kinds of things. See also Matt. 6:19-24.

Israel continued to be afflicted with this sinful habit as Ezekiel mentions the idols that she had set up in her heart, hundreds of years later. Those idols had multiplied and had caused Israel to stumble into increasing forms of sin, thus continuing her estrangement from God. (Ez. 14:1-11)

Sinful leanness of soul reveals itself in our value system, in the heart-idols that we serve each day. Whether outwardly and publicly or inwardly and secretly, God sees our sin. The only "cure" is repentance and a return to walking with God in obedience.

For Prayer Today
-    Confess anything that has replaced God as "#1 in your life and ask for His daily guidance and grace to live for Him.

Personal Notes and Responses

ETERNAL ENCOURAGEMENTS #164

Symptoms of Soul Sickness – Part 3

"...And he gave them their request; but sent leanness into their soul...They forgat God their saviour, which had done great things in Egypt; wondrous works in the land of Ham, and terrible things by the Red sea...Yea, they despised the pleasant land, they believed not his word: but murmured in their tents, and hearkened not unto the voice of the LORD. Therefore he lifted up His hand against them, to overthrow them in the wilderness: to overthrow their seed also among the nations, and to scatter them in the lands." (Psalm 106:15-27)

This story line is found in Numbers 13 and 14 where after the spies gave their report on the land that God had promised them, the people balked at His command and refused to proceed. God said then, "...How long will this people provoke me? and how long will it be ere they believe me..." (14:11) The writer of Hebrews also underscores that it was because they would not trust that God could protect and care for them. They remained in the wilderness because of their unbelief. (Heb. 3:7-19)

In Hebrews 11 is that list of men and women who illustrate how God's people are to "live by faith and not by sight". However, many professed believers live "by sight and not by faith". They see the giants threatening them, and the walls and other obstacles blocking their way. They've read the medical reports, and some have bade farewell to family members and friends. Fear and doubt enter their hearts and take over. They live by distrusting God.

Like Israel, we sometimes forget what God has done and can do so we doubt the wisdom of trusting Him with the details of our lives. We don't believe God will keep His promises; we doubt His trustworthiness. When we do so, we find ourselves living by our feelings, by fear, or by what we might call our fate.

At salvation, we trusted God for our eternity but now we cannot trust Him for our today!

Such unbelief by "believers" is another symptom that our souls are sickly and weak. It becomes evident when we fail to spend time in God's Word and prayer daily. It shows itself as we live in fear and anxiety, uncertain how we are going to handle the surprises and struggles of life. When we find ourselves making decisions based on our own wisdom or the opinions of others, our lack of faith in God may also become obvious.

So, how healthy is your soul today? God so desires that you choose to live by faith, that you trust Him completely with all the details of your daily life. (Proverbs 3:5-7)

For Prayer Today

-   Ask God to deepen your faith in His faithfulness to enable you to trust Him completely with everything every day.

Personal Notes and Responses

Symptoms of Soul Sickness – Part 4

"And he gave them their request; but sent leanness into their souls...They joined themselves also unto Baal Peor, and ate the sacrifices of the dead. Thus they provoked him to anger with their inventions: and the plague brake in upon them. Then stood up Phinehas, and executed judgment: and so the plague was stayed." (Psalm 106:15, 28-31) "And when Phinehas...saw it, he rose up from among the congregation, and took a javelin in his hand..." (Numbers 25:1-18) "For this is the will of God...that ye should abstain from fornication: that every one of you should know how to possess his vessel in sanctification and honour; not in the lust of concupiscence, even as the Gentiles which know not God..." (I Thess. 4:3-8)

A fourth symptom that we are not spiritually healthy is one that runs rampantly through the world today and, sadly, is rather common among those who claim to be God's children. Sexual lust in its varied forms of expression has become enflamed and has toxically infected the souls of millions of people. It is taking what a gracious and loving God gave us to be pure, private, and precious for the marriage relationship and is dragging it through the gutters and sewers of this world, perverting souls and addicting them to a selfish obsession that uses and abuses others and never brings the satisfaction and fulfillment that God intended.

Whenever Israel turned their back on God and His will, there were always very willing religious prostitutes available to them and their lusts. That's what was taking place in Numbers 25, a very dramatic episode with somewhat graphic action intervening and halting the judgment of God, but only after 24,000 had been slain. Phinehas is praised and honored for his righteous action and may be indicative that as we deal with this sinful addiction, sometimes radical "surgery" may be necessary.

Our world tells us we do not need to abstain, that no one gets hurt as we entertain ourselves among "consenting" individuals. But as we play with something God deemed preciously reserved for marriage, by our defiant disobedience many lives are damaged, marriages are destroyed, careers are ruined, diseases spread, and God's judgment hovers over us.

If you are a Christian but are yielding to the temptations of sexual lust in any form, please know that your soul is sick and weakening and that God will discipline you in some way. Take a few radical steps, repent of your sin to God and to those affected by your sin, rid yourself of those websites, ask someone to monitor your entertainment choices, terminate any illicit relationship, invest great value in your spouse and family, get into God's Word daily and ask His help as you seek to walk with Him.

For Prayer Today

- Pray for strength to live a clean life for the Lord and ask God's help for those who are being damaged by this sinful blight in our land.

Personal Notes and Responses

ETERNAL ENCOURAGEMENTS #166

Symptoms of Soul Sickness – Part 5

"And he gave them their request; but sent leanness into their soul...
Yea, they despised the pleasant land...but murmured in their tents...
They angered him also at the waters of strife, so that it went ill
with Moses for their sakes..." (Psalm 106:15, 24-27, 32-33)

So far, from the medical chart of Psalm 106:12-43, we have taken note of the various symptoms that indicate that someone is spiritually unhealthy. We have discovered that a proud, independent spirit ("I don't need God or anyone else!"), idolatrous worship ("I will worship whomever or whatever I please; I will craft my own gods!"), an unbelief in God's Word and His promises, (I don't believe that God will do what He says He will!"), and immoral entanglements ("My sexuality is my own business; no one is going to tell me how to live!") have all made the list of serious symptoms.

We add another one today, that of continuous complaining. Why, that one doesn't sound so bad. In fact, everyone does this and it seems so harmless. Why might this one be of concern?

From the amplified records of several revealing episodes in Numbers 11:1-23, 14:1-38, and 20:1-13, we discover the following serious conditions.

Israel expressed heartfelt disgust with the blessings of God, "despising the pleasant land" that God promised to provide for them. They grew weary of the menu that God was graciously delivering daily in the wilderness. The condition of their hearts was that of dissatisfaction with God's plan and provision for them.

Their hearts' desires were for things left behind in worldly Egypt, for things they were doing without in the wilderness. Gratitude to God was absent; grumbling against Him replaced it.

The contagiousness of these attitudes was insidious as it spread rampantly throughout the camp. A negative and unhappy attitude can easily infect many others and destroy morale, hope, and peace. Gloom and doom are forecasted daily and angry expressions concerning those conditions begin to surface toward those who restrain others from satisfying their own desires.

Let the records show that such complaining does indeed anger God and often aggravates others who are enjoying the blessings of God and who are obeying Him. Such grumbling has indeed brought on the severe judgment of God.

Do not take this symptom lightly. Complaining to others seems as common today as breathing is. Complaints can be heard all day long, like a 24-hour news station that broadcasts our dissatisfaction with the weather, our aches and pains, political situations, judicial processes and decisions, difficult relatives, the clothes we have to wear or don't have, the tweaked order of service in a church, how our favorite sports teams are faring, etc. So much of this is petty and immature, like whining while dining, but on it continues. God calls it sin.

Remember, we are admonished to "Do all things without murmurings and disputings..." (Phil. 2:14-16) and that includes... everything!

For Prayer Today
- Ask God to examine your soul for this symptom, then to cleanse you, and to fill your heart with sincere gratitude to Him.

Personal Notes and Responses

ETERNAL ENCOURAGEMENTS #167

Symptoms of Soul Sickness–Part 6

"...And he gave them their request; but sent leanness into their soul...They did not destroy the nations, concerning whom the LORD commanded them: but were mingled among the heathen, and learned their works. And they served their idols: which were a snare unto them...Thus were they defiled with their own works... Therefore was the wrath of the LORD kindled against his people..." (Psalm 106:15, 34-40) "...Hath the LORD as great delight in burnt offerings and sacrifices, as in obeying the voice of the LORD? Behold, to obey is better than sacrifice...for rebellion is as the sin of witchcraft, and stubbornness is as iniquity and idolatry." (I Sam. 15:10-23)

When the nation of Israel originally defied God and refused His plan for them, God yielded to their wishes but allowed the consequences of their rebellion to play out in their lives. In this piece we find that what I call "incomplete obedience" began to characterize their estranged relationship with God.

They began to obey God in some things but not in all things. Perhaps they'd disobey Him for a short time, then decide to become obedient. They always had good excuses for their disobedience. They didn't wipe out all their depraved and diseased enemies because they thought it wiser to make them slaves and to heavily tax them. They didn't kill all the animals because they could then use them as sacrifices in worship. It seemed wiser to them to mingle and marry into other ways of life instead of all that separation business.

A word to parents today who are seeking to teach their children obedience. Delayed obedience is not obedience. (Numbers 14) Partial obedience is not obedience. (I Samuel 15) Whiney or angry obedience is not obedience. Obedience is "doing all that I am told to do when I am told to do it, happily". Israel habitually did the very opposite and God called it rebellion.

A most dramatic episode of this condition happened during King Saul's reign (I Samuel 15:1-23). Saul had justified his habit of partial obedience to God's commands so much that when Samuel arrived to rebuke him and to declare his consequential judgement, He argued with the prophet that he had indeed obeyed God. But partial obedience was rebellious disobedience in God's eyes and the kingdom was taken from Saul that day.

Could believers today be guilty of such "partial obedience". Well… we know that God commands us not to forsake the assembling of ourselves together as some do (Heb 10:24-25), but we attend church just sporadically… We know that we are not to withhold forgiveness from others who have wronged us (Eph. 4:31-32) and we forgive most people, just not the ones who have so deeply wounded us… We know we should be giving to God first and generously (II Cor. 8-9) but we have a lot of bills and debts to pay so… we do what we can when we have something left over… We know we are never to lie (Col. 3:9-11) but sometimes, not often, but sometimes it seems to our advantage to tell a little "white one"…

Such activity which can become habitual is a sure sign that we are not spiritually healthy and are drifting far from God's Word. Consequences will follow.

For Prayer Today
-    Pray Psalm 139:23-24 from your heart to the Lord.

Personal Notes and Responses

ETERNAL ENCOURAGEMENTS #168

The Cure for Soul Sickness

"If we confess our sins, he is faithful and just to forgive us our sins, and to cleanse us from all unrighteousness." (I John 1:9)
"Now I rejoice, not that ye were made sorry, but that ye sorrowed to repentance...For godly sorrow worketh repentance salvation... ye sorrowed after a godly sort, what carefulness it wrought in you, yea, what clearing of yourselves, yea, what indignation, yea, what fear, yea, what vehement desire, yea, what zeal, yea, what revenge! In all things ye have approved yourselves to be clear in this matter." (II Cor. 7:9-11)

In a recent series we have seen from Psalm 106 that when Israel rebelled against God's plan for them that He often gave them their request but sent leanness (weakness, illness) to their souls. Such spiritual sin-sickness resulted in a variety of sinful practices and the deaths of multitudes. But we also read that whenever Israel turned back to God, He forgave their sins and restored them to harmony with Him.

The legitimate question is, "Can a true believer today who has wandered far from God be likewise forgiven and restored to fellowship with God?" The eager answer is "YES!", but it is only due to the fact that because all our sins were covered at the cross, God can be both faithful and just in forgiving and cleansing us from all our sin. So, how does this actually happen? Let me suggest two components to it.

First, there is the matter of **"confession"** which involves something that we "**say**". We say the same thing that God says about our misbehavior. He calls it "sin" and so must we. We acknowledge that we have sinned against our Father. We do not excuse it, explain it, or defend it. We plead guilty before God. God then immediately and thoroughly forgives and cleanses us from it all. Wow!

Second, there is the matter of **"repentance"**, which will produce some things that we will **"do"**. Repentance involves a change in direction of our mindset and actions, doing a 180, and heading in the opposite direction from where we had been going. It takes us back toward God, into His Word, involvement in the church, a gradual growth in holiness, and an active service to God.

Often, we hear a person **say** ("confess") that he has dealt with his sin and been forgiven but we often become suspicious when there is seen no directional change in that life. Note in the II Cor. 7 verses above that the disobedient believer sorrowed over his sin and repented of it and the evidence of that change of heart and direction was abundant. My, what diligence it produced, what effort to clear oneself of their guilty past, what fresh indignation and hatred for sin surfaced, what reverential fear of God, strong desire and zeal in that new and godly direction was evident! The evidence that a life had been changed and restored was very convincing. And Paul and that church forgave him and rejoiced in what God had done.

When all of that happens in the life of a believer, great victory can continue and fellowship with God and His family will be enjoyed.

For Prayer Today
- Pray for genuine revival to take place in our families and churches as sinners confess and repent of their sin and enjoy forgiveness and fellowship again.

Personal Notes and Responses

Booster Shots of Joy – Dose 1

"Rejoice in the Lord always: and again, I say, Rejoice" (Phil.4:4)
"...And the multitude rose up together against them: and the magistrates rent off their clothes, and commanded to beat them. And when they had laid many stripes upon them, they cast them into prison, charging the jailer to keep them safely: who, having received such a charge, thrust them into the inner prison, and made their feet fast in the stocks. And at midnight Paul and Silas prayed, and sang praises unto God: and the prisoners heard them. And suddenly..." (Acts 16:16-34)

Jesus predicted that His followers would come to experience a special brand of joy that no one would take away. (John 16:16-24) The Spirit of God is busy in our lives producing that fruit of joy. (Gal. 5:22-23) But sometimes we allow the painful challenges of life to displace such joy as we struggle with the difficulties of our daily lives.

Might there be some booster shots available? Shots of real joy that can carry us through our stress-filled days? I am suggesting in this latest brief series that this is possible. As Paul penned the book of Philippians, he mentioned joy at least 15 times in these 4 short chapters and often revealed some special reasons and motivations for joy. And he wrote this while he was again imprisoned!

How could he respond with joy and recommend it so often while his suffering continued and his future seemed so uncertain? I believe it was because he stayed focused on the Lord and on what God had done and was doing in his life. He allowed his daily circumstances to remind him of God's presence and of the incredible things that God had done in his past.

For instance, as he wrote this brief letter, Paul found himself again incarcerated by a formidable government that stood in opposition to everything Paul cherished and was trying to accomplish.

But this imprisonment probably reminded him of his first visit to Philippi (Acts 16) and of his arrest and beatings there. He rehearsed in his mind how he and Silas were then roughly thrown into the inner prison and uncomfortably locked into the stocks with their backs deeply bruised and bleeding. Then, with joy, he recalled the mighty earthquake and the amazing rescue and conversion of the jailer and his family. And just like he and his co-worker could pray and sing praises to God in those conditions, so he could now, as a prisoner again, write to his friends with a clear emphasis on his joy and what should be theirs.

So, with this "introductory booster shot", can you rejoice in what you have seen God do in your life during past episodes of trouble? Can you even chuckle with how your Father provided timely and surprising resources for your need? Can you rejoice in knowing that He is still caring for you?

For Prayer Today
- Ask the Lord to remind you of His past faithfulness to you and then spend time rejoicing in prayer or to others about those special times.

Personal Notes and Responses

Booster Shots of Joy – Dose # 2

"I thank my God upon every remembrance of you, always in every prayer of mine for you all making request with joy, for your fellowship in the gospel from the first day until now...even as it is meet for me to think this of you all, because I have you in my heart; inasmuch as both in my bonds, and in the defense and confirmation of the gospel, ye all are partakers of my grace." (Phil. 1:3-7)

As we begin to look into the "cabinet" of Scripture labeled "Philippians" to locate motivational jolts of joy, we see that the imprisoned apostle Paul first mentions joy in connection with those who were both participants and partners with him in the spread of the gospel.

When he thought of his friends in the church at Philippi, he recalled his early days of preaching the gospel there and how several of them responded by faith almost immediately. Then they became partners with him in sharing that gospel message with others as the foundations of that local church fellowship began to grow. They remained in that fellowship of the gospel as they prayed for Paul's ministry and continued to communicate the salvation message to others. The memory of all that brought him great joy.

In spite of being exceedingly busy and exhausted lately, I have been rejoicing greatly. On Sunday I learned of a lady who recently came to Christ and just one day later openly declared a dramatic change that God had already made in her heart. This morning I read a chaplain's report of a long-term resident in one of our centers, who responded by faith to the gospel last month and the evidence of it became immediately obvious to others there. We know of a young couple who are using hospitality to bring together some adults for a meal and Bible discussions around the gospel. We support and pray often for friends of ours who are scattered around the globe as they communicate the gospel message to others and we frequently hear of exploits and impacts of God's grace at work in lives.

Whether we are personally actively involved in communicating this life-giving message of good news to others, or are playing a supportive role as we pray for other's endeavors, the news of God's powerful work in people's hearts should spark genuine joy in ours. Really, there is nothing quite as exciting as having opportunities to talk about our Savior and then to see God do a miraculous work in someone's life. If you are a believer in Christ, do not miss the joy of partnering with someone who is involved in this mission of grace and love. Being so involved and then the memories of it will bring great joy.

Jesus said, "…And he that reapeth receiveth wages, and gathereth fruit unto life eternal: that both he that soweth and he that reapeth may rejoice together…" (John 4:35-38)

For Prayer Today
-   Pray for someone you know who is sharing the good news of salvation with others. Ask them for specific requests and then rejoice with them as you hear of God at work.

Personal Notes and Responses

ETERNAL ENCOURAGEMENTS #171

Booster Shots of Joy – Dose # 3

"But I would ye should understand, brethren, that the things which happened unto me have fallen out rather unto the furtherance of the gospel...Some indeed preach Christ even of envy and strife; and some also of goodwill: the one preach Christ of contention, not sincerely, supposing to add affliction to my bonds: but the other of love, knowing that I am set for the defense of the gospel. What then? Notwithstanding, every way, whether in pretense, or in truth, Christ is preached; and I therein do rejoice, yea, and will rejoice." (Phil. 1:12-18)

This booster shot may stimulate a little pain and may even draw a bit of blood.

Unfortunately, as Paul discovered and still exists today, the preaching of the true gospel of Christ can be delivered by questionable methods and for a variety of somewhat suspicious motives. Sometimes how it is declared can even do damage to the cause of Christ and to those who seek to represent Him.

Some were into the gospel ministry for selfish reasons, maybe seeking personal wealth or prominence. Some did so out of envy or jealousy, perhaps of those who had more "success" than they had. Some may have included in their sermons critical or deriding statements about the apostle Paul, seeking to bring him greater persecution and affliction. Some were phonies, just posing as legitimate preachers of the gospel.

Amazingly, instead of defending himself or getting bitter or critical toward these people, Paul indicated that, as long as they were declaring the true saving gospel of Jesus Christ, he could rejoice continually in that, regardless of their motives and methods. Ouch!

Across the religious landscape today our freedoms are obvious as many religious systems can be found. Many of them are newer churches that employ different ministry methods, contemporary styles of worship, informal dress, different liturgies, and even non-traditional service days and times. For some of us, it is easy to be critical and judgmental of them, even though many of them are preaching the clear gospel of Christ. Many of our evangelical missionaries today are using creative methods, "tent-making" efforts, starting small businesses, a lower-keyed relational evangelism approach, wheelchairs and water pumps, etc. Some of these lose church support or take on considerable criticism for their cross-cultural creativity, though their gospel preaching remains true and primary.

One great source of Paul's joy was that the gospel was being declared by others, regardless if their motives were not pure or their methods were identical to his or not. Let's not allow our criticism of others rob us of the joy over the worldwide declaration of the gospel of Christ in our day.

People are hearing the good news of Christ's saving grace today through quite a variety of media and methods. Technology has breached the walls and curtains of formerly closed countries. Ministries large and small, traditional and contemporary, are being used of God to bring multitudes to salvation. Can we not rejoice and continue to rejoice in all of that? I certainly believe that we can.

For Prayer Today
- Express genuine joy to God every time you hear of the gospel being preached and people coming to Christ.

Personal Notes and Responses

Booster Shots of Joy – Dose # 4

"...For I am in a strait betwixt two, having a desire to depart and to be with Christ; which is far better: Nevertheless to abide in the flesh is more needful for you. And having this confidence, I know that I shall abide and continue with you all for your furtherance and joy of faith; that your rejoicing may be more abundant in Jesus Christ for me by my coming to you again." (Phil. 1:23-26)

Life is so very hard. So many people's lives, health, family, and future plans are being shattered. Many folks are very lonely and feeling abandoned. Life has become rather joy-less for many.

In this series our quest has been to discover how Paul could experience such great joy when he was again incarcerated and his plans again were in serious jeopardy. Knowing also that he could be executed at any time, he still wrote with hope and joy. His expressed desire was that his release would allow him to travel again and bring great joy to others who were eager to see him and to receive his continued personal ministry to them.

Even believers today seem to be despairing of their very lives, wondering, "What is the meaning of life? Of what good am I? Is life really worth living? Does anyone care about me?" The answer to such queries is that we live in order to love and serve God and to love and serve others. As we do so, we will know often special bursts of joy and blessing beyond comparison to anything else as in "It is more blessed to give than to receive (Acts 20:35). Paul knew that if he was free to travel again, that his visits would bring great joy to others. In Phil. 2:19-30, he indicated that, in the meantime, he was sending both Timothy and Epaphroditus to visit the Philippians so that "when you see him (them) again you may rejoice, and I may be less sorrowful."

As a believer in Christ, do you realize that you can administer abundant doses of joy to others with a personal visit or other kind

352

of personal contact with them? God has so designed His family that they are to care for one another, meeting needs, investing time and love into others for their benefit and for God's pleasure.

My wife and I have always been happily content to spend much of our time together being just us! Perhaps more so at this time and place of our lives. Covid issues have re-enforced that position for most of us. Yet, whenever we leave our little cocoon to invest love in others, our lives are enriched, our world is brightened, and we find that even a little bit of loving care has an overwhelmingly positive and long-range effect on others. Joy in abundance!

Let's not miss this daily opportunity to spread joy to others personally. Some of it will splash back on us, as well!

For Prayer Today
- Ask God to remind you to send some joy to someone today, in some personal way.

Personal Notes and Responses
_____

ETERNAL ENCOURAGEMENTS #173

Booster Shots of Joy – Dose # 5

"Finally, my brethren, rejoice in the Lord...For we are the circumcision, which worship God in the spirit, and rejoice in Christ Jesus, and have no confidence in the flesh...Rejoice in the Lord always: and again I say, Rejoice...But I rejoiced in the Lord greatly, that now at the last your care of me hath flourished again..." (Phil. 3:1, 3; 4:4, 10)

In this final segment of this series from Philippians we note a fifth source of joy for the apostle Paul, even when his situation was seriously discouraging or dangerous. He found great joy in simply knowing and trusting Jesus Christ. Having and enjoying such a personal relationship can likewise be the source of great joy for us, as well.

Commanded Notice his insistence about this personal source of joy. He isn't just testifying about it; he is commanding it. This is an imperative, not a suggestion. He orders his readers to "rejoice in the Lord." We are to be joyfully delighting in the awesome privilege of knowing our great Savior. This is worship, declaring our love for Him and our gratitude for Him. The more we focus on Him instead of on our circumstances, our problems, or our fears, the greater joy we will know.

Caring Note also, Paul's appreciation of Christ's personal involvement in his daily life (4:10-20). He had just received a "care package" from the Philippians but says, *"...I rejoiced in the Lord greatly,* that now at the last your care of me hath flourished again." He acknowledged that Christ, His Savior, was also His real supplier, provider, caregiver, and strength for all he needed every day. He reassured his friends that Christ desires to be all of that for them as well. Do you recognize His direct involvement in meeting all your needs daily and rejoice as He does so?

354

Continuous Thirdly, we must acknowledge the incessant nature of this rejoicing. It is to go on continuously. It should become habitual. We are to rejoice in the Lord *always*. We are to be rejoicing in our Savior without ceasing! These are not circumstantially induced sudden jolts of joy that come and go as were some of his other sources. This should be the regular condition of believers who truly love the Lord Jesus Christ and acknowledge Him gratefully, moment by moment of each day.

I suggest that having a personal relationship with Christ should be the over-riding joy of our lives. Under that umbrella of delight will also be found all the joys of loving each other in the family of God, the excitement over the gospel being preached and souls being saved, and even the past memories of our service for Christ and those who participated with us in such ministry. In Paul's other writings you will find even more reasons for genuine joy to be overflowing your heart each day.

Jesus said, "These things I have spoken to you that My joy may remain in you and that your joy may be full." (John 15:11)

For Prayer Today
    REJOICE – IN THE LORD!

Personal Notes and Responses
_____

Family Traits of God's Family Tree – Part 1

"But as many as received him, to them gave he power to become the sons of God, even to them that believe on his name: which were born, not of blood, nor of the will of the flesh, nor of the will of man, but of God." (John 1:12-13) "...that which is born of the flesh is flesh; and that which is born of the Spirit is spirit...Ye must be born again...For God so loved the world, that he gave his only begotten Son, that whosoever believeth in him should not perish, but have everlasting life..." (John 3:1-18)

It is always interesting and sometimes amusing how in many close-knit families, the entire family, over time, looks like each other, thinks like each other, and acts like each other. In Long Island, NY we had a neighbor whose teenage son, when he would mow the lawn, had a bit of a hop with each step he took. I had never seen that unique stride before anywhere until one day his dad was mowing the lawn and, sure enough, there it was again!

With this devotional I want to begin another short series about the "family of God". When we trust Christ as our Savior, we become "children of God" and He becomes our Heavenly Father. We can even refer to Him as "Abba", a term of endearment like, "Daddy" (Rom. 8:16-17). And this heavenly family has a number of traits that will, over time, become very characteristic of all of God's children, so much so that others should identify us publicly as part of that family.

To begin, the first and main characteristic highlighted in the verses above is that all of God's family members are *believers in Jesus Christ as Savior.* In fact, the actual birthing process, that second and spiritual birth that is needed takes place when we turn from our sin and believe in Christ. By God's grace, we understand our need as sinners and we place our trust in the One Who died on the cross, suffering our punishment, and rose to be our Savior. This is the only way into God's family, by placing our faith, our belief in Christ to save us.

We enter the family of God, not by physical birth or by our own personal efforts and good works, but by the grace of God and His only way of salvation through Christ (Eph. 2:8-9; Rom. 6:23). You might be deeply religious, a very moral person, an upstanding citizen but none of those things can birth you into God's family. Only Jesus Christ can do that when you personally trust in Him as your Savior.

As children of God by faith, we then learn to "walk by faith and not by sight" (II Cor. 5:7) for "the just shall live by faith..." (Heb. 10:38-11:6). We grow to believe all His promises, trusting Him for all we need in life. There are no unbelievers in this family. God's family believes in Him, depends, and relies on Him. It is a foundational family trait.

For Prayer Today

- If you are indeed a member of God's family, thank Him again for welcoming you in, and ask Him to help you to walk by faith in every area of life.

Personal Notes and Responses

Family Traits of God's Family Tree – Part 2

"For as the body is one, and hath many members, and all the members of that one body, being many, are one body: so also is Christ. For by one Spirit are we all baptized into one body..." (I Cor. 12:12-13) "...There is one body, and one Spirit, even as ye are called in one hope of your calling; one Lord, one faith, one baptism, one God and Father of all, who is above all, and through all, and in you all. (Eph. 4:3-6)

I will quickly agree that this family trait is one that does not surface visibly very often but is true, nevertheless. Believe it or not, there is an inherent unity that exists in the family of God. It is a spiritual oneness that exists based on spiritual truths and realities that are shared together.

This unity is not unanimity, where everyone agrees with each other and would always vote unanimously on things. This is not uniformity where everyone takes an identical outward form, wearing whatever matching uniform or flying whatever banner that is expected to provide a striking visual image. No, this one-ness is an inward and spiritual oneness that unites us together and is uniquely built on several realities.

We have all been birthed into the same family, God's family. We don't all live in the same house but we all have the same Father. We are part of one family. We belong to each other. (I Cor. 12:12-27)

We have all subscribed to several foundational truths that bind us together. We believe the Bible is God's Word, that Jesus is God and the only Savior, that salvation is not by works but by God's grace through faith. These and other doctrines unite us together in agreement.

Then there is that sense of family we experience at all those "unexpected family reunions". Sometimes, it only takes a few words or a feeling that these strangers might be "kin". As we discover that it is true, immediately there is a camaraderie, a sense of family that is present. That same sense should be experienced at church or whenever believers gather.

Unfortunately, this spiritual unity is often not visible, disguised by our differences and disagreements within the family. Family fights are not infrequent. Though some doctrinal distinctives necessarily set some apart from others, other areas of differing positions and preferences, or personal hurts and lack of forgiveness often drive people into seasons of sad and serious estrangement from the family.

Which is why Paul urges family members to be "...with all lowliness and meekness, with longsuffering, forbearing one another in love; endeavoring to keep the unity of the Spirit in the bond of peace." (Eph. 4:1-3) Even Jesus prayed, "...that they all may be one; as thou, Father, art in me and I in thee, that they also may be one in us: that the world may believe that thou hast sent me..." (John 17:20-23)

Did you catch that last line? If God's family would display more unity, others might believe that Jesus is God and be saved. Do we realize that our family divisiveness can drive people away from the Savior? (See also John 13:34-35.)

For Prayer Today
-    Pray that God's family would display more love and peace among its members so that others would become "relatives".

Personal Notes and Responses

ETERNAL ENCOURAGEMENTS #176

Family Traits of God's Family Tree – Part 3

"Go ye therefore, and teach all nations..." (Matt. 28:18-20) "I am debtor both to the Greeks, and to the Barbarians; both to the wise, and to the unwise. So, as much as in me is, I am ready to preach the gospel to you that are in Rome also." (Rom. 1:14-15) "...For by one Spirit are we all baptized into one body, whether we be Jews or Gentiles, whether whether we be bond or free... For the body is not one member, but many..." (I Cor. 12:12-27) "...For as we have many members in one body, and all members have not the same office: so we, being many, are one body in Christ, and every one members one of another. Having then gifts differing according to the grace that is given to us..." (Rom. 12:3-8)

In this series we have noted that two of the characteristics of God's family are that all are believers in Christ and that all are united together in a real spiritual unity. A third trait is that this family features a lot of diversity. There are no purely identical twins in this family.

Christ's command to preach the gospel and to make disciples from every nation on earth provides for great ethnic or national variety. People from every economic background or social class are represented. People bring differing personalities, talents, passions, and abilities into the family. At salvation God also provides unique spiritual gifts to His family, with each person receiving some spiritual drive and ability to serve the family uniquely. Men and women add their unique distinctiveness, and everyone together is quite a mosaic of God-designed differences and uniqueness.

What makes the family of God unique is that these inherent differences are not to provide for internal conflicts and contentions (though sadly, that does happen), but are uniquely crafted by God individually so that each part of the family fits together with all other parts, that their differences uniquely contribute to the benefit of the whole family. Just as a husband and a wife bring incredible differences into their union and over time contribute greatly to each other, so does the family of God. (Please read I Cor. 12:14-27 on this.)

These individually unique people are welcomed and integrated into this universal family for the glory and plan of God. As we work together, our differences become assets, not liabilities, and become necessary to the health of the family and especially to each local assembly of family members. No one should declare that he is not needed by the family or that she does not need some other family member. All are needed and are important; all are to contribute and to care for one another. Paul says it again in the following passage. Don't miss it.

"…from whom the whole body fitly joined together and compacted by that which every joint supplieth, according to the effectual working in the measure of every part, maketh increase of the body unto the edifying of itself in love." (Eph. 4:12-16)

For Prayer Today
- Ask God to use your special uniqueness to benefit your local family of believers and to make you willing to call on others to help you in times of need.

Personal Notes and Responses

Family Traits of God's Family Tree – Part 4

"And he gave some, apostles; and some, prophets; and some, evangelists; and some, pastors and teachers...till we all come in the unity of the faith, and of the knowledge of the Son of God, unto a perfect man, unto the measure of the stature of the fullness of Christ: that we henceforth be no more children, tossed to and fro, and carried about with every wind of doctrine by the sleight of men, and cunning craftiness, whereby they lie in wait to deceive; but speaking the truth in love, may grow up into him in all things... even Christ..." (Eph. 4:11-16) "...but grow in grace, and in the knowledge of our Lord and Saviour Jesus Christ..." (II Peter 3:18)

In addition to faith in Christ, spiritual unity, and great diversity, a fourth characteristic of the family of God is a steady growth toward spiritual maturity. We are birthed into this family as infants but we are not to remain as such. We are to grow and mature, to develop motor skills and abilities, and a personality and mentality that is modeled by Jesus Christ.

It is very sad and heart-wrenching when we find little children who never develop beyond childhood limitations. They remain totally dependent on those around them and are often incapable of contributing much to others but a greater capacity of love and care for them.

Sadly, in God's family, there seem to be many who claim to be children of God but who never seem to mature beyond the desires and dependencies of little ones. Many can be heard to be whining and complaining often. Some appear interested more in themselves than in God or others. Many remain ignorant of Bible truths, nor do they have much appetite for them. Many are easily entertained by the childish modules that this world dangles in front of them. They remain very selfish and petty, often fighting, envying, etc. (I Cor. 3:1-4)

Scripture acknowledges the presence of such people but questions their "legitimacy". Though within any family all stages of growth and development are present at any time, in God's family each one should be moving through the maturing process with the resources and help that our Father provides.

Our text today indicates that God has provided the family with spiritual leaders who lovingly provide doctrinal truth by which people can grow and mature. Babies begin with the milk of the Word (I Peter 2:1-2) but then they develop on to more nutritious fare with the more solid meats of the Word (Heb. 5:12-14). They mature in their knowledge of God and of His grace and can discern and defeat the attempts of others to deceive them with false teachings or destroy them with sinful lusts. They learn to study the Scriptures to continue to grow and become equipped for every good work (II Tim. 2:15-16; 3:14-17).

Yes, we all began as newborns, but have we been feeding on God's truth daily so that we've been learning, growing, and maturing in His family? Are we a part of a good Bible teaching church? Can we recognize how our Father has been growing us?

For Prayer Today
-    Ask the Lord to grow and mature you more each day as you feed on His Word.

Personal Notes and Responses

ETERNAL ENCOURAGEMENTS #178

Family Traits of God's Family Tree – Part 5

"And he gave some, apostles; and some, prophets; and some, evan-gelists; and some, pastors and teachers; for the perfecting of the saints, for the work of the ministry, for the edifying of the body of Christ...in love..." (Eph. 4:11-16) "Therefore, my beloved brethren, be ye steadfast, unmovable, always abounding in the work of the Lord, forasmuch as ye know that your labour is not in vain in the Lord." (I Cor. 15:58)

This series has developed around the truth that most families exhibit and pass on certain traits or characteristics that help to identify them. This is true of the family of God as well. Scripture tells us the things that should characterize the children of God, and as we walk with Him in obedience, those features will surface.

So far, we have noted that the members of this family are all firm believers of Jesus Christ for their salvation. They are all united tightly together by spiritual truths and realities. There is great diversity among them. And, all are growing and developing from spiritual infancy toward maturity and Christ-likeness.

Today's featured trait is that this family is very busy in the work of the ministry, busy investing in the lives of others for their growth and encouragement. These family members are not in some spiritual unemployment line awaiting another check from the government. They are not wasting their time overly entertaining themselves with the toys of this world. They are not bored or lazy. They are busy serving the Lord and His people.

This busyness may involve many activities:
1. **They may be studying,** "as a workman that needeth not to be ashamed, rightly dividing the word of truth," (II Tim. 2:15) and to be "...throughly furnished unto all good works." (II Tim. 3:16-17)

2. **They may be soldiering** – "endure hardness, as a good soldier of Jesus Christ..." and does not "...entangleth himself with the affairs of this life..."(II Tim. 2:3-4) as he seeks to please His Commander and through witnessing, rescue others from the enemy. (II Tim. 2:24-26)

3. **They may be serving** others in a variety of ways. The work of the "ministry" is the work of "service". We are commanded to serve one another by loving, encouraging, building up, teaching, forgiving, giving, admonishing, visiting, helping, and praying for one another faithfully. (Gal. 5:13-14)

The family of God is busy, employed daily in the work of maturing and building up one another. Once God's children begin to mature, they realize that life is not about them but is about serving God and others. And what a joyful and rewarding work this can be. (I Cor. 3:5-15; John 4:34-38; Phil. 4:1)

"And they continued steadfastly in the apostles' doctrine and fellowship, and in breaking of bread, and in prayers...continuing daily with one accord in the temple, and breaking bread from house to house, did eat their meat with gladness and singleness of heart, praising God..." (Acts 2:42-47) "For we are his workmanship, created in Christ Jesus unto good works...that we should walk in them." (Eph. 2:10)

For Prayer Today

- Ask God to make you a faithful worker in His family. Ask Him to give you a special ministry of helping or encouraging someone today.

Personal Notes and Responses

Family Traits of God's Family Tree – Part 6

"Behold, what manner of love the Father hath bestowed upon us, that we should be called the sons of God...In this the children of God are manifest, and the children of the devil: whosoever doeth not righteousness is not of God, neither he that loveth not his brother. For this is the message that ye heard from the beginning, that we should love one another. Not as Cain, who was of that wicked one, and slew his brother...We know that we have passed from death unto life, because we love the brethren...Hereby perceive we the love of God, because he laid down his life for us: and we ought to lay down our lives for the brethren..." (I John 3:1-23)

During our 19 years in West Virginia I became acquainted with several renditions of the horrendous saga of two famous and related families. I learned that if you want an example to follow of two loving families, do not choose the Hatfields and McCoys! Perhaps in similar fashion, John tells us that for examples of brotherly love, do not mimic brothers Cain and Abel.

In this final segment of this series, I highlight the fact that God's family should be marked and well-known as a tightly knit family that demonstrates supernatural love for one another. (John 13:34-35)

We were birthed into this family because a loving God provided the supreme sacrifice for our sins, thus enabling our welcome into the family by His grace through faith. (John 3:16; Eph. 2:8-9) With this manner of love, the Father calls us His children.

In I John 3:10-11 it is our righteous lifestyle and our love for our spiritual family that distinguishes us from the family of Satan. We are commanded to "love one another" which becomes further assurance that we are indeed children of God (3:11-15). Such love should be patterned after Christ's love for us; it ought to be personally sacrificial, even willing to lay down one's life for the family

(3:16). Upon discovery of a need in a brother or sister's life, our love should respond quickly to meet that need from our resources (3:17). Our love for each other should not just be frequently verbalized but acted out with honest deeds and service (3:18).

It is to be with love that we serve one another (Gal. 5:13). It is in love that we teach and speak the truth to one another so the whole family can be edified in love (Eph. 4:11-16). Our love should be tough enough in knowledge and discernment, not accepting or approving things that are not excellent or righteous but willing to admonish or correct one another with love (Phi. 1:9-11; II Cor. 2:3-8; Rom. 15:13-16). This birthmark of God's love should be evident to all (John 13:34-35).

The family of God is to be characterized by faith in Jesus Christ, spiritual unity, great diversity, a growing maturity, a busy work ethic, and lots of supernatural love for one another, by which we may be recognized and properly identified.

Do others know to whose family you belong?

For Prayer Today
-      Pray for the spiritual health of the family of God.

Personal Notes and Responses

What about Grace is So Amazing?

"For the grace of God that bringeth salvation hath appeared to all men, teaching us that, denying ungodliness and worldly lusts, we should live soberly, righteously, and godly, in the present age...that being justified by his grace, we should be made heirs according to the hope of eternal life." (Titus 2:11-3:7) "For by grace are ye saved through faith; and that not of yourselves: it is the gift of God; not of works, lest any man should boast." (Eph. 2:8-9)

In a skit I participated in many years ago, we had a suspicious wife demanding of her husband, "Ok, who is this woman named Grace and why are you always talking about her?!"

Ah yes, that "Amazing Grace" of whom (which) we also sing frequently. In fact, many people of varied backgrounds testify in song of its wonders at all kinds of occasions. But so many of them do not understand how amazing it really is.

In this beginning of a five-part series I want to use the letters, G R A C E as an acrostic to help us unpack the wonders of this theme of God's grace.

First of all, the term "grace" is directly connected to the term "gift". It has been defined as the totally undeserved goodness of God that is offered to sinful mankind. It is undeserved favor, unearned blessings from God. Free gift!

In Ephesians 2:8-9 it is contrasted with works. Salvation is not a result of works or of man's effort. It is a gift from God. It is totally free to the recipients; we could not earn or deserve it. What we do earn and deserve in life, because of our sin, is death and the condemnation of God. (Rom. 6:23) But a loving God paid completely for our salvation and thus offers it freely to us by His grace, as His gift to us.

In normal life, no one works for a gift. They do not invest money in trying to win or to purchase a gift. It is not a reward, a wage, or a prize. It is something provided freely to us by someone else. Often when that happens, we respond with surprise or denial, protesting that they should not have done this, that we do not deserve it. That it wasn't necessary.

Actually, most of that is true of God's grace. It should surprise us to realize all that God is offering to us when we deserve an eternity separated from God and His goodness. It is true that we do not deserve it. But it is necessary. We do need it, desperately.

What should our response be? We should humbly acknowledge our sinfulness and with gratitude receive God's free gift of grace by trusting Jesus Christ to save us and to make us a child of God. (John 1:12-13)

When we speak or sing of the grace of God, we are rejoicing in this incredible gift that a gracious God is providing for us through Jesus Christ our Savior. Sadly, the majority of people continue to reject and refuse this gift. Have you received it?

For Prayer Today
- Thank God for His amazing grace and ask His help in talking to others about it.

Personal Notes and Responses

So, What About Grace is So Amazing? -Part 2

*"...There is **none righteous**, no, not one: there is none that under-standeth, there is none that seeketh after God. They are all gone out of the way, they are together become unprofitable; there is none that doeth good, no, not one...But now the **righteousness of God** without the law is manifested...even the **righteousness of God which is by faith of Jesus Christ...being justified freely by his grace** through the redemption that is in Christ Jesus...to declare, I say, at this time **his righteousness**..." (Rom. 3:9-26) ."... Abraham believed God, and it was counted unto him for righteousness..." (Rom. 4:3-5) "... For if through the offence of one many be dead, much more the grace of God, and the gift by grace, which is by one man, Jesus Christ ...For as by one man's disobedience many are made sinners, so by the obedience of one shall many be made righteous...that as sin hath reigned unto death, even so might grace reign through righteousness unto eternal life by Jesus Christ our Lord." (Rom. 5:15-21)*

Ok, I know that the stream of connected verses above can seem very confusing. Please read them again, very slowly this time and much of the confusion can be dispelled.

We are attempting to discover why God's grace is described as amazing. The letter **"G"** reminds us that His **grace** is a free **gift** from God offered and granted to those who admit they are undeserving sinners and who trust in Jesus Christ to save them. By God's grace through faith, sinners can be forgiven and saved. Amazing!

The letter **"R"** speaks of **righteousness**, the state of being right with God. The Bible is clear that we are conceived and born as sinners who continue to sin daily and pile up increasing loads of the just judgment and condemnation of God. As such we are under His wrath and hell awaits our arrival one day.

Except for the grace of God. This gift of grace also provides righteousness for us, not our own, but the very righteousness of Christ. When we come to Christ for salvation, our sin is charged to Him and His righteousness is credited to our account. We become immediately "justified", (declared officially righteous) and acceptable to Him forever! Amazing!

All our personal efforts to live righteously fall far short. But God graciously provides His righteousness through Christ when we come to Him and are saved. By His gracious Spirit, He also provides grace to help us gain victory over temptations and sin and to live righteously as we grow in Him. (Titus 2:11-12; Rom. 6:17-23; II Cor. 5:17) Our spiritual DNA is transformed from a sinful one to one that is right with God. Previously servants of sin, we are now servants of righteousness!

"For he hath made him to be sin for us, who knew no sin; that we might be made the righteousness of God in him." (II Cor. 5:21)

Isn't that amazing? I think you'll agree. All of this is part of God's grace! Wow!

For Prayer Today
- Thank God for His righteousness provided to you and ask Him to help you live righteously each day for Him.

Personal Notes and Responses

So, What About Grace is So Amazing? – Part 3

*"Therefore being justified by faith, we have peace with God through our Lord Jesus Christ: by whom also we have **access** by faith into this grace wherein we stand..." (Rom. 5:1-2) "For He, Himself is our peace who has made both one and has broken down the middle wall of separation...And came and preached peace to you which were afar off, and to them that were nigh. For through him we both have **access** by one Spirit unto the Father..." (Eph. 2:11-19) "...according to the eternal purpose which he purposed in Christ Jesus our Lord: in whom we have boldness and **access** with confidence by the faith of him." (Eph. 3:11-12) "...Let us therefore come boldly unto the throne of grace, that we may obtain mercy, and find grace to help in time of need." (Heb. 4:16)*

In attempting to unpack much of what is included in the nature of grace, we have discovered that **GRACE** is a gift from God, as is the salvation that God's grace provides. We have noted that **GRACE** provides unrighteous sinners with righteousness; Christ righteousness is credited to us! We have been justified, declared righteous!

Thirdly we see that **GRACE** gives us special access into areas that previously were forbidden to us.

1. We were once the children of the devil; now we are the children of God! We are to address Him as Father or Abba. We, as His children, are also heirs of God and joint-heirs with Christ! (I John 3:1-2, 8, 10; John 8:44; Rom. 8:14-17)
2. We were once enemies of God but are now allies of God, reconciled to Him and to other members of the body of Christ. (Rom. 5:10-11; Eph. 2:14-16; II Cor. 5:17-18)
3. We were once far off, separated from God and spiritually dead but now have been made alive, brought near,

and are united to Him, through Christ. (Eph. 2:1-16; I
Cor. 12:12-13)

4. We were once strangers and foreigners but are now fellow
    citizens with the saints and members of the household of
    God. (Eph. 2:19-22)

Because all of the above changes take place at the moment of salvation, we then are given ACCESS to God and to all His resources
that He has provided for us.

1. We have access to "much more" grace, much more of His
    gracious generosity as indicated in Rom. 5:2, 9-10, 15, 17,
    20-21; James 4:6.

2. We have access to God Himself, through Christ, as we
    pray often, to express our love and gratitude to Him and
    to request of Him what we need. (Heb. 4:14-16; Matt. 7:7-
    12; James 1:5-8; 4:1-3) Because we are now His children,
    He is eager to respond to us as our Father. (Rom. 8:14-17)

I am so often amazed that I have this access to the Creator-God of
the universe; that He is so available to me. I can speak to Him at any
time and He hears and responds. He communicates to me through
His written Word. He is involved deeply in my life in a personal way.

And all of this is because of His amazing grace!

For Prayer Today

-   Talk to God as a child to your Heavenly Father. Don't hesi-
    tate; you do have access to Him.

Personal Notes and Responses

So, What about Grace is So Amazing?–Part 4

"And God is able to make all grace abound toward you; that ye, always having all sufficiency in all things, may abound to every good work:" (II Cor. 9:8) "...Therefore...Take no thought for your life, what ye shall eat, or what ye shall drink; nor yet for your body, what ye shall put on...for your heavenly Father knoweth that ye have need of all these things. But seek ye first the kingdom of God, and his righteousness; and all these things shall be added unto you." (Matt. 6:25-33) "But my God shall supply all your need according to his riches in glory by Christ Jesus." (Phil. 4:19) "The LORD is my Shepherd; I shall not want...Surely goodness and mercy shall follow me all the days of my life..." (Psalm 23) "...casting all your care upon him, for He careth for you." (I Peter 5:7)

G.R.A.C.E. Gift freely given. **R**ighteousness of Christ received. **A**ccess to God granted. And now, a fourth facet of God's grace is His amazing **C**are that He provides for His children. (This is, perhaps, my favorite aspect of His amazing grace; it is the most noticeable, at least. I have found it practically, in my face, every day! And I am so overwhelmed by it and so very grateful.)

God, in His grace, not only provides many spiritual blessings and assurances, but He, amazingly, seems very committed to invade our lives daily with physical blessings, answers to prayer, rearranged circumstances, and He surprises us often with His gracious goodness. He convincingly reveals that He cares for us and will oversee and guide us in the messiness of life with supernatural attention to us.

As our good Shepherd, He promises to provide protection, sustenance, guidance, restoration, and life eternal in the house of the Lord. (Psalm 23) Spiritual blessings and physical blessing are enumerated also in Psalm 103 as part of God's gracious care of His own.

So many believers still don't recognize this area of His grace since they do not acknowledge Him in all their ways, every day. They don't have amazing "God-sightings" because they never trust Him with daily matters and needs. They never see His fingerprints on daily circumstances because they are not praying for, expecting, or looking for them.

The Bible's promises are often punctuated with actual accounts of God's miraculous and timely provisions for His people. A timely ram caught in a thicket (Gen. 22), protection of a baby in a river where other babies were drowned (Ex. 1-2), ready-to-eat meals and quiet rest for a despairing prophet who was at the end of his rope (I Kings 19), a miraculous windfall of oil and funds for a desperate widow (II Kings 4), the feeding of the 5,000+ from a child's lunch (John 6), were all enthralling stories that captured our attention in our early years. But God has not changed.

Over almost 47 years of marriage, Debra and I have frequently experienced God's faithful and miraculous provision for our needs. Sometimes incredibly abundant and uniquely delivered. We know that God loves to do this for His children. I hope you know that, too.

For Prayer Today
- Talk to God today very specifically about your needs and worries; cast them upon Him.

Personal Notes and Responses

ETERNAL ENCOURAGEMENTS #184

So, What about Grace is So Amazing? – Part 5

*"...that whosoever believeth in him should not perish, but have **eternal** life. For God so loved the world, that he gave his only begotten Son, that whosoever believeth in him should not perish, but have **everlasting** life." (John 3:15-16) "My sheep hear my voice, and I know them, and they follow me: And I give unto them **eternal** life; and they shall never perish, neither shall any man pluck them out of my hand. My Father, which gave them me, is greater than all; and no man is able to pluck them out of my Father's hand. I and my Father are one." (John 10:27-30) "... and I shall dwell in the house of the LORD forever." (Psalm 23:6) "The wages of sin is death but the gift of God is **eternal** life through Jesus Christ our Lord." (Rom. 6:23)*

This final segment in this series highlights a fifth amazing characteristic of the grace of God – its duration. It is eternal. It is forever. It is everlasting. There is no end to it. This is true for the following reasons.

1. The actual **price of our salvation** has been "paid in full" ("It is finished!") at the cross by our Savior. Our salvation is not based or dependent on our works, our merit, our family heritage. Jesus provided full and free salvation and gave it to us as a gift when we trusted in Him. The wrath of God on sin was completely satisfied by Christ's death and shed blood and we face no longer any condemnation or wrath from Him. (Heb. 10:11-14; Rom. 8:1)

2. The **promises of our salvation** clearly declare that it is everlasting. What God has begun in our lives at salvation He will continue it all the way to glory. (Rom. 8:29-30) He has saved us from the "guttermost" and guarantees to take us all the way to the "uttermost". (Heb. 7:25)

3. The **power of our salvation** is the very power of God. He is the One who keeps us saved. (I Peter 3:3-5; John 10:28-30; Rom. 8:28-39; Eph. 1:17-19) No other power, person, principality, or anything can ever annul our salvation or separate us from Christ's love.

4. The **prospect of our salvation** includes a future glorified (totally perfected) state, with an eternal inheritance received, and a forever in a new heavens and new earth where they will be no sin, suffering, tears, or death and where we will enjoy our God and His forgiven family forever! (Rom. 8:16-17; Eph. 1:7-14; 2:4-7; I Peter 1:3-5; Rev. 21-22)

So, what about grace is so amazing? It is a free **Gift** from God in which we receive the **Righteousness** of Christ and unique **Access** to God who demonstrates His Fatherly **Care** of His children daily and will keep His promises to us forever. It is a gift that will last forever; it is **Eternal** salvation from our eternal God! Incredible!

Alright, now. Are you ready to sing? Join me – "Amazing grace how sweet the sound…When we've been there ten thousand years…!"

For Prayer Today
> If you are truly amazed at God's grace, ask Him to help you live daily in a way that shouts, "Thank you!" to Him.

Personal Notes and Responses

Topical Index

(Subject/Eternal Encouragement #)

CPSIA information can be obtained
at www.ICGtesting.com
Printed in the USA
LVHW032028120522
718627LV00012B/1278